KORZYBSKI AND...

KORZYBSKI AND ...

Edited by

COREY ANTON AND LANCE STRATE

INSTITUTE OF GENERAL SEMANTICS

New York

Published by:

INSTITUTE OF GENERAL SEMANTICS
www.generalsemantics.org

First printing

Cover & Interior Book Design by Scribe Freelance

ISBN: 978-0-9827559-7-6

Published in the United States of America

LIBRARY OF CONGRESS CATALOGING-IN-PUBLICATION DATA

Korzybski and-- / edited by Corey Anton and Lance Strate.
  p. cm.
 Includes index.
 ISBN 978-0-9827559-7-6 (alk. paper)
1. Korzybski, Alfred, 1879-1950. I. Anton, Corey. II. Strate, Lance.
B945.K74K67 2012
 191--dc23
                    2012036682

CONTENTS

ACKNOWLEDGEMENTS

MANY PEOPLE, ORGANIZATIONS, and institutions need to be thanked and recognized for their help in bringing this collection together. We need to acknowledge a host of academic associations and organizations, including the National Communication Association, The Media Ecology Association, the Institute of General Semantics, The Eastern Communication Association, The International Communicology Institute, and the Semiotic Society of America for the public contexts and intellectual forums in which many of these ideas first appeared. These venues have allowed for many of the contributors to share earlier drafts and gain valuable feedback on their papers. We wish to express deep thanks to the Institute of General Semantics for the kind permission to reprint Zhenbin Sun's essay, here titled, "Korzybski and Friedrich Nietzsche" (originally published in *ETC*, Oct. 2011, pp. 414-440), and Thierry Bardini's essay, here titled, "Korzybski and Cyberculture," first published as "When the Map Becomes the Territory: Korzybski and Cyberculture," *General Semantics Bulletin*, 76: 37-49, 2009/2010. We want to thank all of the contributors for their patience and understanding during the long time it took to get this collection to print, and we also wish to express our gratitude to all authors for their willingness to alter titles and make modifications to their papers for inclusion in the volume. Without such talent, flexibility, and generosity, this collection would not exist. We also need to recognize and thank Bruce I. Kodish for his inspiration, and his contribution to this volume, and his various forms of assistance behind the scenes.

At Grand Valley, we wish to thank and acknowledge the Faculty and Development Grant money that aided in conference travel and the additional funding from the Center for Scholarly and Creative Excellence and the Pew Teaching and Learning Center. We also wish to thank Grand Valley State University, especially Provost Gayle R. Davis and Dean Frederick J. Antczak, and the School of Communications, for the Winter 2012 sabbatical release for Corey Anton, which greatly aided in the completion of this project. At Fordham University, we thank Provost Stephen Freedman, Dean Isabelle Frank, and the Department of Communication and Media Studies.

We both want to express our gratitude to our families, friends, and many colleagues who have been supportive and helpful during this long process. On a personal note, Lance wishes to acknowledge the support and forbearance of his family, Barbara, Benjamin, Sarah, and Betty Strate, and his dog, Dingo,

VIII ■ KORZYBSKI AND . . .

may he rest in peace. Corey wishes to acknowledge the continued support and care of Valerie V. Peterson as well as friends and family for their boundless encouragement.

CHAPTER 1: SITUATING ALFRED KORZYBSKI

Corey Anton and Lance Strate

I.

SITUATING ALFRED KORZYBSKI is a rather daunting feat. This is partly because of the wide range of his influences, the vast scope of his claims, and the sweeping implications of his work. All potentially place him in dialogue with countless individuals and yet locate him at the heart of contemporary concerns regarding the wild variety of humanity's possible futures. Korzybski also defies quick and easy placement because his aspirations were so much more than scholarly. He was not merely an academic or a scientist but was equally, if not more deeply, a public intellectual, a social activist, a humanitarian. As someone who was alive and well during the progressive education movement, Korzybski sought to bring a kind of general education to the masses. He wrote impassioned letters to Robert Maynard Hutchins which, among other things, make quite evident one of the main differences between their views: Korzybski demanded a *teachable system*. And yet, despite his strong desire for developing and disseminating such a system, and his personal yearnings for more direct and practical instruction regarding "semantic reactions" and "consciousness of abstracting," Korzybski's texts are somewhat labyrinthine and intimidating. His work is in fact so broad and inclusive that it today can easily be identified as a forerunner of contemporary theory and scholarship in the areas of language studies, neuroscience, cognitive science, applied psychology, sociology, cybernetics and systems theory, communication studies, media literacy, and media ecology.

At the very least, we might begin to situate Korzybski by simply acknowledging that he was a grand synthesizer—as is well attested to by the list of authors to whom *Science and Sanity* was dedicated. He was a scientific realist with optimistic leanings, someone who not only believed that a saner and more adult phase of humanity is possible but also that he would be among those who would help shepherd it in. One of the main strengths of Korzybski's overall orientation is that it sought to help people improve their evaluations of their neurosemantic and neurolinguistic environments, with the effect being a saner, more rational world. Korzybski yearned for a more humane and mature society and actively created the means and methods to help bring it about. Still, for all of his practicality, Korzybski was a wide-ranging thinker and philosopher of language and the human condition. His work has been so influential that it makes good sense, now with the clarity of hindsight, to consider some of the ways that his influence still can be felt, and to take up some of the ways that his work still needs to be appraised and developed.

Korzybski was born in 1879, at a time when Poland was part of the Czarist Russian empire. A member of a noble family, Count Korzybski wanted to study at university to become a mathematician, physicist or lawyer, but his father wanted him to become an engineer. It was not until he was 18 years old that he discovered that his parents' earlier choice to place him in a realschule, which offered a more scientific emphasis than the Gymnasium, with a traditional emphasis on classics and humanities, would prevent him from entering a university program of study which focused on his great ambitions. Doing as his parents wished, he resigned himself to study chemical engineering, which he studied as an undergraduate at Politechnika, Warszawska. As he continued his studies, mostly on his own, and he was an absolutely voracious reader, he came to idolize Albert Einstein. Other major influences included mathematicians Cassius J. Keyser and Henri Poincaré, psychologists William Alanson White, Ivan Pavlov, and Sigmund Freud, and philosophers Bertrand Russell, Alfred North Whitehead, Ludwig Wittgenstein, Josiah Royce, and indeed Aristotle, however much he styled his approach and system as non-Aristotelian. But perhaps his greatest influence was the First World War, where he served in the Czar's army, and was wounded several times. Sent to North America, and electing to remain in the United States, Korzybski published his first book, *Manhood of Humanity: The Science and Art of Human Engineering*, in 1921 (in 1950, shortly after his death a second edition of *Manhood of Humanity* was published, in which the subtitle was eliminated). In this work, Korzybski reasoned that forms of life could be classified based on how they obtain energy. He classified plants as *chemistry-binding* (based on their capacity for photosynthesis), animals as *space-binding* (based on their mobility in contrast to plant life), and the human species as *time-binding*, based on our ability to capture and store knowledge and pass it on to our progeny, to accumulate learning from one generation to the next, to build on what previous generations have accomplished, and thereby to make progress. Arguing that scientists engaged in the most effective form of *time-binding*, Korzybski put forth a utopian vision of a society governed and administered by scientists, one where the scientific method applied to all aspects of human life, for the greater good of all.

Following the publication of *Manhood of Humanity*, Korzybski engaged in an extended period of writing and research which included studying psychiatric methods firsthand at St. Elizabeths Hospital in Washington, D.C. He then published his magnum opus, *Science and Sanity: An Introduction to Non-Aristotelian Systems and General Semantics* in 1933 (and subsequently in four more editions, the last two posthumously, the most recent in 1993). In this work, he noted that what set humans a class apart, and made our time-binding possible, is language and symbolic communication, which he categorized as a form of abstracting. He situated these activities on a higher level than sense perception, and therefore further removed from an actual reality of which we can never have direct knowledge, although we can construct verbal and nonverbal maps that are more (or less) structurally similar to the environment, and therefore more (or less) predictive. Sense perception brings us closer to actual reality, which is why modern science is based on the empirical method. But perception remains a form of abstracting and without language it is impossible to develop a consciousness of abstracting, the goal of Korzybski's system, to which he gave the name *general semantics*.

Korzybski characterized general semantics as a non-Aristotelian system, arguing that after more than two millennia, it was time to move past Aristotle's approach to logic. Korzybski stressed the importance of non-identity, arguing that no two phenomena in the universe are entirely identical, and that all phenomena are unique events in spacetime. He especially warned of the danger of mistaking words for things, and symbols for reality. He famously reminds us that, "*the map is not the territory*," and "*whatever you say a thing is, it isn't*." To the Principle of Non-Identity he added the Principle of Non-Allness, that we can never say all there is to say about any phenomena, or perceive all there is to perceive about any aspect of the world (just as maps must always be incomplete and selective representations of a territory). He also included a third principle, the Principle of Self-Reflexiveness, noting that not all words refer to phenomena in the world. Some words, that is, refer simply to other words, and there can be words that refer to words that refer to words, and so on *ad infinitum*, at least in theory. We can make statements about the world, but we also can self-reflexively make statements about statements, statements about statements about statements, etc.; we can ask questions, ask questions about questions, and questions about questions about questions, etc. Self-reflexiveness takes us higher up in levels of abstraction, and can be the cause of confusion when levels are confused (as made clear by Alfred North Whitehead and Bertrand Russell, 1925-1927). But self-reflexiveness is also the key to higher levels of human consciousness.

Korzybski's system emphasized a non-elementalistic and therefore holistic approach to relating to the environment, an approach that depicted the *organism-as-a-whole-in-an-environment*, as he put it. Through the application of these and other concepts, including familiarity with the structural differential as a model of the process of abstracting, emphasizing the extensional over the intensional (e.g., facts over opinions), the use of devices such as indexing (thing$_1$ is not thing$_2$), dating (thing^{1984} is not thing^{2004}), and etc., (as a reminder of non-allness), awareness of the problematic nature of the verb *to be* (the "*is* of identification" and the "*is* of predication"), along with various other exercises aimed at heightening awareness, training perception, and raising consciousness, Korzybski hoped to enable individuals to take control of their own semantic reactions (i.e., responses to stimuli), improve their ability to evaluate statements, messages, and percepts, and thereby become better human beings. In this way, the goal was sanity for individual and society alike, and through sanity, progress, not just in science and technology, but social progress, political and economic progress, and moral progress.

An inkling of Korzybski's early teaching method can be gleaned from the transcript of his lectures on general semantics given at Olivet College in Michigan, which was published under the title of *General Semantics Seminar 1937* in that same year (with two posthumous editions following, the most recent in 2002). Despite the fact that he lectured and conducted seminars without an academic position, he gained a loyal following, and with the support of his students, was able to set up the Institute of General Semantics (IGS) in 1938 in Chicago. In the years that followed, he offered regular seminars, lectures, and also personal counseling for his students. In 1942, a group of his students founded the International Society for General Semantics (which merged with the IGS in 2004), and began publishing the journal, *ETC: A Review of General Semantics* the following year. There was a great deal of public interest in Korzybski and general semantics at that time, no doubt fueled in part by the Great Depression and the Second World War, and a number of popularizations of his work did much to spread the word about his ideas, which enjoyed great influence in many areas of study and practice. Following the war, Korzybski was forced to relocate the Institute to Lakeville,

Connecticut, and finances remained a concern for the Institute and for him personally. In 1948, he published an abridged version of his main work under the title of *Selections from Science and Sanity* (posthumously modified over eight printings, transfered to CD-ROM, and now in a second edition published in 2010).

Korzybski passed away on March 1, 1950, as the IGS was just readying for publication the first issue of its own journal, the *General Semantics Bulletin*, and, in 1952, the Institute established an annual Alfred Korzybski Memorial Lecture. Interest in Korzybski and general semantics declined during the late 20th century, so much so that in 1990, when two of Korzybski's closest associates, M. Kendig and Charlotte Schuchardt Read, compiled and published Korzybski's various articles and papers under the title of *Collected Writings, 1920-1950*, it received little in the way of fanfare or exposure. The 21st century is likely to witness a reversal of fortune, however, as signs of a nascent revival of Korzybski's ideas and goal have been seen in recent years, notably the publication of Lance Strate's *On the Binding Biases of Time*, Corey Anton's *Communication Uncovered*, and Korzybski's first full length biography written by Bruce I. Kodish, all published in 2011.

II. KORZYBSKI AND...

In conceiving of a collection of essays with the common designation of "Korzybski And..." we realize that we could just as easily have settled on the title, "Korzybski Etc." Indeed, the phrase *et cetera* is Latin for *and the others*, and in a more general sense, we use it to mean *and so forth*, or more elaborately as, *and other unspecified persons and/or things of the same or similar class*. As an extensional device, the *etc.* reminds us of the Principle of Non-Allness, which applies to persons as well as to things, so that in the well-known words of John Donne, *no man is an island*, no individual exists in isolation, unaffected by and with no influence on others. It is the very essence of Korzybski's concept of time-binding to recognize that all of our accomplishments rely upon the work of those who came before. Even the greatest, most original of thinkers are, in a certain sense, dwarfs standing on the shoulders of giants. Following Einstein's theory of relativity, Korzybski's general semantics is based on the fundamental understanding that our knowledge of the world, and indeed our very being, exists only in relation to other phenomena. And so, in this volume, we set out to explore Korzybski in relation to others, Korzybski in the context of other thinkers and intellectual movements. To this end, our aim is to go beyond *Korzybksi Et Cetera, Korzybski And Unspecified Others*, and instead present a series of specific relationships, *Korzybski And. . .*

The types of relationships can be divided chronologically into those whose work preceded Korzybski's, his contemporaries, and those who came after. Along the way, we also will consider those whose ideas, methods, etc., influenced Korzybski; those whose work was influenced by Korzybski, whether directly as his students, colleagues, etc., or indirectly through his writings, teachings, etc.; and those whose works offer significant parallels to that of Korzybski, providing opportunities for comparison, and contrast.

Our anthology begins, Chapter 2, with Bruce I. Kodish's essay on "Korzybski and Gottfried Leibniz." Kodish explores how Korzybski's *Science and Sanity*, a book that deals with the dreams and ideals of Man and the problems of human happiness from a peculiar mathematical perspective, owes a significant debt to Leibniz. This debt is not only for Leibniz's development (along with Newton) of the calculus, which over the years had so inspired Korzybski, but also for the dreams of Leibniz—various schemes and speculations Leibniz proposed over his lifetime to advance mathematics, science, and society.

In Chapter 3 we turn to Zhenbin Sun's, "Korzybski and Friedrich Nietzsche," where Sun offers a comparative study of Nietzsche and Korzybski's thought on several philosophical and linguistic issues, including their mutual critique of Greek metaphysics and their own received worldview; their deconstruction of logocentricism; parallels in how they understand the nature of language and its relationship to thought and reality; and how they relate to structuralism and poststructuralism, respectively.

In "Korzybski and Charles Sanders Peirce," Chapter 4, Isaac E. Catt provides a new paradigm for theory construction, one that reflects the influence of both general semantics and semiotic phenomenology. Catt's discussion, which includes a robust critique of positivist conceptions of human communication, centers on the relevance of these two schools of thought to postmodern intellectual discourse. It furthermore outlines "communicology," the science of embodied discourse, as the proper context for the whole of human communication research.

In Chapter 5, Corey Anton explores some overlaps and intersections between the ideas of Korzybski and Martin Heidegger. He shows how both thinkers directly combat elementalism by bringing about changes in language practices and reckon with the uniquely human situation by turning attention to the nature of time and temporality. Comparing Korzybski's three classes of life and account of time-binding to Heidegger's tri-part account of being (e.g. extants, lives, and exists), Anton opens a long overdue dialogue by identifying some key commonalities (and also some critical divergences) between these two thinkers.

Jean-Yves Heurtebise, in Chapter 6, addresses the relationship of Korzybski to French Structuralism. He draws parallels between Korzybski's *Science and Sanity* and contemporary French philosophers such as Henri Bergson and Gilles Deleuze to suggest a common theoretical framework. By re-considering Korzybski's central idea that the only content of knowledge is structure, this chapter provocatively explores the potential "structuralism" of Korzybski's philosophy.

In Chapters 7 and 8, William Henry Sharp considers the relationships between Korzybski and two scholars well known within general semantics: Stuart Chase and S. I. Hayakawa. Sharp, in Chapter 7 intimately documents some of the relationship dynamics between Korzybski and Chase, including how Chase's initially enthusiastic reception of *Science and Sanity* came to popularize the term "semantics," and how a later falling out led to Chase's eventual estrangement from Korzybski. In Chapter 8, Sharp suggests that whereas Chase helped Korzybski's work gain recognition, Hayakawa played an even more significant role in the development of general semantics. Unfortunately, Sharp claims, neither Chase nor Hayakawa really appreciated Korzybski's intellectual contribution to the field of communication studies. Both said more about themselves than about GS, and, according to Sharp, we need more bright scholars going back to Korzybski's text while also becoming more extensional.

Martin H. Levinson, in Chapter 9, "Korzybski and Albert Ellis," outlines the many ways that Ellis, originator of Rational Emotive Behavior Therapy (REBT) was influenced by and indebted to general semantics. Levinson spans ideas such as: "the 'is' of predication," the use of E-Prime, the importance of precise thought and language, the value of constructive change, and the role of multi-valued orientations. Levinson also includes speculation about what Korzybski might have thought of REBT today.

Chapter 10, "Korzybski and New Trends in Psychotherapy," by Ramiro J. Álvarez, examines the influence of and parallel currents to Korzybski in contemporary psychology and psychotherapy. Identifying thinkers such as

Albert Ellis, George Kelly, Paul Watzlawick, Humberto Maturana, Eugene Gendlin and Ira Progoff, Álverez emphasizes the general trend toward larger, more holistic, "colloidal" conceptions of persons-acting-in-particular-environments, and he suggests that therapy and everyday life come to coincide for those who would enlarge their lives by growing more extensional.

Lance Strate, in Chapter 11, explores parallels between Korzybski and Marshall McLuhan. Among the common chords we find: Korzybski's Non-Aristoleanism and McLuhan's orientation to "grammar" in the classical sense of the word, their mutual recognition of post-Newtonian, post-Euclidian world views, and their mutual recognition of the importance of language in perception. Strate ultimately advocates an ecology of mediating and an ecology of abstracting, an ecology of knowing; one that incorporates form and technology, the inner landscape and the outer environment, the map and the territory, the medium and the message.

Chapter 12, "Korzybski and Cultural Studies," by Geraldine E. Forsberg examines the many uses and developments of Korzybski's ideas regarding consciousness of abstracting. Outlining both Korzybski's "Structural Differential" and Hayakawa's "Abstraction Ladder," Forsberg shows the applicability of theorizing the role of abstracting, with its attention to different senses of space and time, to media studies, to television, and to cultural studies broadly and globally defined.

In Chapter 13, "Korzybski and a New Visual Language," John S. Caputo, Robin Wynyard and Heather M. Crandall address the work of Korzybski in terms of its connections to painting and literary theory, more specifically contemporary authors and painters such as Maurice Merleau-Ponty, Robert A. Heinlein, Jorge Borges, and Mark Rothko. They illustrate how Heinlein mistakenly believes he can capture the reality of Korzybski's thought, without realizing how a fictive text plays with the reader in setting up oppositions and binary concepts. They argue that Borges and Rothko offer more complimentary and resonant mutli-valued orientations, ones that provocatively trace different layers of abstracting and reflexivity in literature and painting respectively.

In Chapter 14, "Korzybski and Cartography," Bini B.S. examines the analogy, "Map is not the Territory; Word is not the Thing Defined" by considering it in relation to Korzybski's idea of time-binding. Bini explores various theoretical and philosophical nuances of time-binding by examining its application and reference to language and other means of communication, representation, perception and comprehension. Her analysis highlights factors that impact the circulation and transmission of knowledge and she ventures into the contemporary cultural, political, and disciplinary implications of Korzybski's notion of time-binding.

Thierry Bardini, in Chapter 15, "Korzybski and Cyberculture," explores the direct and indirect influences that Alfred Korzybski's work had on contemporary cyberculture. He considers Korzybski's influence on William S. Burroughs, A.E. van Vogt, Philip K. Dick, and the 1980s genre of cyberpunk literature. He also shows how Korzybski's influence on Gregory Bateson, among other cyberneticians of the first hour (such as McCulloch and Northrop), and Neil Postman, contributed in shaping one of the leading modes of thought in this domain (e.g. "media ecology"). Ultimately, Bardini illustrates how Korzybski's legacy in contemporary culture far exceeds the slogan "the map is not the territory."

Finally, in Chapter 16, Deborah Eicher-Catt reflexively turns our attention to the ellipsis in her chapter, "Korzybski and . . . ," where she re-considers "*ellipse*" and "*et cetera*" by rendering a semiotic phenomenological interpretation of their discursive contours. This interpretation reveals their qualitative nature as *figures* (*or tropes*) *of speech* rather than as mere stylistic devices. As such, she shows how *tropes of speech*, in their mediating capabilities as phenomenological semiotic enactments or *bodily gestures*, highlight what Korzybski identifies as our *psycho-logic*. Moving Korzybski's work well beyond a narrow social science perspective, she outlines his contributions to a "reflexive human science."

III.

The present collection, given space and time constraints, has omitted many thinkers whose ideas intersect with Korzybski's and whose work could have been engaged and expounded upon. Indeed, so many connections, intersections, and divergences could have been explored, but by necessity were omitted that we welcome future scholarship along the following lines. We find it easy to imagine future research delving into Korzybski and his influences, perhaps none more deserving than Aristotle himself, whose name appears first in the lengthy list of dedications in *Science and Sanity*. Socrates and Plato are also included, and a more general consideration of Korzybski and the philosophers of antiquity might be in order. Another line that might have been explored and still could be examined more fully is the connection between Korzybski and the stoics. In many regards Korzybski's orientation to happiness and effort can be traced back to stoic philosophy, the writings of Epictetus in particular. But not just moral philosophy, for we also find many ideas on logic and language that predate Korzybski by about 2000 years and then run concurrent with and independent of GS: Seneca writes:

> 'Mouse' is a syllable. Now a mouse eats its cheese; therefore, a syllable eats cheese. Suppose now that I cannot solve this problem; see what peril hangs over my head as a result of such ignorance! What a scrape I shall be in! Without doubt I must beware, or someday I shall be catching syllables in a mousetrap, or, if I grow careless, a book may devour my cheese! Unless, perhaps, the following syllogism is shrewder still: 'Mouse' is a syllable. Now a syllable does not eat cheese. Therefore a mouse does not eat cheese. What childish nonsense! Do we knit our brows over this sort of problem? Do we let our beards grow long for this reason? Is this the matter which we teach with sour and pale faces? (2002, p. 317)

We find within the ancient stoics early concerns regarding the discrepancy between map and territory, between words and things. Such orientations can be found much later within the work of Spinoza. Consider *How to Improve Your Mind*, where Spinoza provides a line of thinking that predates Korzybski by about 300+ years. Spinoza writes, "…thus a circle is different from the idea of a circle. The Idea of a circle is not something having a circumference and a centre, as a circle has; nor is the idea of a body that body itself" (1956, p. 36).

Korzybski also lists Descartes, and general semantics might well be termed a non-Cartesian system for its opposition to the elementalism of mind-body dualism, and considerations of Korzybski and Kant, Korzybski and Locke, and Korzybski and empiricism, would also be in order. The work of the 19th century American philosopher Josiah Royce had a major impact on Korzybski's thought, and research on that relationship would be of great importance to advancing Korzybski studies. The pragmatist philosophy and semiotics of Charles Sanders Peirce was acknowledged by Korzybski to be a parallel non-Aristotelian system, and a comparative study would be an important area of further research, as would an examination of the influence of

Ernst Cassirer, Alfred North Whitehead, Bertrand Russell, and Ludwig Wittgenstein. Certainly, Susanne K. Langer's arguments concerning symbolic form, which take issue with the emphasis on propositionality and discursive symbols of the logical positivists, would provide an important point of contrast with Korzybski's system based on scientific language.

Scientists and philosophers of science alike would also be important subjects for further study. Certainly, no one looms larger on the Korzybski map than Albert Einstein, whose work Korzybski believed he was complementing, and whose approval he desperately sought. Charles Darwin as well should be included here, for his non-Aristotelian biology emphasized change over time. Other possibilities include Niels Bohr, Max Planck, Henri Poincaré, and Werner Heisenberg, and among the philosophers, John Dewey, Karl Popper, Stephen Toulmin, Thomas Kuhn, Ernest Nagel, Hilary Putnam, and W. V. O. Quine. Korzybski's keen attention to physiological processes and the neuro-linguistic physiology of perception aligns much of his work with contemporary phenomenological research as well as easily places him in dialogue with contemporary neuroscience. At a minimum, Korzybski, neuroscience, and phenomenology all share a concern with combating naïve verbal realism. A consideration of Korzybski's work in relation to scholars of perception such as Adelbert Ames, Fritz Heider, and J. J. Gibson, as well as the neuroscience of António Damásio would also be welcome. Cognitive science would be another area ripe for further study, especially in regard to Douglas Hofstadter, whose emphasis on recursion parallels Korzybski's analysis of abstraction and self-reflexiveness. Moreover, Korzybski, especially given his early, utopian vision of a society governed by science might be compared to similar notions put forth by Thorstein Veblen (who also stressed the importance and irrationality of the symbol in human life), to the dystopias of Aldous Huxley and George Orwell (whose speculations about the relation between language and thought are consonant with Korzybski's own), and the utopian ideas of Edward Bellamy. Indeed, there is no doubt that Korzybski grappled with the socioeconomic arguments and utopian projections of Karl Marx, and this would certainly merit further investigation.

Additional study might also consider points of overlap and intersection between Korzybski and Mikhail Mikhailovitch Bakhtin. Much of Bakhtin's early work on ethics—how ethical demands are made upon each of us because we are radically non-substitutable, non-interchangeable and are located within a unique unfolding of space and time—resonates with Korzybski's appreciation of non-identity and the eventfulness of reality. Both Bakhtin and Korzybski claimed Einstein as a significant influence; both sought to develop accounts of humanity and agency compatible with the latest developments in physics. Like Bakhtin, Kenneth Burke roams across the boundaries of philosophy, and rhetoric and literary theory, and his work stands in contrast to Korzybski's for its emphasis on the irrational and the dramatistic. Burke, however, was influenced by Korzybski's critique of identity relations, and his views on rhetoric in particular are written in response to and reaction against Korzybski. In literary theory proper, the work of I. A. Richards (along with C. K. Ogden) parallels Korzybski's in many important respects, and is especially ripe for comparative study. More recently, Jacques Derrida's deconstruction owes a major debt to Korzybski, and further study of his influence among the French structuralists and poststructuralists would be in order. Korzybski can also be seen as pre-Postmodern. His notions of mapping and recursivity predate the contemporary concern with self-reference and self-referential systems. Jean Baudrillard, who also works with the map-territory metaphor, and questions of symbolic exchange, would make for another interesting point of comparison. In the literary world, we might include further work on William S. Burroughs, Korzybski's student, and Robert Anton Wilson, and science fiction writers A. E. van Vogt, and Frank Herbert, all of whom reflect the direct influence of Korzybski and general semantics, as well as other authors whose work bear some relation to Korzybski's, such as James Joyce and Jorge Luis Borges.

Korzybski's concern with therapy and sanity should not be downplayed, and therefore it would be essential to consider his relation to psychologists, such as Ivan Pavlov, whose work on signals and symbols informs Korzybski's notion of semantic reactions, and Sigmund Freud, whose views on symbolism also contributed to Korzybski's system; William Alanson White is another significant psychotherapist singled out by Korzybski. A study of Gregory Bateson's relationship to Korzybski would be of great significance, as Bateson both extended Korzybski's work, and provided a complementary perspective that also served as a critique of Korzybski's shortcomings, particularly in not paying enough attention to relational factors. Bateson's approach to therapy served as the foundation for relational therapy, and the brief therapy associated with Paul Watzlawick and his colleagues, and Bertrand Frohman, and further investigation of these interconnections, and their association with theories of the social construction of reality, would prove fruitful. Korzybski's influence on Fritz Perls, Paul Goodman, and Gestalt therapy is also worthy of further investigation, and on Richard Bandler, who took the name of his approach, Neuro-Linguistic Programming, directly from Korzybski. Another intriguing avenue would be the investigation of the claims made by L. Ron Hubbard as to Korzybski's influence on his development of dianetics, and Scientology. Moreover, although linguistics scholars generally disavowed any connection to Korzybski, there is much potential in an examination of the relationship between his work and that of linguistic relativists such as Edward Sapir and Benjamin Lee Whorf, the cultural-historical psychology of Lev Vygotsky and Alexander Luria, the generative grammar of Noam Chomsky, the theory of metaphor of George Lakoff and Mark Johnson, and the relational approach to linguistics associated with Deborah Tannen.

Additionally, Korzybski's multilingual background and high levels of multidisciplinary literacy were a vital part of his means for getting a handle on his own semantic reactions. To the degree that literacy and print facilitate a distanciation and detachment that enabled Western people to, as McLuhan would suggest, "act without reacting," we might with considerable gain examine the earlier context and/or ground from which and against which Korzybski's sensibilities grew. Future research might consider Korzybski's program of helping people increase their consciousness of abstracting, showing how this relates to the advent of the scientific age, by comparatively re-reading the writings of Lucian Lévy-Bruhl, Sir James George Frazer, and other turn of the century anthropologists. Such work might illuminate and clarify the many different kinds of "identifications" that have characterized human thought at different times and places, especially prior to the modern scientific world-view. Consider, as one simple illustration, the insights of anthropologist Dorothy Lee, where she reveals the Western, "modern" prejudice regarding the possible de-contextualization of both words and things. She writes,

> In Western thought, a symbol is usually something which "represents," which "fits"...This conception of the symbol as something distinct from and applicable to, can be held because of a mode of thinking according to which it is possible and desirable to abstract elements from a total situation, and to separate idea or form from substance. (1959, p. 78)

Her point is that the total situation includes the symbol and the symbol is not a discretely separate item that can be given or assigned value arbitrarily. Each symbol participates in the situations in which it occurs and it accrues its meaning only by such participation. She goes on: "When 'primitives' are said to be incapable of distinguishing the word from the *thing*, or to confuse an object with its name, I suspect that what we have is rather the recognition of this participation of the symbol in the thing" (ibid., p. 84). It was literacy writ large, lay literacy and the widespread sensibilities of literacy that neutralized speech and gave it the appearance of a self-standing independent thing. As Dorothy Lee contends, words are not empty and neutral labels that stand independently and simply refer to or designate items in the world. They always emerge, occur, and are always taken from situations, and they retain some residue of meaning from their participation in all of the situations in which they have participated. So the word "apple" not only carries all of its significant meanings from botany, nutritional labels, and the grocery store. It carries meaning from its use in expressions such as "an apple a day keeps the doctor away" or "apple polisher," referring to the way students may be overly obsequious to their teachers, or to the "poison apple," or even to the "forbidden fruit" by which "eyes are uncovered," and also to all of the many ways that actual apples have participated in situations and have accordingly gained a value other than that conveyed "by themselves."

Korzybski considered the term *anthropology* as a potential alternative to *general semantics*, and other scholars in the discipline of anthropology whose work might serve as topics of comparative study include Margaret Mead (a close associate of Gregory Bateson), Edward T. Hall, and Clifford Geertz, who stressed the semiotics of culture. Future scholarship should continue to explore the ways that Korzybski's project accomplishes what is sought in so many different forms of Eastern thought. One might make the argument that Korzybski's work, from a fully scientific orientation, culminates into a kind of Zen or Buddhist life-practice. Consider some of the obvious parallels. Much of Korzybski's thought attends to the process nature of the world, its impermanence. He teaches non-identification and offers strategies to become more aware of the once-occurrent world that is always so different than the maps to which we commonly cling. Korzybski's Structural Differential neatly aligns with Buddhist traditions that stress the importance of the distinction between the silent level and verbal levels and also aligns with schools of direct pointing within Zen. His style of awareness /consciousness raising (especially regarding semantic reactions) powerfully rivals various Buddhist exercises by which persons train to become more focused on their reactions to events, to become more cognizant of confusing thoughts about events for events themselves. As many Buddhist orientations are designed to help people become more aware of their identifications and symbolic attachments and increasingly open to the forever-changing nature of the reality including themselves, future work might more thoroughly advance and develop these kinds of intersections.

Korzybski's work anticipates, is consistent with, and to some extent informs the development of systems theory, and its origins in Claude Shannon's information theory, and Norbert Wiener's cybernetics, suggesting the possibility of a study focused on Shannon, Wiener, and also Bateson, along with pioneers of systems theory such as Ludwig von Bertalanffy and Ervin Lazlo, and also to Fritjof Capra, whose work on physics, systems, eastern philosophy, and ecological thinking pulls together mainy of the strands associated with Korzybski. The Chilean biologists Humberto Maturana and Francisco Varela come to very similar conclusions in their work on autopoiesis as Korzbyski arrives at in *Science and Sanity*, stressing the *structural coupling* between the map developed within the system and the environment that exists outside of the system, and the connections and relations between these two bodies of work would be a very significant area of further study. Niklas Luhmann's sociological study, based on Maturana and Varela's notion of autopoiesis, draws significantly on Korzybski's work as well, and is worthy of continued study. Chaos and complexity theories also hold much potential for further study, including Benoit Mandelbrot's fractal geometry, and chemist Ilya Prigogine's dissipative structures.

We likewise can imagine future research exploring how Korzybski's work relates to the field of communication, to communicology scholars such as Richard Lanigan, and especially to the media ecology intellectual tradition. Neil Postman's long association with general semantics, which includes his ten-year stint as editor of the general semantics journal *ETC*, would clearly be of interest, as would exploration of the Korzybski-connection regarding his colleagues, Christine Nystrom and Terrence Moran, the media ecology program that they created, and the students who came out of that program, such as Joshua Meyrowitz and Paul Levinson. Other media ecology scholars would also be worthy of further consideration, notably Walter Ong. As a few brief but telling examples, Ong provides solid arguments regarding the role that Learned Latin played (and subsequently, the role that print writ large played) in widening the split between knower and known. In a related way, scholars ought to consider at length the role that Korzybski's Structural Differential plays in giving visual values and orientations to the relations between the unseen event-level, the non-verbal level of experienced objects, and various levels of talk about abstracted objects, taking the objects and utterances and giving them graphic simultaneous representation. Scholars, too, might look to the "July 1944 Lecture Blackboard Notes" in which Korzybski gives graphic, iconic, and visual representation to many of his key ideas. Eric Havelock too would be of interest, as he discusses the fact that the verb "to be" is not used to represent passive status within the oral culture of ancient Greece, and only takes on that more abstract meaning after the introduction of the alphabet. Jack Goody's work on writing and the creation of lists, as well as more generally on literacy's impact on the organization of society, would also be of interest here, as would Harold Innis's various insights on the written word, and Robert Logan's arguments concerning *The Alphabet Effect*. Lewis Mumford was aware of Korzybski's work, and his grappling with the role of science and technology in society, as well as his writings on the preeminence of symbols in human existence, would be an excellent subject for further research.

Because Korzybski's work touches on so many different aspects of human life and knowledge, the individuals and topics we mention above represent nothing more than a preliminary scan of possibilities. And because, as Korzybski would remind us, there is always more to be said on a subject than we have already said, and because time does not stop and therefore new potential partners for "Korzybski and" study will continue to appear, the opportunities for continued research are all but inexhaustible. And we are confident that as such scholarship continues to unfold, it will become increasingly clear that Alfred Korzybski was one of the most important intellectuals of the 20th century, and for the 21st century as well.

REFERENCES

Anton, C. (2011). *Communication Uncovered: General Semantics and Media Ecology*. Fort Worth, TX: Institute of General Semantics.

Kodish, B. I. (2011). *Korzybski: A Biography*. Pasadena, CA: Extensional Publishing.

Korzybski, A. (2010). *Selections from Science and Sanity* (2nd ed.). Fort Worth, TX: Institute of General Semantics. Original work published 1948.

Korzybski, A. (2002). *General Semantics Seminar 1937* (3rd ed.). Brooklyn, NY: Institute of General Semantics. Original work published 1937.

Korzybski, A. (1993). *Science and Sanity: An Introduction to Non-Aristotelian Systems and General Semantics* (5th ed.). Englewood, NJ: The International Non-Aristotelian Library/Institute of General Semantics. Original work published 1933.

Korzybski, A. (1990). *Collected Writings, 1920-1950*. Englewood, NJ: Institute of General Semantics.

Korzybski, A. (1950). *Manhood of Humanity* (2nd ed.). Lakeville, CT: The International Non-Aristotelian Library/Institute of General Semantics. Original work published in 1921.

Lee, D. (1959). "Symbolization and Value," In *Freedom and Culture*. New York: Prentice Hall.

Seneca. (2002). *Epistles 1-65*. Translated by Richard M. Gummere. Cambridge, MA: Harvard University Press.

Spinoza, B. (1956). *How to Improve Your Mind*. Translated by R. H. M. Elwes, with Biographical notes by D. D. Runes. New York: Philosophical Library.

Strate, L. (2011). *On the Binding Biases of Time and Other Essays on General Semantics and Media Ecology*. Fort Worth, TX: Institute of General Semantics.

CHAPTER 2: KORZYBSKI AND GOTTFRIED LEIBNIZ[*]
Bruce I. Kodish[**]

It was the summer of 1921 and Alfred Korzybski,
traveling in California with his wife Mira, had been dreaming.

IN JUNE 1921, the publishing company E. P. Dutton brought out Alfred Korzybski's first book, *Manhood of Humanity*, in which he introduced the notion of time-binding, his new functional definition of human life, his initial effort in providing a foundation for a "science of man [humanity]."[1] In the book's final pages, he had presented a dream for the future of humanity, which seemed to expand upon some of the old Polish ideals he had grown up with:

> In humanity's manhood, patriotism—the love of country—will not perish—far from it it will grow to embrace the world, for your country and mine will be the world. Your "state" and mine will be the Human State—a Cooperative Commonwealth of Man—a democracy in fact and not merely in name...guided...by scientific men, by honest men who *know*.
> Is it a dream? It *is* a dream, but the dream will come true. It is a scientific dream and science will make it a living reality.[2]

How to bring about this dream? In the book, Korzybski had made an admittedly vague proposal for "the establishment of a new institution which might be called a Dynamic Department—Department of Coordination or a Department of Cooperation" (whether wholly governmental, or not, didn't seem quite clear). He wrote: "Its functions would be those of encouraging, helping and protecting the people in such cooperative enterprises as agriculture, manufactures, finance, and distribution."[3]

Now that *Manhood of Humanity* had been published, Korzybski wasn't planning to dwell on this or any other social, economic, or political applications of the time-binding notion. He hoped that others would do so. His need to figure things out in the most comprehensive way—what he called his "innate abstractness"—one of the main factors driving him to write *Manhood*—was still driving him. It was leading him now to explore and uncover the foundation of time-binding, its underlying mechanism.[4] Since he

27

seemed inclined to see the broadest theory as potentially the most practical, he had confidence that this might actually lead to some far-reaching social benefits.

What lay at the foundation of time-binding? It seemed to him that the very mathematical spirit that he had tried to apply in developing his definition of Man, exemplified time-binding at its best. He had given this spirit—the spirit of rigorous thinking—more attention in his original manuscript. But in the editing process, he had moved it into the background. In the published book, much of his discussion of mathematics had either been deleted or moved to an appendix or footnote. Now he wanted to move time-binding to the background—as it were—and to shift his focus to this mathematical side. He felt strongly that by digging into the foundations of mathematics and the physico-mathematical sciences, he would be digging to uncover the roots of time-binding itself.

Much of the deleted material was contained in a single manuscript of *Manhood* that he had loaned some time before to an acquaintance in New York City. Perhaps he still needed this draft for the work he anticipated doing. (With some difficulty, he finally managed to get it sent to him several months later.) Yet, he had also begun to find deeper issues in his theory that he simply hadn't written about or at least hadn't been able to treat with much clarity. He had already established that "Language no doubt is an essential instrument or vehicle of time-binding."[5] But how did it work to impede or improve progress? Perhaps there were problems with some of the language he himself had been using. How did this all relate to mathematics? His friend and mentor Cassius J. Keyser, Adrain Professor of Mathematics at Columbia University, had introduced him to the theory of dimensions and the theory of types. He felt that mathematical analysis using these and other approaches could "bring order in the confusion of wrong language and wrong logic in the affairs of men."[6] But how? In broad terms, he knew what he was aiming for. If *Manhood* contained his "special theory," to use an analogy with Einstein's work on relativity, he was now aiming to formulate a more "general theory." But what did he need to do to get there?

As an engineer with an especially strong practical bent, he expected his general theory to have application to people's lives—practical application that Bertrand Russell and Alfred North Whitehead, among other formulators in the foundations of mathematics, had not been able to demonstrate. Such a *practical* general theory was the thrust of the new book he was planning. He had already started to work on it before the spring publication of *Manhood*. John Macrae, Vice-President and managing head of E. P. Dutton, had an option to publish it. The book would deal with the dreams and ideals of Man and the problems of human happiness from Korzybski's peculiar mathematical perspective.[7] Korzybski had hoped to be able to get it out within four to five months (it would take 12 years) and already had a title— *When Dreams Become True: The Mathematical Theory of Life*.[8] (The evolving book's title would over the years undergo numerous changes to finally become *Science and Sanity*.)

The initial title referred to Korzybski's dreams but also alluded to the dreams of Leibniz. Among the many historical figures studied by Korzybski, Gottfried Wilhelm Freiherr von Leibniz (1646–1716) looms as one of his greatest conscious and acknowledged influences. Years later, he would include him (he spelled his name with a "t," i.e., "Leibnitz") in the list of those to whom he dedicated his second book. This was not only for Leibniz's discovery/invention (along with Newton) of the calculus, which over the years had so inspired Korzybski.[9] The dreams of Leibniz—various schemes and speculations Leibniz proposed over his lifetime to advance mathematics, science, and society—stirred Korzybski as well.[10]

Leibniz's Dreams

To what extent Korzybski knew of Leibniz's work before meeting Keyser remains unknown. But Keyser had referred to Leibniz and his dreams in his own writings. Undoubtedly by the summer of 1921, Korzybski had at least seen these references in his readings of Keyser's work. In Leibniz, Alfred sensed a kindred spirit and he went on to study Leibniz's life and work. Leibniz was born at the tail-end of the Thirty-Years War in Germany. Although he received a doctorate in jurisprudence and had been offered a university professorship, Leibniz spent most of his professional life in the service of German princes, first the Elector of Mainz, and then two successive Dukes of Hanover. These latter patrons deemed that the most significant task that Leibniz—one of the greatest intellects in human history—could perform was to write a chronicle of the Hanover family. (The family is now mainly known because of its connection to Leibniz.) In his 'spare time', among other accomplishments, Leibniz managed to invent the differential and integral calculus (independently of Isaac Newton), founded the disciplines of symbolic logic and analysis situs, i.e., topology (although he failed to develop either of these to any significant extent), and carried on extensive scientific-philosophical and diplomatic activities and correspondence throughout Europe.

Perhaps at least in part because of the era of European disharmony that he had been born into, Leibniz was obsessed with dreams of universalism and unification. One of his dreams was that of universal peace in Christian Europe. He had floated a scheme for unifying the Protestants and Catholics (at least in Germany) after more than a century of conflict since the start of the Reformation. The scheme never got off the ground. He also wanted to unify the various areas of knowledge. He wrote that "The entire body of the sciences may be regarded as an ocean, continuous everywheres and without a break or division."[11] He felt strongly that the sciences were the "greatest treasure of mankind."[12] In addition, his experience as a mining engineer in the Harz Mountains of Germany may have reinforced his conviction about the necessity of uniting theory and practice in order to gain the greatest benefit from this treasure.

As the Duke of Hanover's librarian, he had access to texts from all over Europe and even China. As an inventor cum mathematician cum scientist he had been stimulated and encouraged by his meetings with some of the age's best "natural philosophers." These experiences fed further dreams of the unification of the sciences and scientists. While living in Paris and visiting London, he had become a member of both the French Academy and the Royal Society of London. This inspired him to work at establishing other societies in Europe for the sharing and dissemination of scientific knowledge. In this regard, he helped found the Prussian Academy in Berlin and before his death in 1716, corresponded with Tsar Peter the Great, in an effort to found a Russian Academy in St. Petersburg.

Scientific unity could be promoted in other ways too. Leibniz dreamt of a universal encyclopedia. Even at the end of the 17th Century he was worrying about the effects of the "...horrible mass of books which keeps on growing" and "the indefinite multitude of authors."[13]

> ...[W]ith books continuing to increase in number, we shall be wearied by their confusion...some day a great, free and curious prince, a glorious amateur, or perhaps himself a learned man, understanding the importance of the matter, will cause to

undertake under the best auspices what Alexander the Great commanded Aristotle to do with the natural sciences,...namely that the quintessence of the best books be extracted and joined to the best observations, not yet written, of the most expert in each profession, in order to build systems of solid knowledge for promoting man's happiness. ...Such a work would be a most durable and great monument of his glory and constitute an incomparable debt which all mankind would owe him.[14]

Leibniz speculated that such a system could lead to new discoveries "...by examining each science with the effort necessary to discover its principles of discovery, which once combined with some higher science or general science (namely, the art of discovery), may suffice to deduce all the rest or at least the most useful truths without needing to burden the mind with too many precepts."[15]

Idols of the 'Mind'

A universal encyclopedia of knowledge and a general science of discovery would, in Korzybski's terms, necessarily accelerate the time-binding power of Man by helping to extend the methodology of science and mathematics to more and more areas of human life. First, however, a great deal of the 'deadwood' blocking the rate of time-binding would have to be removed from the 'tree of culture'. As Korzybski wrote in *Manhood of Humanity*:

> Metaphysical speculation and its swarming progeny of blind and selfish political philosophies, private opinions, private "truths," and private doctrines, sectarian opinions, sectarian "truths" and sectarian doctrines, querulous, confused and blind— such is characteristic of the *childhood* of humanity. The period of humanity's *manhood* will, I doubt not, be a scientific period—a period that will witness the gradual extension of scientific method to all the interests of mankind—a period in which man will discover the essential nature of man and establish, at length, the science and art of directing human energies and human capacities to the advancement of human weal in accordance with the laws of human nature.[16]

As Korzybski was not the first to hold such a dream of scientific and cultural advancement, neither was Leibniz. Sir Francis Bacon (1561-1626), had gotten there before. Bacon had championed the move away from dry medieval scholasticism toward the modern experimental study of nature. He had proclaimed that "Knowledge is Power" and had hoped to usher in "The Great Instauration"—a golden age of science-based progress. Before Leibniz, he sought to create a universal encyclopedia of knowledge. And he too had written about a general science, an art of thinking and discovery, that he hoped to advance. In his 1620 work, *Novum Organum,* he had presented this new system of thought, hoping to replace or at least expand on the logic of Aristotle. This would require recognizing and dealing with,

> Four species of idols [sources of error which] beset the human mind, to which (for distinction's sake) we have assigned names, calling the first Idols of the Tribe [intrinsic to general human nature, perception, etc.], the second Idols of the Den [intrinsic to each individual's idiosyncracies and training], the third Idols of the Market [related to language], the fourth Idols of the Theatre [related to doctrines and beliefs]."[17]

In *Manhood of Humanity* Korzybski had quoted at length from Bacon's discussion of these idols. Bacon's idols seemed to Korzybski to summarize some of the major impediments to human understanding and successful time-binding which characterized the childhood of humanity. To clarify the mechanism of time-binding, Alfred would need to make a less 'literary', more exact formulation of how the 'idols' of the 'mind' were formed.

The Dream of A Universal Language

The dreams of Leibniz, known as a 'rationalist', in some ways extended and refined those of the 'empiricist' Bacon. But for Leibniz, a mathematician, an intrinsic part of his dream included a proposal for a "universal language" or "universal characteristic" growing out of mathematics. Alfred, as a lover of mathematics and a good mathematical 'journeyman', seemed very much in tune with Leibniz here.

As early as Pythagoras and Plato, people had wondered at the 'miracles' of mathematics and seen it as a model for other areas of thought. By the 17th century significant parts of natural philosophy, i.e., the science of mechanics and astronomy, were beginning to yield to mathematical treatment with astonishing success. It surely seemed, as Galileo commented, that the Almighty had written the book of nature in the language of mathematics. Leibniz was convinced that "there is nothing which is not subsumable under number"[18] if we only knew how to do it. Number had exactness, and exactness—the inevitablility of correct conclusions—appeared as the holy grail. Why? Because when rightly understood it would lead to agreement—universal agreement.

Even the simple operations of arithmetic might in a certain sense be made more exact through mechanization. In pursuit of this, Leibniz had designed and built the first four-function calculator. Leibniz also found that in other areas of mathematics, operations could at least be facilitated by an apt notation, such as the symbolism that he designed for calculus (still used today).

Could anything like this be done for traditional logic and the even more inexact areas of knowledge and everyday language? Leibniz seemed to think so. As he put it in his 1677 essay "Preface To A General Science," his "universal characteristic" entailed developing a new language for the perfection of reason. This language would allow people to express themselves with the exactness of arithmetic and geometry. With it, arguments and errors would dissolve as conversation would come to resemble calculation. Possibility or pipe dream? Leibniz thought he could do it. But ultimately he didn't succeed in his long-term project of mathematizing everyday discourse. However, the vision did inspire a large portion of his work. His founding of the discipline of symbolic/mathematical logic, even though he was not able to carry it very far, is considered by many to be the closest he got towards the goal of a universal characteristic.

More than 100 years later, the English mathematician George Boole, formulated the first system of mathematical logic, in his 1854 book, *Investigation of the Laws of Thought*. (Boole expressed delight when he learned that he had in fact followed in Leibniz's footsteps.) According to Keyser, Boole's work initiated a revolution in mathematics and logic, by showing their deep relationship. Russell and Whitehead and others had built and were building upon it. Korzybski had had many discussions with Keyser about these developments and, as 1921 advanced, was immersing himself in this work. He felt and knew its importance. But the work—with its high level of abstractness—seemed remote and forbidding, not anything like a universal language that could be applied to everyday life. For example, from the elaborate and exotic apparatus of their algebraic symbology, Russell and Whitehead had spent several hundred pages in Volume I of *Principia Mathematica* simply getting to the point of showing how to demonstrate the truth of $1+1=2$. Alfred felt that there was something in what they had done, and in the other books he was studying, that *was* relevant for living life. He wanted to draw it down to earth—make it practical for the man, woman and child in the street.[19]

This was the project he was dreaming about and developing in the summer of 1921, as *Manhood of Humanity* was getting publicized. He wanted to topple if he could the idols that impeded people's ability to time-bind. He had accomplished the first step. People now had the formulation of time-binding by which they could clearly and consciously view themselves as time-binders. Mathematical logic and the exact physico-mathematical sciences seemed to hold the key for the next step—to liberate the time-binding mechanism.

In his new book, Alfred hoped he could bring to life an updated version of the dreams of Leibniz, Bacon and others. Building from the notion of time-binding and from the revolutionary new mathematics and science of the early 20th century, Korzybski was groping to construct a methodological foundation for a science of humanity. So far, he had worked most of his life as a troubleshooter—while growing up on his family's farm, later managing some of his family's business, then during the war as an intelligence scout and artillery inspector for the Russian army, etc. He was continuing his career of troubleshooting now, but on a much more general scale

NOTES

A Note on the Notes and Documentation:

"AKDA" in the reference notes below refers to what I have labeled the Alfred Korzybski Digital Archives, a digitized version of the thousands of microfilmed documents and letters housed in the Alfred Korzybski Archive at Columbia University's Butler Library Rare Book and Manuscript Collection in New York City. I could not have provided the details of factual narrative, excerpted here from the book *Korzybski: A Biography*, without the close and careful study of these and other archival materials now scattered amongst several different locations and individuals. The raw digitized pdf files I received from the Institute of General Semantics in 2005 (one pdf for each microfilm screen) required further digital processing by me to be of use. The individual pdfs were collated by me into larger files that correspond to the numbered microfilm rolls at Columbia and their corresponding hard-copy folders of documents. I have annotated a large proportion of these expanded pdf documents, which I hope will be of future use to other researchers interested in Korzybski's life and work. In the notation below, "AKDA 11.388" refers to the document numbered 388 in the sequence of digitized pages of microfilm roll number #11.

*Excerpted, and reworked for this book, from *Korzybski: A Biography*, © 2011.

** As an independent scholar, Bruce I. Kodish has specialized in studying, writing about and teaching the implications and applications of Alfred Korzybski's work and in exploring its history. Bruce has spent nearly seven years writing-researching the first book-length account of Korzybski's life and work, which contains many never-before-told details of Korzybski's extraordinary career. Bruce was a student and close associate of many of the foremost scholar-teachers at the Institute of General Semantics (IGS), including Charlotte Schuchardt Read, Allen Walker Read, Robert P. Pula, Stuart A. Mayper, Kenneth G. Johnson, Thomas E. Nelson, Susan Presby Kodish, and Milton Dawes, during the Institute's post-Korzybski but still quite korzybskian heyday in the final decades of the 20th Century. He served for many years on the staff of the IGS seminar-workshops and the General Semantics Bulletin. He received a PhD in Applied Epistemology/General Semantics from the Union Institute and University in 1996. With his wife Susan Presby Kodish, he wrote the renowned introduction to korzybskian general semantics, *Drive Yourself Sane: Using the Uncommon Sense of General Semantics*, recently published in its Third Edition. Susan and Bruce received the Institute's prestigious J. Talbot Winchell Award in 1998 for their "... many contributions severally and together to the wider understanding of general semantics as authors, editors, teachers, leaders."

[1] Time-binding consists of "the potential for each generation of humans to start where the last generation left off; the potential for individuals to learn from their own and other people's experiences; the potential to become aware of this ability; this allows for the formation of cultures and the ability to study

cultures, etc.; based upon the characteristic human ability, involving language and other symbolism, to transmit information across time." From the "Glossary" in Kodish and Kodish 2011, p. 217.

[2] Korzybski 1921, p. 199-200.

[3] Korzybski 1921, p. 200. See pp. 200-203 for more detail on Korzybski's Dynamic Department proposal.

[4] AK to C.J. Keyser, 6/20/1921. AKDA 11.335-338.

[5] AK to V.S. Sukthankar, 6/12/1921. AKDA 11.388

[6] AK to Keyser, 6/6/1921. AKDA 11.409-411.

[7] Key for Korzybski's practical endeavor was the fundamental view of mathematics that he shared with Keyser—mathematics, logic (ultimately included as a part of mathematics), and science were all—as Korzybski would bluntly put it—'man-made and nothing but.' But even as a human product, a form of language and human behavior, mathematics qualified for both men as the prototype of rigorous human thinking, "unsurpassed," as Keyser would write, "as means in the study of mind." [Keyser 2001 (1922), p. 412.] (Korzybski would designate the physico-mathematical sciences in this way as well.) Korzybski and Keyser thus represented a distinctly minority view about the foundations of mathematics, opposing the notion of the separation of logic/mathematics from psychology that Gottlob Frege and Bertrand Russell helped popularize. For Frege and Russell, mathematics did not reveal much if anything about human thinking. Following Frege, "psychologism" became a term of disapproval wielded against those like Keyser and Korzybski who *did not* accept that mathematics/logic was completely 'objective' and independent of human 'minds'. On the contrary, Keyser and Korzybski could be called 'psychologists', even 'grammarians', of mathematics—grammarians in the sense that Marshall McLuhan would later use the term, to refer to those concerned with the human, communicative effects (understanding, interpretation, agreement, and their opposites) of the variegated structurings of a medium, in this case the medium of mathematical language. See Strate.

[8] AK to Keyser, 6/6/1921. AKDA 11.409-411.

[9] "It is not an exaggeration to say that the calculus is one of the most inspiring, creative, structural methods in mathematics. There is little doubt that the analysis of the foundations of mathematics, and their revision, was suggested by a study of the methods of the calculus. *It is structurally and semantically [evaluationally] the 'logic' of sanity* and, as such, can be given ultimately without technicalities by the present $\bar{A}$*[non-aristotelian]*-system and semantic

[evaluational] training, with the aid of the Structural Differential [a training model of the experiencing process that maps how humans abstract, i.e., accumulate and transmit knowledge]." Korzybski 1994 (1933), p. 574.

[10] Indeed, Korzybski noted twice in *Science and Sanity* that the system presented in it implied a theory of universal agreement that would allow "the dreams of Leibnitz" to become "a sober reality." Korzybski 1994 (1933), pp. 52, 287.

[11] Leibniz, "The Horizon of Human Knowledge [After 1690]," in Weiner, p. 73.

[12] Leibniz, "Precepts For Advancing The Sciences And Arts" [1680], in Wiener, p. 33.

[13] Ibid., pp. 29–30.

[14] Ibid., p. 32.

[15] Ibid., pp. 39-40.

[16] Korzybski 1921, pp. 44-45.

[17] Bacon qtd. In Korzybski 1921, pp. 42. Although Korzybski did eventually have a great deal to say about language, his general theory would deal with all of the idols that Bacon mentioned, not just the ones of the Market (i.e., language).

[18] Leibniz, "Towards A Universal Characteristic [1677]," in Weiner, p.17.

[19] Leibniz, in expressing his dreams of 'universal agreement', etc., had imagined the possibility of somehow algebraizing 'thought', so that with a 'perfect' language, involving some kind of impersonal, formulaic, and step-by-step procedure (an algorithm), people could sit down and say "Let us calculate" in order to settle a dispute or work out a problem. Ultimately, Korzybski, in pursuit of Leibniz's dreams, would produce something quite different. Rather than a 'logical' algorithm, the educational and 'grammatical' (in the McLuhanistic sense) methods he produced—involving the Structural Differential and other techniques and devices that embodied his theory—seemed closer to a set of psycho-logical heuristics: behavioral guidelines for becoming more extensional (oriented to facts) and for reaching agreement with others at a particular time and place. (Billy Vaughn Koen defines a *heuristic* as "anything which provides a plausible aid or direction in the solution of a problem" but may remain "unjustified, incapable of justification, and potentially fallible." [p. 28] For Koen, heuristics constitute the core of engineering method, and indeed of all human methods of problem solving: "To be human is to be an engineer." [p. 7] Korzybski would likely agree.) Even in mathematics,

Korzybski would conclude that you couldn't have a 'perfect language'—at least one inherently free of all ambiguity—as Leibniz had seemed to suggest. Considering language as a joint product of abstracting human nervous systems, each individual would inevitably abstract differently and give different values to words and other symbols and events. Agreement had to be worked at by people in a given context [Korzybski 1994 (1933), p. 134]. Korzybski's heuristic approach to agreement and method—non-formulaic and personal—reflected this. To follow Korzybski's method you would have to internalize a set of standards and use them to self-reflexively inquire into your own reactions (linguistic and otherwise) and those of others—i.e., 'put them up' on the Structural Differential. From there new possibilities could emerge for modifying your reactions and adjusting to the reactions of others. (For more on the Structural Differential and other extensional devices and techniques developed by Korzybski and his students, see *Drive Yourself Sane* and, of course, *Science and Sanity* and Korzybski's *Collected Writings*.)

References

Keyser, C. J. (2001). *Mathematical philosophy: A study of fate and freedom.* Honolulu, Hawaii: University Press of the Pacific.

Kodish, S. P. & Kodish, B. (2011). *Drive yourself sane: Using the uncommon sense of general semantics* (3rd ed.). Pasadena, CA: Extensional Publishing.

Koen, B. (2003). *Discussion of the method: Conducting the engineer's approach to problem solving.* New York/Oxford: Oxford University Press.

Korzybski, A. (1921). *Manhood of humanity: The science and art of human engineering.* New York: E.P. Dutton & Company.

Korzybski, A. (1950). *Manhood of humanity* (2nd ed.). Lakeville, CT: The International Non-Aristotelian Library Publishing Company.

Korzybski, A. (1994). *Science and sanity: An introduction to non-aristotelian systems and general semantics* (5th ed.). Brooklyn, NY: Institute of General Semantics.

Merz, J. T. (1948). *Leibniz.* New York: Hacker Press.

Strate, L. (2007). "War and peace among rhetoric, grammar, and dialectics:

On Marshall McLuhan's the classical trivium." *EME: Explorations in Media Ecology,* 6(3), 221–226.

Wiener, P.I. (Ed). (1979). *Leibniz selections.* New York: Charles Scribner's Sons.

CHAPTER 3: KORZYBSKI AND FRIEDRICH NIETZSCHE

Zhenbin Sun

AT THE OUTSET, THERE are sharp differences between Nietzsche and Korzybski: the former is a distinguished critic of Platonic philosophy, a poet, philologist, and philosopher with an unusual style of writing, a thinker whose influence on Western intellectual history was not popularly recognized in the English-speaking countries until the 1960s, and a pioneer of the linguistic turn and poststructuralism/postmodernism, while the latter is a founder of general semantics, a builder of a "non-Aristotelian system" that tries to synthesize diverse areas of human knowledge, a scholar whose work gave rise to the "general semantic movement" in the 1940s and 1950s, and a practitioner of altering people's way of thinking and acting by changing their linguistic behavior. At a deeper level, however, Nietzsche and Korzybski share at least one common position, that is, to deconstruct the ancient Greek philosophical tradition as a basis of Western culture by illuminating the harmful pseudo-identity between the law of reality and the law of language. It is the deconstructive insight and function that marks both Nietzsche and Korzybski's contribution to contemporary scholarship. Many scholars have acknowledged this in similar ways. Foucault (1973), for example, believes that Nietzsche is actually the first thinker who not only treats language as a central issue of philosophy, but also deconstructs philosophy by displaying the identity between language and metaphysics.[1] Breazeale (1976) observes that Nietzsche is "practically and theoretically concerned with problems of language to a degree unparalleled among serious thinkers of modern times" (p. 301). Wilcox (1982), Schrift (1985), and Crawford (1988) argue that Nietzsche's theory of truth, value, and knowledge is inseparable from his philosophy of language. On the other hand, Ogden (1935) claims that Korzybski's work "presents a revolutionary thesis" (p. 82) as well as a wealth of materials that may "clarify a world view" (p. 84). Chase (1938) stresses Korzybski's "stubborn attempt to find out how words behave, and why meaning is so often frustrated" (p. 7). Postman (1988) characterizes Korzybski and general semantics as revealing the relationship between the world of words and the world of non-words as well as how people use words to abstract and symbolize reality.

41

This chapter is a comparative study of Nietzsche and Korzybski's thought on several philosophical and linguistic issues. It consists of four sections: the first one focuses on their critique of Greek metaphysics and their own worldview; the second centers on their deconstruction of logocentralism; the third explores how they understand the nature of language and its relationship to thought and reality; and the fourth inquires into their similarity and difference by comparing structuralism with poststructuralism. The chapter suggests that although Korzybski does not acknowledge Nietzsche's influence on studies of language, the latter actually sheds more light on the relationship between language, thought, and reality than anyone Korzybski does give credit to; compared to Korzybski's pragmatic endeavor in changing people's linguistic behavior, Nietzsche's philosophical investigation has been proved more powerful and far-reaching in altering people's way of understanding and coping with language; and in the final analysis, Korzybski can be said to be a promoter of structuralism and Nietzsche a forerunner of poststructuralism.

Traditional Metaphysics and New Worldview

In reading Nietzsche and Korzybski, one finds that they share interests in some basic themes, advance a number of similar ideas, and even employ the same key words.[2] Both of them, for example, apply new achievements of natural sciences to their own research; both take a psychological approach to philosophical and linguistic issues; and both seek for answers to theoretical and practical problems in light of mankind's nature. However, the first and foremost similarity is manifested in three respects: critique of ancient Greek metaphysics; analysis of the basic laws of logic; and discussion on the relationship of language to thought and reality.

As we know, Nietzsche's philosophical investigation is based on an inquiry into nihilism. "What does nihilism mean? *That the highest values devaluate themselves*" (Nietzsche, 1968, p. 9). By "highest values" Nietzsche means the ultimate substances, including Christian God and Plato's Idea, and all kinds of idealism that provide human life with basis, aim, and meaning. In Nietzsche's view, Greek philosophers, mainly Socrates and Plato, construct a metaphysical system. This system denies human senses and instinct as well as the changes of various things, making realities unreal; on the other hand, it creates "God", "Idea", and an eternal world, making unrealities real (Zhou, 1990, p. 29). The very nature of Greek metaphysics is nihilistic because it is based on three fundamental values: morality, reason, and being. While morality is promoted to control human senses in the name of God and reason is employed to replace mankind's instinct in the name of science, being is said to be the very essence and final cause of the universe. Yet, in Nietzsche's view, the senses and instinct are vital to life; to deny the senses and instinct is to devaluate the essence of life and to devaluate the essence of life is nothing but the root of nihilism. Moreover, nihilism features a "real world" "constructed out of the contradiction to the actual world" (Nietzsche, 1990a, p. 49). While the real world is characterized by such concepts as "stable," "organized," "perfect," and "transcendental," the actual world does not possess these features. To Nietzsche, the "real world" is nothing but "a *moral-optical* illusion" (1990a, p. 49); the actual world "is not an organism at all, but chaos" (1968, p. 379); "it is essentially a world of relationships" (1968, p. 306); it is full of energy (1968, p. 550); and it is always in a state of becoming (1968, p. 281). Since Greek metaphysics is against the very nature of human life and so of the actual world, it must lose its value. Nihilism is rightly the appearance as well as the outcome of Greek metaphysics' decline.

Like Nietzsche, Korzybski makes great effort to undermine Greek metaphysics. His book *Science and Sanity* (1941)[3] attempts to build up "a general science of man" (p. 38), or a non-Aristotelian system,[4] which not only embraces all human functions including language, mathematics, science, and "mental" ills (p. 38), but trains ordinary people to handle their thought and behavior with sanity in all walks of human life. To compare the Aristotelian system with his non-Aristotelian system, Korzybski draws a table of differences between the two. Among them, the following four factors are more crucial, they are: (1) the old system deploys subject-predicate methods, the new system employs relational methods; (2) the old one orients to permanent substance, the new one orients to ever-changing process; (3) the old stresses the sameness and two-valued causality/certainty, the new emphasizes the non-identity and infinite-valued causality/probability; and (4) the old focuses on static absolutism, the new centers on dynamic relativism (pp. xx-xxii). One can see clearly that all these factors are tightly related to the nature of the world as well as the relationship between thought/knowledge and reality/existence, a fundamental issue of special concern to ancient Greek philosophers. Because Aristotle's doctrine systematically and creatively summarizes and elaborates key propositions of metaphysics, epistemology, and logic and thus stands for the cream of ancient

Greek philosophy, Korzybski aims his critique at Aristotle's doctrine and argues that "for more than 2,000 years our nervous systems have been canalized in the inadequate, intensional, often delusional, aristotelian orientation" (p. xviii). And because over the past 2,000 years Western culture, particularly Western system of knowledge, has based itself on Greek philosophy, it is necessary for him to advance a non-Aristotelian system and bring a framework-shift to Western cultural tradition by reinterpreting the relationship between logic/grammar and thought/reality.

To be sure, Nietzsche and Korzybski's critique cannot be separated from their worldview. Where Greek philosophers believe in an ultimate substance, i.e., a capitalized being, that is final, absolute, and independent from but giving rise to various things, Nietzsche (1968) rejects such kind of being and suggests that becoming is the essence of the world and even the world itself; as a becoming the world is eternally changing, eternally self-creating, and self-destroying (p. 550). To be specific, becoming cannot be ascribed to atoms or monads (p. 380); it is incapable of being expressed by language (p. 380); it has no final state as its aim (p. 378); its state is not ordered (p. 379); it is beyond value (especially moral) judgments (p. 378); and its development is not lineal. In contrast, becoming is not the key concept Korzybski uses to interpret the essence of the world; instead, he claims that "The *event* is the most elementary notion" for the world consists of events rather than objects (p. 667). Unlike objects, which refer to space only and thus are three-dimensional, events refer to both space and time and thus are four-dimensional (p. 755). That means, events are associated with process (p. 205) and process is characterized by the infinity of the appearance and possibility of events (p. 206); moreover, events belong to the unspeakable objective level. To my understanding, nevertheless, becoming and event as two notions share the same features and can be used to define one another. While a world of becoming is a world of events, a world of events is full of changes and possibilities; while becoming is associated with and manifested in events, events display becoming as infinite activity and creativity.

Interestingly enough, both Nietzsche and Korzybski's worldview is shaped in promoting quantum physics (although they may not share the same definition of that term) while objecting classical mechanics. In thoroughly reviewing ancient Greek metaphysics, Nietzsche strongly criticizes atomism and mechanism. This is because where there are atoms, there would be an eternal unity; this unity provides constant with a base and gives metaphysics a home. According to Nietzsche, there are no such things as atoms, monads, and durable ultimate units in the world (1968, p. 380); what truly exists is, in his view, a cumulated center consisting of non-material but active quanta, and the relation among quanta is tensional and discontinuous (Zhou, p. 208). Because of the activity, tension, and discontinuity, the world is relational and always in the process of changing and becoming. On the other hand, when introducing the result of his investigation, Korzybski claims that the non-Aristotelian system he formulated is "the first to express the very scientific tendency of our epoch, which produced the non-Euclidean and non-Newtonian (Einstein and the newer quantum theories) systems" (p. 7). Elsewhere in his work, he emphasizes "repeatedly the 'organism-as-a-whole principle" (p. 101), which is against the traditional principle that treats the world as elementalistic, separated, static, and solid.

Critique of Logocentralism

Nietzsche and Korzybski's worldview may not be entirely revolutionary since ever-changing and process, as onto-cosmological concepts, have been stressed by philosophers such as Heraclitus and Whitehead. However, what differentiates Nietzsche and Korzybski from other scholars is the very fact that they systematically and critically review the laws of logic in terms of the aforementioned characteristics of the world, illuminating the metaphysical and linguistic implication of these laws as well as their physiological and psychological root. In deconstructing logocentralism, nobody's work is as enlightening and effective as that of Korzybski and especially Nietzsche.

Generally speaking, Nietzsche and Korzybski's review of logic focuses on three issues: the origin and function of logic, the essence of causality, and the problem of identity. Regarding the first issue, Nietzsche makes four points. First, logic comes not from transcendental principles, but from the need for survival. In order to make quick and necessary decisions or "to comprehend the actual world... to make it formulatable and calculable for us" (1968, p. 280), mankind has to transform complicated, changing, and different things into simple, fixed, and identical ones by means of certain tools. Second, these tools are originally images and words (1968, p. 275), which eventually change into regular formulas as they are repeatedly used "to classify phenomena into definite categories (1968, p. 280). Third, as a set of categories and formulas, logic is necessary for serving life-praxis; it functions well in facilitation and expression; thus, it is first seen as an effective tool and later recognized as truth (1968, p. 291). Fourth, logic becomes a vital method and component of metaphysics when it is normally employed to infer an eternal world and evaluate the actual world; consequently, logic is treated no longer as a tool for achieving an end, but as a measure of value upon which even the end is evaluated. "This is the greatest error that has ever been committed, the essential fatality of error on earth" (1968, p. 315).

On the other hand, the main point Korzybski makes about logic and its origin and function is that as the laws of thought, logic in fact represents "the relation between the structure of primitive languages and the structure of the 'philosophical grammar' formulated by Aristotle" (p. 200). By "primitive languages" he means those symbolic systems that fail to structurally reflect the changes, differences, and process of the world.[5] And by "philosophical grammar" he means the categories and formulas of thinking. In his view, what these categories and formulas do is to mislead people in understanding and acting upon the world. One may wonder in what way(s) logic and language mislead thinking and behavior. The answer can be found in Nietzsche and Korzybski's analysis of causality.

Causality is certainly an important law that people regularly follow when they try to understand an event, assuming that a subject is "responsible for something that happens and for how it happens" (Nietzsche, 1968, p. 296). Yet, Nietzsche claims that "There are neither causes nor effects" for an event actually appears as a "necessary sequence of states" that does not imply a causal relationship between them (--that would mean making their effective capacity leap from 1 to 2, to, 3, to 4, to 5)" (1968, p. 296); in other words, an event is itself both the cause and the effect. If the law of causality is simply "a deception" as Nietzsche labels it, why do people believe in it so consistently and for so long a time? He points out two main reasons: one psychological, the other linguistic. Psychologically, whenever mankind encounters something unfamiliar and thus feels disturbed or dangerous, he appeals to something familiar or experienced, which is associated with his "selected and preferred kind of explanation;" then, he thinks of the familiar as the cause of the unfamiliar since his explanation helps him cure his fear and gain control over the situation (1968, p. 297; 1990a, p. 62). Here we face a sharp contrast: while Kant treats causality as a transcendental category, Nietzsche sees it as mankind's oldest psychophysiological habit. Linguistically, the syntactic structure of subject-predicate leads people to assume a doer who and whose intention is the subject/cause and a deed that indicates the attribute and effect of the subject. In Nietzsche's words, whenever noticing something we always "seek an intention in it, and above all someone who has intentions, a subject, a doer: every event a deed" (1968, p. 294). To many of us, this is a very logical and natural way of thinking; but to Nietzsche, this is a great stupidity (1968, p. 295). For what really exists is nothing but events that unite doer-deed, cause-effect, and subject-attribute. He takes the following example to explain his point: lightning and flashing actually belong to the same event; yet, when someone says "lightning flashes," he is indeed separating flashing from lightning. He is so doing simply because the grammar he follows asks him to set a subject/cause for flashing and to think of flashing as the attribute/effect of lightning even though here he mistakes an active becoming as a fixed being (1968, pp. 288-289). Through this example Nietzsche argues that causality is derived not from the ultimate being but from our language; it is the grammar we follow that gives rise to causality.

Similarly, Korzybski rejects the traditional notion of causality since it is against the newer quantum mechanics and the structure of the world. Particularly, he makes the following points. First, causality originates in three factors: mankind's experience, the habits of thought, and the structure of language. Second, the cause-effect relationship is not an accurate reflection of the world, "but a rash limiting generalization from probability." Third, all events are serially related rather than causally connected. And fourth, in an ever-changing world not only is a supposed effect produced by many possible causes, but the relations of the antecedents are hardly to occur again (pp. 215-217). Apparently, the first three points echo Nietzsche's ideas, but do not gain the same detailed analysis that Nietzsche conducts. Thus, one can comprehend the three points by reviewing Nietzsche's theory. What interests us is the two authors' attitude toward "cause" and "effect." In the case of Nietzsche, although causality is useful in the early stage of mankind's survival and cognition, as a whole it is a vital error because it misinterprets the actual world and contributes to the formation of metaphysics and morality; hence, it should be abandoned. Korzybski, however, does not suggest the cause-effect category be given up completely, but replaced by an infinite-valued notion of causality. By "infinite-valued causality" he means: (1) for a given effect there are many causes rather than only one; (2) the cause-effect relation is bound to many possibilities, so we cannot assume an absolute origin or consequence; (3) there is no such kind of thing as the "same cause" or "same effect," the sameness comes from the nervous system's abstraction of the facts outside our skin. These ideas undermine traditional understanding of causality and develop Nietzsche's critique. But, one may ask: under the condition that Korzybski has believed the use of "cause" and "effect" in daily life leads to "a great deal of absolutism, dogmatism, and other harmful semantic disturbances" (p. 216), why does he reserve the cause-effect category? From the Nietzschean point of view, no matter how the infinite-valued notion is different from the two-valued notion, the contradiction between the connotation of causality and the nature of all events cannot be removed.

While the two authors do not have the same attitude toward causality, they do hold the same position on the notion of identity. It is safe to assert that the most insightful and powerful criticism of logic lies in Nietzsche and Korzybski's discussion of identity. This is the area where issues in ontology, epistemology, and logic are tied to language and fundamental problems can be convincingly (re)interpreted through grammatical rules.

Identity as a law of logic means that everything (either an object or a concept) is identical with itself, i.e., A = A. This is a necessary condition for making logical thinking and inferences (Nietzsche, 1968, p. 277): to understand a thing through a concept, one has to assume the thing remains the same in different spatial-temporal situations; hence, one can use the concept to deal with it in both psychological and behavioral ways. However, this condition is to Nietzsche fictitious because there are no identical cases or "nothing is really equal" in the actual world (1974, p.171) and "whatever is real, whatever is true, is neither one nor even" (1968, p. 291). Usually, Nietzsche reviews the meaning of identity through three terms: "same," "equal," and "even." We can understand them as stressing different respects of identity while maintaining the same concern: the first term focuses on the appearance of things; the second stresses the quality and quantity of things; and the third centers on the state of things. Since Nietzsche has described the world as eternally changing, creating, and destroying, it is natural for him to deny identity as an ontological and epistemological principle.

Of course, Nietzsche's criticism of identity does not stop at revealing what identity is not or how it is against reality. Instead, he further investigates its physiological, psychological, and linguistic origin. In the first place, he points out that the basis of logic is to make different things equal; this basis is itself illogical, meaning the laws of logic do not come from the realm of logic; and the root of logic can only be found in mankind's experience of dealing with daily problems. "Those, for example, who did not know how to find often enough what is 'equal' as regards both nourishment and hostile animals—those, in other words, who subsumed things too slowly and cautiously—were favored with a lesser probability of survival than those who guessed immediately upon encountering similar instances that they must be equal" (1974, p. 171). That is to say, identity is not derived from the nature of the world, but from mankind's will to equality and "*the will to equality is the will to power*" (1968, p. 277). In the second place, he reveals the psychological mechanism of making the unequal equal: first, our understanding of the world is based on our "inner experience," which is the function of memory and perception; second, memory refers to remembering, remembering is a process of assimilation and classification that emphasizes what is already familiar and experienced (1968, p. 289) while leaving out differences (1968, p. 274); third, perception is in fact the result of assimilation and equalization, the same ordering and equaling force the rules in our inside and outside experience (1968, p. 273); fourth, "In *our* thought , the essential feature is fitting new materials into old schemas (= Procrustes' bed), *making* equal what is new" (1968, p. 273). In the third place, he argues that all metaphysical and logical issues are generated not in an eternal substance, but in the language that mankind uses (1968, p. 303); as words create concepts, grammar creates logic. The two philosophical notions "subject" and "object," for example, come rightly from the two syntactical items "subject" and "object." To Nietzsche, it is because we believe in grammar and the grammatical subject that we believe in an absolute substance, be it "the soul," or "God," or "thing-in-itself" (1966, p. 67). Since grammar defines the necessity and legitimacy of the subject-predicate structure, we are trained or enforced to recognize an eternal and identical subject and its counterpart: an object of the same character. And as far as we want to communicate, we have to encode and transmit messages in terms of grammatical rules and consequently think of the ever-changing events as firm and simplified matters (1968, p. 306).

It is significant to mention that Korzybski's objection to identity is also based on the syntactic structure of subject-predicate and its function in thought and communication. He claims that the very nature of the logic formulated by Aristotle is a kind of philosophical grammar, which characterizes a primitive language (p. 89). In his view, the primitive language: (1) centers on a subject-predicate; (2) adds to the world of non-words what it does not have; and (3) is unable to correspond to the reality structurally. He argues that "From the use of a subject-predicate form of language alone, many of our fallacious anti-social and 'individualistic' metaphysics and *s.r.* [semantic reactions] follow" (p. 57). And in his eye, the law of identity exemplifies the problems growing out of the primitive language; it not only replaces the realistic non-identity with a false identity but also prevents sanity in knowledge, thought, and behavior. So, his general semantics treats identity as a primary issue.

Korzybski observes that in our schoolbooks we still preserve identity as the most fundamental law of thought, which is defined as "absolute sameness" or "everything is identical with itself" (pp. 194-197). As a matter of fact, however, there is no identity between (1) words and things, (2) different things, and (3) the "same" thing in different times or situations. For example, "one may not step in the same river twice, not only because the river flows and changes, but also because the one who steps into it changes too" (Johnson, 1946, p. 23). Moreover, because the meaning of words is determined by the context in which they are used and because no two contexts are exactly the same, "*no word ever has the same meaning twice*" (Hayakawa, 1978, p. 54). He further analyzes the reason behind the non-identity and thinks of it as threefold. First, what words amount to are statements on objects or events, and any statement is verbal in nature; yet, the nature of objects or events is empirical rather than verbal (p. ix). Second, the word that represents a thing is an abstraction of the thing, it leaves out "many important characteristics of the thing" (p. xxii) so as to maintain its sameness over time; however, "In a world of process and non-identity it follows that no individual, 'object', event, etc., can be the 'same' from one moment to the next" (p. xxxi). Third, words are elementalistic instead of relational, they split "what in actuality cannot be separated" (p. xxx); things like mind/body, emotion/intellect, and space/time are empirically and innately related to one another; it is in language that they are changed into isolated elements.

Then, why is the non-identity easily replaced in people's daily communication by the false identity? The answer, according to Korzybski, lies in the lack of discrimination between the "is" of predication, the "is" of existence, and the "is" used as an auxiliary verb (p. 93). Under this condition, he repeatedly stresses one point: as maps are not the territories they represent, "words *are not* the things spoken about" (p. 50); and more importantly, he promotes a set of extensional devices that people can utilize to make their semantic responses structurally match the universe. The devices include: Indexes—e.g., car_1, car_2, showing "the uniqueness of every person or event;"

Dates—e.g., Smith[1920], Smith[1940], reminding "changes over a period of time;" Etc.—e.g., "It is clear, soft, attractive, etc.," indicating "any statement can *not* cover *all* the characteristics of a situation;" Quotes—e.g., "reality," "reliable," designating "a term is not to be trusted;" and Hyphens—e.g., "space-time," "psycho-somatic," bringing "to awareness the interconnectedness of the complexities in this world" and "their inseparability" (Read, 1984, p. 69). The first two devices are directly aimed to solve the problem of pseudo identity.

In his study of Nietzsche and philosophy, Deleuze (1983) makes the following claim: "No one extended the critique of all forms of identity further than Nietzsche" (p. xi). This can be verified in both the width and depth that Nietzsche's theory reaches. In the history of Western ideas, Nietzsche is one of the first thinkers to criticize Platonic philosophy from a linguistic point of view. While other philosophers take the laws of logic for granted and base their own philosophy on these laws, he illuminates the physiologic root of causality and identity, traces their psychological character and development, displays their linguistic orientation, reveals their effect on the formation and function of Western metaphysics, and analyzes their vital influence on people's understanding of reason, truth, and knowledge as well as people's thought and action. Moreover, Nietzsche is probably also the first thinker who explores the key role that "is" plays in the development of Western philosophy. He points out that "is" not only changes differences into sameness, but also gives rise to the ultimate being: a metaphysical existence; although this being "is an empty fiction," since it was formulated by the Eleatics, change, mutation, and becoming have been "taken merely as proof of appearance" while unity, identity, substance, and cause are seen as the essence of the world; this concept is so powerful "for every word, every sentence we utter speaks in its favour" (1990a, pp. 46-48)!

Regarding the falsity of identity, Korzybski shares with Nietzsche similar understanding. Nevertheless, the focus of his critique is not on the root, character, development, and orientation of identity and its function in philosophy; instead, he is more concerned with how to free semantic reactions from the restraint of identity and make language use match or represent the nature of the world. As he asserts, the aim of general semantics is "of two kinds: (1) scientific, leading to a theoretical, general structural revision of all systems, and (2) purely practical, such as can be grasped and applied by any individual" who has gained some training in general semantics (p. 45). It is for fulfilling this aim that he advances a non-Aristotelian system to replace the

Aristotelian doctrine and creates the extensional devices to cure cognitive ills and linguistic wrongdoings, including the belief in identity. Apparently, the extensional devices mark a significant difference between Nietzsche and Korzybski: the former orients more to undermining Greek metaphysics through a critique of identity, the latter makes more efforts in achieving sanity by altering people's linguistic attitude and behavior. When scholars in the 1930s and 1940s still separated semantics from pragmatics and did not take language use into account of meaning, Korzybski had investigated language by tying together its meaning and usage. This demonstrates a significant insight and merit of his theory.

Language, Thought, and Reality

Up to this point, we should be able to realize that Nietzsche and Korzybski's worldview and criticism of logic is closely associated with their analysis of the very nature of language and its relationship to thought and reality. Yet, it is necessary to mention that in the case of Korzybski the nature and relationship is reviewed in terms of mankind's abstraction of the outside world and language's misleading to thought and behavior; in the case of Nietzsche, on the other hand, the nature and relationship is investigated in terms of the metaphorical development of language and the linguistic root of reason.

According to Postman (1988), "One of Korzybski's most interesting and fundamental creations was a model of the abstracting process" (pp. 139-140). This model refers to "the structural differential" in Korzybski's theory, suggesting that the way we understand the world is an abstracting process consisting of four levels of response. He takes "apple" as an instance to describe the process. The first level is the neurological response; at this level our senses are stimulated by an apple as a scientific object. The second is the perceptual response; at this level the specific object is transformed into an ordinary object by our lower nervous system. The third is the psychological response; at this level our higher nervous system changes the ordinary object into a mental picture. And the fourth is the verbal response; at this level the mental picture is defined and conceptualized by the term "apple" (p. 384). Korzybski explains this model through three points. First, each of the four levels of response focuses on a category: scientific objects, ordinary objects, labels, and descriptions (p. 406). Second, the last two levels involve language: while psychological response appeals to words, i.e., linguistic labels, verbal response unfolds along with concepts, i.e., intellectual judgments such as descriptions, inferences, and interpretations (p. 406). Third, abstraction takes place in both lower and higher orders: the former is to abstract objects by means of language and the latter is to review abstractions of objects through language (pp. 426-433).

Probably, his most concise explanation of the nature of the abstracting process is made in this passage: "we abstract whatever we and the instruments can; then we summarize; and, finally we generalize" (p. 377). Here all the three key words he uses, i.e., "instruments," "summarize," and "generalize" relate to language. While no abstraction is independent from a certain instrument, the most important one is language. It is language that directs abstracting: as far as we want to control over the world psychologically and semantically, we have to rely on language; even the meaning of the outcome of any other abstracting utilizing a different instrument is defined in language. Furthermore, since our response to, and eventually our knowledge of, the world of non-words is mediated and formulated by language, the objects we deal with do not appear as what they are in their original manner, but as what language projects them to us. As for summarizing, it refers to describing an object by filtering out many of its unique characteristics. When summarizing, we not only make the object simpler and thus easier for us to handle, but also fit it in the label we already have in hand. In so doing, an apple appears similar to many other apples and meets our definition of apple as a term. That means, to summarize is to inductively build up the similarity of objects at the expense of their differences. As for generalizing, it refers to interpreting various objects in light of the same character. When generalizing, we think of an object identical not only to itself in diverse spatial-temporal contexts but to other objects of the same category. In so doing, an apple changes from a kind of fruit into a symbol, which in turn stands for all individual apples no matter how different they are from each other. In other words, to generalize is to deductively ascribe objects the same attributes embodied in a term.

Since Korzybski believes that language is the primary instrument we use to understand and act upon the world, it is unavoidable for him to inquire into the nature of language and its relation to reality. Does the structure of language match the structure of the actual world? This is a question Korzybski repeatedly asks in his work. When contrasting and comparing the Aristotelian system and non-Aristotelian system, he actually describes the difference between two structures. To him, the world is dynamic, relational, diverse, ever-changing, non-lineal, four-dimensional, infinite-valued, etc.; yet, whenever we abstract, we order things at different levels, and the very nature of ordering is to abolish factual differences among things and to achieve metaphysical identification (p. 404). He argues that the way we abstract is determined by "the structure of language we habitually use" (p. xviii) and the "elementalistic, splitting, structural characteristics of language have been firmly rooted in us through the Aristotelian training. It built for us a *fictitious animistic world*" (p. xxx). What he suggests is that the structure of language is opposite to that of the world and its grammar leads us to (1) blur the differences between the world of words and the world of non-words; (2) ignore changes of the same thing over time; and (3) cut off the relationship of one thing to others. Under this condition, we should establish consciousness of our abstracting process and transform the structure of our language.

Regarding the relation of language to thought and reality, Nietzsche makes some original and enlightening points. Among others, the following one deserves special attention: knowledge is a function of metaphor; to know is to translate an unfamiliar situation into a familiar one. Generally speaking, Nietzsche uses the term "metaphor" in two senses: first, it means the linguistic identity of things that are actually not the same; and second, it regards any transference from one sphere to another (Schrift, 1985, pp. 374-375). The first usage can be interpreted as relating to the constitution of concepts and the second to the process of cognition. Undoubtedly, language consists of terms and many of them are thought of as names; as names they are used to designate classes of things; so, the process of naming is the process of constituting concepts. For example, we only see in real life individual leaves and no two leaves are exactly the same in color, size, and form. When using the word "leaf" to denote individual leaves, however, we omit all differences among them and put all leaves in one category, assuming they share the same character. In so doing, a word becomes a general name, i.e., a concept. As Nietzsche claims, "the concept 'leaf ' is formed through an arbitrary abstraction from these individual differences, through forgetting the differences; and now it gives rise to the idea that in nature there might be something besides the leaves which would be 'leaf'—some kind of original form" (1982, p. 46). What he tells us here is that there exists an essential gap between "leaf" as a symbolic reminder and as a physical matter; the former is indeed a metaphor of the latter.

Then, how does metaphor create knowledge or make knowing possible? Nietzsche answers this question by introducing a model of three-stage transformation: it starts from a nerve stimulus, which is transformed into a mental image: first metaphor; in turn, the image is imitated in a sound or word: second metaphor; and finally, the sound or word is reformed into a concept: third metaphor (1968, p. 275; 1982, p. 46). "In this series of metaphorical translations (nerve impulse-image-sound/word-concept), what Nietzsche isolates is an expressive transference through four experiential spheres: physiology, intellect, acoustics-linguistics, and abstraction. Each is marked by a selective, creative carrying over from one 'language' to another" (Schrift, p. 375). That means, to know is to project our experience formed in one sphere to a thing in another sphere; our past experience measures this thing and gives meaning to it; once we complete transferring the thing from one sphere into another, we announce we have gained knowledge of it. Even the most metaphysical notion of being, says Nietzsche, is derived from the human experience: to breathe (quoted in Schrift, p. 375); thus *Knowing is nothing but working with the favorite metaphors*" (Nietzsche, 1990b, p. 51).

One can compare Nietzsche's four experiential spheres (ES) to Korzybski's four abstracting levels (AL) through the following table:

Nietzsche	Korzybski
ES1: a stimulus — *leaf*	AL1: a particular object — *apple*
ES2: a mental image — *picture of a leaf*	AL2: an ordinary object — *apple*
ES3: a sound/word — *"leaf"*	AL3: a psychological picture — *apple*
ES4: a concept — *"leaf"*	AL4: a verbal definition — *"apple"*

This table indicates that: (1) both models refer to mankind's cognitive process consisting of four steps; (2) both start from an objective thing (be it an event or object) and end at a conception of the thing; (3) both recognize a mental picture of the thing as a bridge between the thing and its conception; (4) the former includes a word but lacking "lower nervous centres" which produce the ordinary object, and vice versa. Closely looking at the two models, however, the difference is not too substantial to be compatible. According to Korzybski, the "ordinary object" grows out of the lower level of abstraction; its distinctive features have been left out while its similarities to other objects are spotlighted. It becomes "ordinary" because it has been treated as a familiar and hence repeating as well as fixed impression. This familiar, repeating, and fixed impression is what Nietzsche means by a "mental picture." The second step is necessary in transformation or abstraction, but not exclusively human since some animals could form such kind of object as well. It is the third step (i.e., the higher level of abstraction) that differentiates mankind from animals. While on the surface a sound/word may not be the same as a psychological picture; the two are in fact interchangeable for a word is nothing, according to Nietzsche, but "The image of a nerve stimulus in sounds" (1982, p. 45). So, even though the two authors employ different terms, the two models of transformation/abstraction express some similar ideas.

Certainly, besides recognizing the similarities of the two models, one should also be aware of their differences. The most significant difference lies in the fact that Korzybski's model stresses that the abstracting process is conducted at both non-verbal and verbal spheres, while Nietzsche's model focuses on the genesis and development of language. As mentioned earlier, Korzybski suggests that abstraction can proceed in different orders; the lower order starts from a real apple as a scientific object and ends at a concept of apple. But, we can also start abstracting from the word "apple" as a stimulus and end at a statement of apple as a word; moreover, our abstraction can also start from the statement of "apple" and end at an evaluation or interpretation of that statement. In these cases, we use language to think about language instead of objects. The purpose for Korzybski to address the diverse order of abstraction is twofold: (1) to display the self-reflexive character of language as a kind of instrument of abstraction; (2) to reveal a vital source of mental illness or insanity. Those who confuse the world of words and the world of non-words are by and large not aware of the different levels and orders of abstraction. On the other hand, Nietzsche's model indicates that language originates in the stimuli of the world mankind lives in; those stimuli that repeatedly occur become fixed psychological images; when these images are marked by and bound to certain recognizable sounds, words come into being. As the function of these words is to serve mankind's survival and communication, their connection to what they symbolize is merely metaphorical (i.e., arbitrary). Moreover, words are not transformed into concepts until their meaning and relation to objects and other words is carefully examined and popularly recognized. That means, in the beginning or for quite a long period of time language is used under the conceptual level; and Nietzsche does believe concepts and reason come much later than language (1968, p. 220, p. 283; 1982, p. 482).

It is important to note that Nietzsche's examination of reason is of special significance for it reveals the effect of language on thought in general and on philosophy in particular. As a philosophical concept, reason is in many cases used interchangeably with rationality and has three usages and three features as well. First, it refers to a metaphysical entity. Second, it designates a set of epistemological rules and measures. And third, it means the human faculty of making right choices. According to the classical or foundationalist model of reason or rationality, those beliefs, decisions, and acts that are rational must be "universal, necessary, and determined by rules" (Brown, 1988, p. 5). Here, by "universal" it is meant that based on the same information different individuals will arrive at the same solution to the same problem. The "necessary" refers to a logical connection between premises and a conclusion. And the "rules" are laws that regulate thinking and establish relations between propositions. Although Nietzsche deliberately gives no definition to reason (and many other philosophical concepts), we can still see he covers all the three usages of this term in different contexts; and his critique of the traditional notion of reason can be comprehended along with the three features of rationality.

First of all, where does the universal come from? To seek a universal solution, one has to assume a universal starting point plus a universal way toward the universal solution. And all these universalities are not possible unless there is something constant. It is this constant that makes things themselves and identical with themselves over time and space. Only under this condition can these universalities be achieved. According to Nietzsche, reason amounts to this condition because reason is "a source of revelation concerning being-in-itself" (1968, p. 311) and "the road to the constant" (1968, p. 317). What he argues here is that ontologically reason manifests itself as a metaphysical entity and epistemologically reason leads beliefs, decisions, and acts to the constant universality (or the universal constant, they are the same thing).

Secondly, why is the necessary necessary? To think rationally is to think logically, and to think logically is to follow and express the scheme of premise/cause-conclusion/effect; "we cease to think when we refuse to do so" (Nietzsche, 1968, p. 283). The necessary is necessary because it is the only way for us to think correctly and to communicate effectively. In short, "*rational thought is interpretation according to a scheme that we cannot throw off*" (Nietzsche, 1968, p. 283). However, even though the necessary is necessary, it is not rational from the viewpoint of Nietzsche's perspectivism because it displays the constraint of language, which misrepresents the actual world, harms the will to power, and prevents people from being aware of the constraint of language.

Finally, what are the rules? They are the laws of causality, identity, and contradiction. These laws are more important than the universal or the necessary for the latter is derived from these laws. It is by following these laws that we classify various things into "subject," "attribute," "activity," "object," "substance," "form," etc., as well as put them in organized relations. However, these laws do not come from the transcendental world; instead, they are rooted in the language mankind creates and uses; in the final analysis, they are nothing but grammatical rules. In other words, although reason in some people's view belongs to a metaphysical entity, that entity in Nietzsche's eye cannot be separated from language; actually, reason itself lives in language. "'Reason' in language—oh, what an old deceptive female she is!" Nietzsche (1990a) says, "I am afraid we are not rid of God because we still have faith in grammar" (p. 48). Furthermore, even if reason can be thought of as a human faculty, the faculty is not free. Insofar as grammar functions, reason can only dance with the shackles of language.

Structuralism vs. Poststructuralism

In his *Science and Sanity* Korzybski does not mention Nietzsche at all; yet, rather than anybody else he gives credit to, from Socrates and Wittgenstein to Newton and Freud, Nietzsche turns out to be the real forerunner of Korzybski's critique of the Aristotelian logic. Korzybski claims that what makes his theory different from the Aristotelian system is his denial of the law of identity and that his general semantics is based on this denial. Several decades before the publication of his work, however, Nietzsche already conducted the same sort of critique and went even further and deeper.[6] From the above discussion, one can see the two writers' similarities in their differences as well as their differences in the similarities. Putting every similarity and difference together, we can observe one tension that ties and explains all the philosophical and linguistic issues this chapter has reviewed, that is, structuralism versus poststructuralism.

Although structuralism and especially poststructuralism as labels for two types of theory, mode of thinking, or thought movement are vague and controversial, they do represent the primary themes, sharp arguments, and significant achievements of the Western intellectual history in the 20th century. Generally speaking, structuralism (1) emphasizes a pattern of homologous relation between things, (2) thinks of the structure as a self-closed system governed by universal rules, (3) seeks objective truth, coherent laws, and scientific status; as a contrast, poststructuralism (1) stresses discontinuity, heterogeneity, innovation, plurality, and openness, (2) thinks of the world as fragmentary and determined by local rules, (3) rejects any standard models of foundation, truth, objectivity, certainty, and system (Piaget, 1970, Frank, 1989; Best & Kellner, 1991).

Korzybski does not claim he is a structuralist; but the term that appears frequently in his *Science and Sanity* and bears extreme importance is "structure." He intentionally interprets reality, language, and knowledge in terms of this concept. As he asserts, language has a structure, which affects semantic reactions (p. xxxvi); "*structure, and structure alone*, is the only link between languages and the empirical world" (p. 50); moreover, "structure, and structure alone, becomes the only possible content of knowledge, and the search for structure, the only possible aim of science" (p. 449); eventually, "only an analysis of *structural* and *semantic reactions*," particularly his non-Aristotelian system, can free people from their "unconscious copying of animals" (p. 37).

Up to this point, nobody will doubt Korzybski's firm belief in structure. Then, what does it mean by "structure?" It "can be considered," says Korzybski, "as a complex of relations, and ultimately as multi-dimensional order" (p. 20). Here "relations" and "order" refer to the ordered connection between elements and the position of the structural elements in a system. Obviously, a system cannot live without elements and the relations and order; furthermore, the relations and order are determined by "structural laws." In this situation, "the only possible aim of science is to discover structure," including the elements, relations, order, and laws of a certain system (p. 29). *Science and Sanity* can be thought of as a structuralist work because it features the principles of structuralism. Methodologically, it respectively treats the world, language, knowledge, and even the nervous system as a structure (or system, the two terms are interchangeable in both structuralism and general semantics); ascribing them the same nature and hence making them reducible to several simple foundations. Ontologically, it suggests that as the world is objective and independent from mankind, our language and knowledge could be objective as well if they structurally correspond with the world; in this sense, the truth-value of language and knowledge is derived from the objective world. Epistemologically, it sees science as the most desirable form of knowledge and seeking and formulating laws as the sole aim of scientific study; whenever structures exist, laws function; knowledge is desirable, possible, and dependable only under the condition that laws are objective, universal, absolute, and eternal.

Three themes exemplify Korzybski's structuralist position and his difference from Nietzsche. They are changing objects vs. static structures; scientific laws vs. humanistic interpretations; and organized and trained speeches vs. free and open speeches. First of all, when Korzybski criticizes the Aristotelian system as well as the false-to-fact identity between language and reality, he shares Nietzsche's viewpoint, emphasizing the relational and changing character of all events or objects. But, when he insists on a structural correspondence between language and reality under the influence of early Wittgenstein (1990), he goes back to traditional metaphysics not only because he still wants to seek the meaning of language from a source that is transcendent to language itself, but also because he has to assume the structure of both language and reality is fixed and dependent on each other; otherwise, objects will be immeasurable and language unmanageable. However, later Wittgenstein (1968) replaces the notion of structural correspondence with the notion of language game. For he realizes that the meaning of language comes not from its relation to logical/grammatical rules or reality, but from its use in real life; the actual use of language is itself a form of human life. Here Wittgenstein stands on the side of Nietzsche, emancipating language from the metaphysical jail and resuming its pragmatic identity. As a matter of fact, at the time Korzybski published his *Science and Sanity*, Wittgenstein's *Philosophical Investigation* had not come out yet. Suppose Korzybski had a chance to read Wittgenstein's later works, would he give up the notion of structural correspondence between language and reality? The answer is most likely negative partially because of his belief in scientific laws.[7]

Needless to say, objectivity is the principle and essence of science. While the world is objective, the laws of the world are objective; consequently, science as the discovery and formulation of objective laws is objective, too. According to Korzybski, "objective" means events or objects are self-established, regulated by their own rules, and independent from mankind's will; furthermore, the laws of the world are objective because they are eternal and universal, those "laws" that "cannot stand the test of invariance" are not laws but "local private gossips, true for one observer and false for another" (p. 286). Surely, when talking about scientific laws, Korzybski does not completely separate them from language for he recognizes laws are represented in the form of scientific "statements." Nevertheless, as far as these statements structurally tally with reality, they are in Korzybski's eye universal truths instead of individual interpretations. By stressing the objectivity of science and laws, he actually denies the function of intersubjectivity (in Husserl's sense[8]) and the openness of laws to intellectual discourse (in Foucault's sense[9]). However, Kohn (1962) convincingly demonstrates in *The Structure of Scientific Revolutions* that science is in nature institutional discourse; while scientific laws appear as paradigms, scientific progress is nothing more than paradigm-shift. In other words, both scientific laws and scientific studies are subject to discursive interpretations, which are neither objective nor universal, but intersubjective and local. This is what Nietzsche suggests in various ways.

To better understand *Science and Sanity,* one should not underestimate the significance of its extensional devices. In addressing the characteristics of his non-Aristotelian system, Korzybski repeatedly claims that this system could work as a handbook training people how to achieve sanity and solve social problems by correctly using language. The major tools he invents to accomplish this task are the extensional devices. Seen from the general semantic point of view, these devices perform two main functions. Theoretically, they demonstrate the structural correspondence between the world of words and the world of non-words. And practically, they make the world of non-words verbally graspable and the world of words meaningful and valuable. What the devices imply is that there is only one correct way to use language; any speech that does not apply them will result in semantic falsity and mental illness. Consequently, the structure of language and the extensional devices are closed to active conversations, their contexts, and speakers' will, emotion, and attitude, while the diverse possibility, rich productivity, and necessary creativity of language and its use is denied, discouraged, and destroyed. As mentioned earlier, it is insightful for general semantics as a theory of meaning to take into account a speech act, which brings up infinite possibilities. But, since structural correspondence is the ultimate principle and criterion, a speech act could not play the key role in the relationship of language to thought and reality; instead, it is imprisoned in a highly closed and restricted area.

In contrast, Nietzsche is neither a structuralist nor a poststructuralist. Rather, he is a forerunner of poststructuralism, exerting great influence on leading poststructuralists such as Derrida, Foucault, and Deleuze.[10] As we know, there were two dominant topics in 20th century Western philosophy: one is the linguistic turn, the other is the end of philosophy.[11] Both of them aim to critically review the Platonic philosophy by exploring its metaphysical root in language and the future direction of philosophy after the linguistic turn. Nietzsche is definitely a crucial thinker who initiates discussions of these two topics. Regarding the first topic, he claims that language not only results in logical laws, but contains the secret of metaphysics. His analysis of how "is" as a word becomes a philosophical concept (being) and a law of thinking (causality) powerfully illuminates the relationship between language, logic, and metaphysics. He even suggests that a particular way of philosophizing is guided by the language philosophers employ. "It is highly possible," therefore, "that philosophers within the domain of the Ural-Altaic languages (where the concept of the subject is least developed) look otherwise 'into the world,' and will be found on paths different from those of the Indo-Germanic peoples and the Muslims" (1966, pp. 27-28).[12]

Regarding the second topic, Nietzsche proposes to replace negative nihilism with positive nihilism. The former designates the decline of Greek metaphysics, which compiles a set of false values (ultimate substance, absolute truth, transcendental principle, etc.), while the latter recognizes becoming and appearance as the essence of the actual world. Clearly, the shift from the Platonic philosophy to a new philosophy is the process of reversing values: as a world of becoming was changed into a world of being and appearance was devalued in traditional metaphysics, the new philosophy should see the world the other way around or resume what has been turned upside down; the world *is* what appears rather than what is behind the appearance and appearance *is* becoming because becoming is inventive, appearance is fluxional (1968, p. 319; pp. 330-331).

Perhaps, we can use Nietzsche's saying to generalize the meaning of and difference between negative and positive nihilism, that is, "Everything is false! Everything is permitted" (1968, p. 326)! What is false? Every value of traditional metaphysics is false. What is permitted? Every appearance or every state of becoming is permitted. Here "permitted" can be construed as "possible," "understandable," and "valuable." It refers to the universe as well as mankind and his relation to the universe. In other words, as the world is a world of becoming, its appearance in mankind's consciousness must be diverse, ever-changing, relative, and incomplete. That means, (1) mankind's understanding of the world shares the same characteristics of the appearance; (2) hence, every interpretation of the universe and mankind is permitted; (3) accordingly, ultimate, absolute, and exclusive explanation of the world is impossible and deceptive. So, Nietzsche's saying bears both ontological and epistemological significance. Actually, his perspectivism unfolds along with the above vein.

In Nietzsche's proposal, a new philosophy is based on five fundamental innovations and one of them is that a perspective theory of affects should center the place of epistemology (1968, p. 255). This theory holds:

> That the value of the world lies in our interpretation (—that other interpretations than merely human ones are perhaps somewhere possible—); that previous interpretations have been perspective valuations by virtue of which we can survive in life, i.e., in the will to power, for the growth of power; that every evaluation of man brings with it the overcoming of narrower interpretations; that every strengthening and increase of power opens up new perspectives and means believing in new horizons—this idea permeates my writings. The world with which we are concerned is false, i.e., is not a fact but a fable and approximation on the basis of a meager sum of observations; it is "in flux, as something in a state of becoming, as a falsehood always changing but never getting near the truth: for—there is no "truth." (1968, p. 330)

In Zhou's (1990) view, at least five points are made in this passage. First, knowing is evaluation or interpretation; interpretation is multiple and mankind's interpretation is just one of all possible interpretations. Second, interpretation is perspective, which associates with horizon, a particular point of observing; that is to say, knowing is always bound to and restrained by the point of observing. Third, the center of perspective or the subject of knowing is mankind's instinct for survival, the will to power, and emotional impulse. Fourth, the view of the world derived from perspective is not truth, but virtual appearance. And fifth, perspective is fluxional rather than static; it is enhanced as the will to power increases (p. 143).

Nietzsche's philosophy has two distinctive features: holistic and human-centered. It is holistic because it treats issues in ontology, epistemology, logic, ethics, aesthetics, religion, and language as interrelated rather than isolated problems. It is human-centered because it investigates these issues through a consistent and thorough framework, i.e., mankind's will to power instead of the aim of Being, God, or Idea. Accordingly, he appreciates ever-changing and various appearances since they stand for creation and innovation as the essence of the universe and human life. He encourages the Dionysian and favors the philosophers in the pre-Socratic period since the Apollonian dominates the Platonic tradition and makes Western culture imbalanced. He thinks the value of the world lies in mankind's interpretation since the meaning of the world manifests in human reactions to the universe. He supports the diversity, relativity, and development of interpretation since knowing is in nature limited, varied, and from local perspectives. All these ideas inspire poststructuralists and are developed in their writings.

Certainly, Nietzsche's understanding and employment of language is a part of his philosophy and vividly displays the two features. He argues that the very function of language lies not in its correspondence to reality, but in its activity in human life; and the use of language is itself a dimension of human life. He values very much the multifunction and creativity of language for each use of "language has the potential for reinforcing or changing the existing value moment, both within the system of language itself, and at the same time, in the broader cultural or moral systems of people" (Crawford, 1988, p. xiv). He believes in the diverse meaning, metaphorical character, and openness of language for "The life of actual language consists in multiplicity of meaning," and "To relegate the animated, vigorous word to the immobility of a univocal, mechanically programmed sequence of signs would mean the death of language" (Heidegger, 1991, p. 144). He suggests resuming the poetic, aphoristic, and emotional genre of language for "The profoundest and least exhausted books will probably always have something of the aphoristic and unexpected character of Pascal's *Pensees*" (1968, p. 229). Moreover, he composes his philosophical work in a non-philosophical mode by using aphorism for our thoughts come to us not merely in the logical manner. He seldom makes a definition to the key words of his writings, but shows their meanings in different contexts; and he uses various rhetorical means such as mockery, self-sneering, analogy, ellipsis, and leap to escape from the restriction of logic/grammar (Zhou, 1990, pp. 113-114). In short, he draws a sharp dividing line between his philosophy and Platonism or linguistic metaphysics not only in theory but in practice as well.

CONCLUSION

The most common point between Korzybski and Nietzsche is that both stress the importance of relational elements and change as the key to systems. This makes them share similar worldview and pay great attention to language and its connection to thought and reality. On the other hand, the most crucial difference between the two authors lies in their ultimate concern: in the case of Korzybski it is the eternal structure and science as the real knowledge of the structure; in the case of Nietzsche it is mankind's relation to the universe and his will to power. While Korzybski tries to emancipate thought and behavior from the Aristotelian system, the eternal structure and scientific laws in his non-Aristotelian system become an ultimate substance and an absolute knowledge; hence, change is not the end, but the means to that structure and knowledge. In this sense, his critique of Aristotelian logic is not complete and thorough and his general semantics includes the remainder of Greek metaphysics, to say the least. This problem is shared by all structuralists and leads to poststructuralists' objection. On the contrary, Nietzsche asserts that becoming is the nature of the universe and mankind and that mankind is different from animals because of his will to power. It is the will to power that makes mankind always on the way to change, innovation, and difference. Seen from the Nietzsche's point of view, the meaning and value of human life and the world is manifested in becoming and diversity as well as established through and displayed in language; as the voice of the will to power, language does not believe any rule or accept any regulation from a transcendent authority; it is its own master and dwells in all fields that it could possibly open up.

NOTES

[1] According to Wolfgang Stegmuller (1970), Franz Brentano, Nietzsche's contemporary and countryman as well as teacher of Husserl and Freud, also investigated the relationship of language to basic metaphysical categories.
[2] Examples include "nervous system;" "quantum;" "mathematics;" "organism;" "animalistic;" "consciousness;" "physiology;" and "relational." In addition,

Korzybski even shares Nietzsche's tone when both of them talk about philosophers.

[3] Throughout this paper all quotations from Korzybski refer to this book.

[4] By "system" Korzybski means "a complex whole of coordinated doctrines resulting in methodological rules and principles of procedure which affect the orientation by which we act and live" (p. lix).

[5] According to Korzybski, the only scientific or non-Aristotelian language is the one that adopts the extensional devices he promotes; therefore, all languages people use in daily life are primitive languages.

[6] *The Complete Work of Friedrich Nietzsche*, an authorized English translation, was published by Macmillan in 1911. It is valuable to know whether or not Korzybski had read Nietzsche before working on his general semantics.

[7] It is highly important to keep in mind that by "scientific laws" Korzybski means not only laws in physics, chemistry, mathematics, but laws in mankind and society as well.

[8] As Duranti argues, "Husserlian intersubjectivity includes a mode of participation in the natural and material world that does not even require an immediately perceivable human presence." See his "Husserl, Intersubjectivity and Anthropology" (*Anthropological Theory*, 2010, no. 1-2, 16-35).

[9] Lessa summarizes Foucault's definition of discourse as "systems of thoughts composed of ideas, attitudes, courses of action, beliefs and practices that systematically construct the subjects and the worlds of which they speak." See her "Discursive Struggles within Social Welfare: Restaging Teen Motherhood" (*British Journal of Social Work*, 2006, no. 2, 283-298).

[10] It does not matter whether or not these thinkers label themselves as a poststructuralist as far as they share Nietzsche's critique of Greek metaphysics.

[11] The two edited books: *The linguistic turn* (1967, University of Chicago Press) and *After philosophy* (1987, The MIT Press) present leading philosophers' arguments on the two topics.

[12] In this sense, the Sapir-Whorf hypothesis is an echo of Nietzsche's suggestion.

REFERENCES

Best, S., & Kellner, D. (1991). *Postmodern theory*. New York: The Guilford Press.

Breazeale, D. (1976). The word, the world, and Nietzsche. *The Philosophical Forum*, 6 (2-3), 301-320.

Brown, H. (1988)). *Rationality*. London & New York: Routledge.

Chase, S. (1938). *The tyranny of words*. Brace, NY: Harcourt.

Crawford, C. (1988). *The beginnings of Nietzsche's theory of language*. New York: Walter de Gruyter & Co.

Deleuze, G. (1983). *Nietzsche and philosophy* (H. Tomlinson, Trans.). New York: Columbia University Press.

Foucault, M. (1973). *The order of things*. New York: Vintage Books.

Frank, M. (1989). *What is neostructuralism* (S. Wilke & R. Gray, Trans.). Minneapolis: University of Minnesota Press.

Hayakawa, S. (1978). *Language in thought and action*. New York: Harcourt.

Heidegger, M. (1991). *Nietzsche* (D. Krell, Trans.). New York: Harper Collins Publishers.

Kohn, T. (1962). *The structure of scientific revolutions*. Chicago: University of Chicago Press.

Korzybski, A. (1941). *Science and sanity*. Lancaster, PA: The International Non-Aristotelian Library Publishing Company, The Science Press Printing Company, Distributors.

Johnson, W. (1946). *People in quandaries*. New York: Harper & Row, Publishers.

Nietzsche, F. (1966). *Beyond good and evil* (W. Kaufmann, Trans.). New York: Vintage Books.

Nietzsche, F. (1968). *The will to power* (W. Kaufmann, Trans.). New York: Vintage Books.

Nietzsche, F. (1974). *The gay science* (W. Kaufmann, Trans.). New York: Vintage Books.

Nietzsche, F. (1982). *The portable Nietzsche* (W. Kaufmann, Trans.). New York: Penguin Books.

Nietzsche, F. (1990a). *Twilight of the idols.* (R. Hollingdale, Trans.). New York: Penguin Books.

Nietzsche, F. (1990b). *Philosophy and truth*. (D. Breazeale, Ed. & Trans.). Atlantic Highlands, NJ: Humanities Press.

Ogden, R. (1935). Book review. *The Philosophical Review*, XLIV (Jan.), 82-84.

Piaget, J. (1970). *Structuralism* (C. Maschler, Ed. & Trans.). New York: Harper Torchbooks.

Postman, N. (1988). *Conscientious objections*. New York: Alfred A. Knopf, Inc.

Read, C. (1984). General Semantics. In M. Morain (Ed.) *Bridging worlds through general semantics* (pp. 63-72). San Francisco: International Society for General Semantics.

Schrift, A. (1985). Language, metaphor, rhetoric: Nietzsche's deconstruction of epistemology. *Journal of the History of Philosophy*, 23 (July), 371-395.

Wilcox, (1982). *Truth and value in Nietzsche*. Washington D.C.: University Press of America.

Wittgenstein, L. (1968). *Philosophical investigations* (G. Anscombe, Trans.). New York: Macmillan Publish Co., Inc.

Wittgenstein, L. (1990). *Tractatus logico-philosophicus* (C. Ogden, Trans.). London & New York: Routledge.

Zhou, G. (1990). *Nicai yu xingershangxue* [Nietzsche and metaphysics]. Changsha: Hunan Jiaoyu Chuban She.

CHAPTER 4: KORZYBSKI AND CHARLES SANDERS PEIRCE
Isaac E. Catt

GENERAL SEMANTICS IS SAID to have "important intellectual allies: pragmatism, social constructionism, structuralism, phenomenology, and others" (Cole). Communicologists no doubt subsume these "allies" under the summary rubric of semiotic phenomenology. A partial list of philosophers and human scientists who explicitly synthesize these different but related traditions in such a manner would include Charles Sanders Peirce (1958), Ernst Cassirer (1953-1957/1925, 1996, 2000/1942), Wilbur Marshall Urban (1929, 1939), Roman Jakobson (1990/1956, pp. 69-79), Maurice Merleau-Ponty (1962/1945), Michel Foucault (1970), Pierre Bourdieu (Catt, 2006), Hubert Alexander (1972/1967) and Carlo Sini (1993; 2009). The list of contemporary scholars in America who explicitly call themselves communicologists and who have contributed significant publications in this vein includes Richard L. Lanigan (1988, 1992, 2007, 2010; ICI website at communicology.org), Frank J. Macke (2010), Deborah Eicher-Catt, (2010a, 2010b; and Eicher-Catt and Catt, 2010), Jacqueline Martinez (2008, 2011), Andrew R. Smith (2002, 2005), Kristin Langellier (2004), Eric Peterson (2010), Igor Klyukanov (2010), and Isaac E. Catt (2010, 2011, 2012; also see Catt and Eicher-Catt, 2012), all of whom conduct research in semiotic phenomenology.

Scholars have routinely credited these connections to General Semantics in one form or another (Rappaport, 1955; Bois, 1963; Read, 1983; Anton, 2008; Strate, 2009; Eicher-Catt, 2010b). Moreover, prominent Alfred Korzybski Memorial Lectures attest to the broad, and some might say generous, interpretations given to General Semantics (for example, Sebeok, 1981; Montagu, 1982). Alfred Korzybski (1933/Preface to the Third Edition, 1948) himself invited these comparisons by demarcating semiotics and General Semantics, even while associating with pragmatism, and explicitly indicating his respect for C. S. Peirce.

Minimally, these readings through various philosophical frameworks, and over a long period of time, attest to the quality of General Semantics as a movement and the endurance of its ideas. However, some claims regarding these inter-paradigmatic intellectual relationships have largely remained at the level of flirtation, as though breaking the ice by suggesting a date might lead to a dangerous romance or, perhaps, termination of a gratuitous infatuation. After all, every flirtation ends once the object of the game is taken too seriously. In fact, the game depends on no follow-through; or, if a different but similar metaphor is preferred, the reverie cannot be made real without a change in conscious communication.

Already a risk has been taken here; for to challenge the game or the dream as such is to break the spell of ataraxy, the *illusio*, as Pierre Bourdieu would have it, the fabrications we silently perpetuate as tacit consciousness in order to maintain our perhaps too casually held beliefs (see Catt 2000; 2001a; 2001b; 2006 and 2010 for an interpretation of Bourdieu's cultural communicology.) I proceed, however, on the assumption that there are other critical readers who, like me, are curious about what General Semantics really has to do with postmodern discourse and how Peirce might be related to it. There are many paths that could be taken to rupture the reverie and get down to business. The one I have chosen is not a zero sum game.

I propose to compare the philosophies of communication at work in Alfred Korzybski's General Semantics and semiotic phenomenology with particular attention given to C. S. Peirce. The interpretation is influenced by both of these human scientists from the very beginning of my task. First, there is much more to be said than I can possibly say here; *etc.* applies. I intend, in fact, to limit my discussion severely, to provide an introductory sketch, a mere outline that is intended to suggest possibilities for further elaboration. Second, I am comparing a Peircean influenced semiotic phenomenology to Korzybski within my own philosophy as a context for both. It is General Semantics and semiotic phenomenology as envisioned by me; Catt's Communicology contextualizes the whole (2000, 2001a, 2001b, 2003, 2006, 2008, 2010, 2011, 2012; Catt and Eicher-Catt, 2010, 2012). This statement is by way of taking responsibility for my interpretations, while not pretending to speak for other communicologists. Furthermore, it is necessary to generalize in order to philosophize; some abstractions of discourse are necessary. A multi-ordinal world is the fate of perception and expression, listening and speaking, and inhabiting discourse as a cultural body. As should become evident, this is an interpretation of discourse already latent in Korzybski and Peirce.

To make sense of the task ahead I employ a traditional theory construction term that, with the notable exception of Edwin Hersch's *From Philosophy to Psychotherapy* (2003), is seldom used these days: *paradigm*. This will provide a means for systematic discussion, and it will reflect the influence of General Semantics and semiotic phenomenology all along the way. Contrary to Thomas Kuhn (1962), however, I shall not argue for a single encompassing paradigm, the positivist's fantasy of integrated theory where language ostensibly mirrors reality. Nor do I argue, on the other hand, for a pointless relativism in the guise of intellectual diversity where everybody's narrative is equally valid and true, with the consequence that a theoretical commitment is never made. Not only is it not a zero sum game; it is not a mere game. Coherent theory is required to truly understand something, anything in fact, because all facts are contextual. The neo-positivist position (like that of some contemporary versions of cultural studies) is built upon implicit truth conditions, and the "facts" are presumed to be the requisite bricks mortared one to another to produce a theory. Contrarily, I maintain, "there are no facts without a frame" (Catt and Eicher-Catt, 2010, p. 25). Therefore, my concept of a paradigm is a step back from research practices (especially the interminable fascination with methods that seems endemic to a technological age) to create a net for making sense, to paraphrase Merleau-Ponty's definition of a concept (2002, p. 53). For theory construction in the human sciences, which is precisely what Korzybski and Peirce were up to, a paradigm commences with philosophical assumptions or meta-theory.

We move in what Gregory Bateson calls a dependent hierarchy (Wilden, 1987; Catt, 2003). (Recall that Korzybski was an important influence on Bateson's theory of communication.) The hierarchy is like a pyramid or a ladder where each higher rung serves as the environment for the preceding one, the bottom rung being the source of the greatest constraints on the ascending order of abstraction and the highest rung being the source of greatest complexity. The highest rung makes the most assumptions (see an elaboration of this idea applied to networks of discourse in Catt and Eicher-Catt, 2010). This is similar to the General Semantics' view expressed in S. I. Hayakawa's (1973, chapter 10) notion of a "ladder of abstraction," which should not be mistaken for an argument against abstraction. The General Semantics case was never against abstraction, the ability for which defines human intellect. The argument was against "dead-level" abstracting (Johnson, 1946, pp. 270-282), where we get stuck on a rung of the ladder and forget the inter-dependency of the hierarchical structure. Hierarchy is intrinsic to the reality of the scientific universe, just as Korzybski emphasized in his many discussions of order in *Science and Sanity* (1933). The point, of course, is to know the location of a construct on the ladder, so as not to become lost in the fog of practices sans theory or theory sans practices, a form of dead-level abstracting in either case. So, descending the ladder is movement from extant *practices* of everyday life and research or *methods* that amount to specifications of methodology; to *methodology* that provides a general framework for conduct in everyday life and research; to a *model* that is a shorthand representation of a theory and depicts the ideal condition of its "truth;" to *theory* that describes the relation of the paradigm's discourse to "reality;" to the *meta-theory* or philosophy on which the entirety depends. This can be depicted as follows:

THEORY CONSTRUCTION TERMS IN A PARADIGM FORM A DEPENDENT HIERARCHY

Practices
(procedures or method, *modus operandi*)

Methodology
(general framework for conduct of every day life as well as research)

Model
(represents what happens when or if necessary and sufficient conditions occur)

Theory
(relation of discourse to "reality," definition of truth)

Meta-theory
(philosophy: ontology, epistemology, logic, axiology)

Theory construction terms are individually and collectively specific to the paradigm and its community of subscribers. *Importantly, members of the paradigm community may not be fully conscious of the fact that their views place them in a paradigm(s) to the exclusion of alternative perspectives.* For instance, higher learning often legislates a point of view while ostensibly merely describing reality. In this way, dubious or even absurd information is sometimes transmitted in uncritical aphorisms, such as: "It is impossible not to communicate;" "Communication is a skill;" "Messages are used to generate meanings;" etc. (see Porter and Catt, 1993; Catt, 1995; Catt and Eicher-Catt, 2010; Catt, 2010, 2011). Repressed is the fact that research and pedagogical practices at the top level are an abstraction of the whole. (Yes, theory is more concrete than method! See Polanyi, 1966; 1969; Innis, 2002). Concrete experiential grounds are located at the bottom level. Codes of conduct are tacit in all behavior, including research. (For a postmodern example, this is a recurring thematic of Bourdieu's Communicology; see Catt, 2006.) To think otherwise is to assume that vacuous perception brings nothing to its object and that *forms* of objects inhere within their intrinsic qualities, a point not only opposed by Korzybski and Peirce, but by the great philosopher of culture, Ernst Cassirer (1953-1957/1925, 1996, 2000/1942). In truth, theory always precedes practices, a tacit level of consciousness (Polanyi, 1966). Theory is first a preconscious experience and only secondarily a formal descriptive act (Catt, 2011). These are, of course, two interrelated levels of consciousness realized and actualized in the perception-expression doublet that is the ground of discourse. As Merleau-Ponty indicated, expression accomplishes perception (1962/1945, Chapter 6). Yet, the expression is recursively productive of perception (Cassirer, 1942).

The top level of the hierarchy is always more complex than it appears because of the paradigm's typically implicit presuppositions, namely, the four dependent levels upon which practices stand. Meta-theory imposes the greatest constraints on the ascending levels, but may remain relatively unconscious, pre-conscious or conscious at the level of practices, depending on the degree of reflexivity built into the theory and the recursivity of the methodology. For example, the top level is relatively unconscious in most positivist-oriented research, regardless of whether qualitative or quantitative data analysis is employed. This is because the social science paradigm (information theory or the message focus dominant in communication study) presupposes itself as the solitary and exclusive standard for determination of the truth about its subject matter. So-called "data-based" or "reality-based" research epitomizes this sort of legislative, autocratic reason (Bauman, 1992, pp. 116-125; Catt, 2008, 2011, 2012).

Perhaps inevitably, there is a dominant community whose members tacitly seek to impose their paradigm view, judging all others by their standards. These standards are the taken-for-granted reality that is exempted from criticism. Particularly, the meta-theoretical presuppositions of a dominant paradigm are deeply held and deeply buried; the underlying philosophy is naturalized and above reproach. As Kuhn indicated, it takes a scientific revolution to upset the system of belief; a major paradigm shift is hard fought ground. A new paradigm is criticized, above all else, for its unacceptably "strange" vocabulary; it is made to appear strange against the implicit yet familiar standard discourse of the dominant view. Redundancy is more highly valued than entropy, though the latter is the source of new ideas. More often than not, new paradigms are objects of fear and trepidation, and steps are frequently taken to blot them out, often by means of not so subtle local politics. Mediocrity of accomplishment in organizational and institutional life is often sustained on this foundation. These matters are highly relevant here, because both semiotic phenomenology and General Semantics radically challenge the prevailing discourse, often produce unexpected controversy, and are not infrequently pronounced deceased intellectual movements by passersby whose motives may not be entirely self-conscious.

Theory and research in the social and human sciences may generally be understood from a paradigm point of view. A given paradigm (neo-positivism, hermeneutics as narration or performance, structuralism, and post-structuralism-semiotics, phenomenology, or semiotic phenomenology, etc.) may be comprehended in depth, and paradigms may be compared and contrasted through the theory construction terminology of the paradigm approach that I propose.

Now, make no mistake, I am arguing, perhaps counter-intuitively, that *practices are the abstractions for which our sets of philosophical presuppositions or meta-theories are the concrete grounds.* Here, I use the term concrete as a synonym for *eidos*, which refers to the *whole*. In this limited sense, I subscribe to the philosophy of Johann Wolfgang von Goethe as interpreted by Ernst Cassirer (1953-1957/1925, 1996, 2000/1942). Support for this perspective may also be found in Carlo Sini (1993) and Robert Innis (1994, 2002) and before both of them Peirce (1958). In Cassirer's particular departure from neo-Kantianism, "the whole is the truth" (Lofts, 2000, p. 169). This view is not entirely excluded where the concept of practices is of paramount concern, for example in Bourdieu (1990; Catt, 2000, 2001a, 2001b, 2006, 2010) and Sini (2009), for the reason that a practice is but the tip of an iceberg. Life (*Lebenswelt*) philosophy and the concept of symbolic formation are not at extreme opposites when it is realized that *empirical* practices are normally built from implicit but cognizable *eidetic* grounds and are devoid of meaning in their absence. Likewise, of course, the *eidos* lacks substance without *empirical* enactment (for an important application of these ideas see Polkinghorne, 2004). In this precise sense, nascent meaning (*form* = sufficient condition) precedes a message (*sign* manifestation = necessary condition), as perception (semiotic code) is the pre-consciousness of every expression (phenomenological experience), and inversely. Of course, this is precisely opposite the positivistic instrumental conception of discourse: the simplistic idea that messages may be used as instruments to generate meanings. This is the dominant view of communication advocated, for example, by the National Communication Association that can be found at (http://www.natcom.org/nca/Template2.asp?bid=531.html). Recall that Korzybski's general argument concerns *semantic* pollution of the human environment, the source for which is always to be found in our philosophical presuppositions! Remember too that Communicology refuses to accept the prevalent *logos* as the only acceptable version of rational discourse (Lanigan, 1994; Eicher-Catt and Catt, 2008, 2010; Catt, 2006, 2008, 2011).

The phenomenon *communication* is at issue and especially the assumptions we tacitly make about the *experience* of this phenomenon whether in our everyday or scientific practices. Predominantly, the study of communication in the United States has *presupposed* its object of inquiry, the repression of which has all but precluded a serious science of discourse (Eicher-Catt and Catt, 2010). Communicology arises, in part, as a response to this unacceptable condition, just as Peirce and Korzybski challenged the positivist's uncritical allegiance to classical assumptions concerning theory and language.

Having set the stage with a paradigm perspective that is already informed by Korzybski and Peirce, my reader will hopefully be satisfied with a brief look at some of the most important considerations as the paradigm view is deployed. Let us begin this short journey with a comparison of Korzybski and Peircean semiotics on the philosophy of communication, that is, meta-theory. Any paradigm's meta-theory minimally consists of ontology, epistemology, logic, and axiology. In the human sciences, where philosophic concepts bump up against the real world, these traditional branches of philosophy are interrelated as the eidetic ground for subsequent ascent into theory, model, methodology, and practices or methods, respectively. We enter, then, into a comparison of two paradigms of communication, General Semantics and semiotic phenomenology.

META-THEORY OF COMMUNICATION

Ontology

What are human beings and what is the relation of communication to the humane? Arguably, this is the area of Korzybski's greatest contribution;

certainly it is his earliest. In *Manhood of Humanity* (2008/1921), he proposes that the worlds of plants, animals, and humans differ. Plant life involves the physico-chemical bindings of nature; animals are space-binders who are condemned to autonomous existences in the *now*, because they do not have a *mind* for time. Gregory Bateson (1972, p. 160) also spoke to this in vivid terms, distinguishing creatures that "eat to live," "the highest human," from the rather more rough humans who "live to eat," and animals that "eat *and* live," because that is their lot. Distinctive to human being is the capacity to learn, to change and pass knowledge on to future generations. Only humans are time-binders. Moreover, only humans can change their experience of time. That fact has become increasingly transparent as technologies of information continue to alter consciousness. Importantly, Korzybski observes that the human capacity is revealed as a *synthesis* of the physical-natural world in which physico-chemical-binding occurs, the movement in space that limits other animals, and, ultimately, the space-time that marks embodied personhood. For humans, it is all of the above, and then some.

For Peirce, like Korzybski, the haecceity of an object of perception does not inhere in the qualities presumed to exist as substance, essence or self-identity of the object, per se. A person is a *token* that is, in some significant sense, the replica of a *type*. The token is not necessary but is "necessarily possible" (Deledalle, 2000, p. 12). What could be called the *tone* of the self is not directly knowable. The attribute that uniquely identifies something, even a person, is its triadic relation. The tone may be considered "Firstness," the token "Secondness," and the type "Thirdness" (Peirce, 1958, para. 313). A sign is definitional of consciousness. Thus, "a sign is something which stands to somebody for something in some respect or capacity" (Peirce in Buchler, p. 99). A person is just such, a sign.

As sign, the person is a triadic relation of quality, fact, and thought. Quality or Firstness (self tone) can only be inferred; it is only knowable indirectly. Quality is a "sheer possibility" of Secondness or fact, the empirical dialogic relation that allows us to conceive of its possible constituent parts (self-other tones). Yet, their relation possibilizes both Firstness and Secondness, tone and token, in Thirdness or type. This admitted interpolation of Peirce for present purposes allows us to see the self as a sign, the other as a sign and both within consciousness considered as *the becoming of the sign* or, simply, *signifying* (Peirce in Buchler, 1955/1940, pp. 74-79). Of direct relevance to the issue of ontology is the identification of Thirdness with thought, and, in particular, of thought with the experience of time. Peirce (Buchler, p. 95) elaborates:

> It seems, then, that the true categories of consciousness are: first, feeling, the consciousness which can be included with an instant of *time*, passive consciousness of quality, without recognition or analysis; second, consciousness of an interruption into the field of consciousness, sense of resistance, of an external fact, of another something; third, synthetic consciousness, *binding time together*, sense of learning, thought. (My italics)

Thought, as conceptualization, is a sense of time. Binding time requires typification or, in other words, what we assume to be "real," as object or part, requires an "ideal," or concept of whole (see Hardy's interpretation of Cassirer, 2006). Ashley Montagu (1982) was entirely correct to associate culture with Korzybski's ontology of time-binding, because culture is essentially an experience of time. Peirce and Korzybski are using the same terminology: "time-binding" in the latter, "binding time together" in the former. Peirce (Buchler, p. 97) surmises his third category by stating that: "This is the consciousness that binds our life together. It is the consciousness of synthesis."

Also vital to the General Semantics account is the post-Cartesian idea that affect and intellect are inseparable. Korzybski's focus is non-A, and particularly on non-elementalism relevant to this point. He is critical of the contrived abstractions and bifurcations of beings from the wholeness of their lived-worlds. Peirce, as well, presents the sign as a *manifestation* of consciousness, which consists in a synthesis of the affective, behavioral and cognitive as the normal order of experience.

Along the way, Korzybski advocates as well an inherent interrelationship of stability and change. This reciprocity is evident in many ways, for example, in the substance of processes and the processes of substances that together comprise reality. Likewise, the nonverbal layers that belie our verbal capacities similarly interact with them to form our *beings* as empirical and eidetic creatures. Korzybski understands that consciousness is layered. We are creative, productive beings capable, Bateson (1972, 279-308; 1942, pp. 81-97) would say, of "deutero-learning" (also see Anton, 2003, pp. 127-152). However, the main concern in General Semantics is to engineer a better human being by better correlating the supernatural or spiritual (semiotic) with the nonverbal reality that lies beneath words (pre-logical experience). The linguistic structures of the former must be made to comply with the nonverbal or preverbal structures of the latter.

That is not the case with Peirce. Rather, the nonverbal has to be understood as an iconic step on the way to the verbal sign, which is its destiny. The very purpose of thought is to induce belief and that of belief to be realized in habits of mind that are formed *in* and *as* signs, and are inconceivable apart from them. The only thought that could ever occur is a *signifying event*. Though, of course, when we consider the person as a sign object, the inference of an icon is itself dependent on an indexical sign, and that upon the further inference of the symbolic sign. The human being is a tri-relative phenomenon of life.

Here, the Peircean ontology of *objects* (there are other types of signs) consists of sign relations: icon, index and symbol. These are respectively *signifying relations* of familiarity, contiguity and continuity (see Deledalle, p. 121). *Familiarity* I interpret to be the level of the person, *contiguity* the social level, and *continuity* culture. I have addressed continuity above; culture transmits itself as time. Contiguity is social contact; society is formed intersubjectively in shared space. Time-space is a synthesis in conscious experience; that is, signs are embodied. The binding of time to space is a function of the realized sign. Therefore, that which we name the human is a synthesis of the semiotic (cultural) and the phenomenological (embodied) in the shared experience of the social matrix (see Eicher-Catt on Sapir's Communicology, 2011; and Ruesch and Bateson, 1951). Peirce states: (Buchler, p. 249) "the word or sign which man uses *is* the man himself . . . man is a sign [sic]." He (p. 249) also says that, "man is conscious, while a word is not . . . men and words reciprocally educate each other [sic]." Or, Deledalle (2001, p. 105) simply puts it: "Peircean semiotics is a semiotics at once of representation [cultural experience], of communication [social experience], and of meaning [personal experience as enactment of the whole]." (Bracketed terms are mine.) He concludes that: "Communication is thus a concrete individual action, an event of and in history; it defines the sense of every act of the same type in a given system of signs . . . The enactment is at the meeting point, always social, of the three paths of the sign" (p.106).

Epistemology

What counts as knowledge and what is the relationship between the knower and the known in these paradigms? This question is contingent on the ontological premise, because knowing is an experience of a knower. According to Korzybski, the nature of human being is *structurally* similar to the nature of the world discovered in physics and chemistry by use of precise mathematical tools. Science has discovered the processual, ever-changing relativity of reality, and that contradicts the static substance orientation of Aristotle, Euclidean geometry, and Newtonian physics. Identities of anything and everything, including human beings, are now inconceivable apart from their *relations*. In fact, it is impossible to *perceive* phenomena alienated from their systemic nests. Yet, the linguistic tools we have inherited do not account for this flux of things. To the contrary, the Western language is anachronistic, tied to the past by an uncritical linguistic history, and thus shackled to an outmoded reality. General Semantics seeks a better symbolic system. *Extensional* devices and techniques exercised at the pragmatic, behavioral level are expected to alter our archaic *intensional* ways of knowing (Korzybski, 1933, pp. 135-136).

Knowledge as shared consciousness is made better by Korzybski, the engineer of the *Manhood of Humanity* and sometime therapist of *Science and Sanity*, by re-cognizing the semantic system and making it better aligned with the reality of things as science understands them in modernity. At first glance, this appears to be the episteme of positivism so characteristic of Korzybski's era. However, things are not quite that simple. General Semantics and phenomenology arose, in large part, as strong reactions to positivistic thinking. Korzybski is critical of the notion that reality can be accurately *reflected*, at least by use of the inherited linguistic structure. Implicitly, he recognizes the power of language to *construe* reality and to thereby mislead us in our attempts to attain communication with others. The first object of knowledge must be the structure of language, the perceptions it delimits, and its behavioral effects. The relation of knower to the known inheres in the use of language. As a practical matter, the relationship can be improved. This begins with the recognition that "all our deeper knowledge must be, and can never be anything but, hypothetical . . ." (Korzybski, 1951, p. 201). Korzybski's epistemology is a reflection on the reflexive condition of language as it functions to filter the relations of persons to their worlds. In other words, knowledge is inherently circular because of language (Korzybski, 1951, p. 200).

In Peirce as well we witness the circularity of knowledge, which I have elsewhere said (Catt, 2001a, 2003, 2006, 2008, 2011), is a recursion of communication to knowledge and then information. In other words, information requires knowledge to be perceived as such, and knowledge requires communication to be meaningful. In the Peircean system, this is a movement from sign "object" to "representamen" to "interpretant" (Peirce in Buchler, p. 99). This may be considered, in the postmodern context, as an originary (using a term borrowed from Merleau-Ponty) critique of information theory, where information is alternately obfuscated with either knowledge or communication. Oddly, both the ontological and epistemological significance of the *experienced phenomenon* of communication are repressed in dominant, contemporary, empiricist-positivist accounts of communication. By their own admission, these accounts are message-information focused and presume communication to be a mere vehicle of thought. Ironically, this disciplinary practice in American communication studies substantially diminishes the significance of its own undertaking. Understood as mere information exchange, that is, the message-perspective, the phenomenon "communication" lacks profundity as an object of science. By sharp contrast, Peirce's conception of communication as semiotic process is deeper, much more complex and philosophically interesting. He surmises that (Peirce in Buchler, 1955/1940, p. 80): "By the third, I mean the medium or connecting bond between the absolute first and last. The beginning is first, the end second, and the middle third. The end is second, the means third. The thread of life is third; the fate that snips it, its second."

Confusion of thought in the information theory account of communication stems from a thorough misunderstanding of the interrelationships between and among message, code and context (Catt, 2003). That is why communicologists, including for instance Pierre Bourdieu, Richard Lanigan, and myself argue that the message is almost never the problem of communication, though that is the usual emphasis in most accounts of "communication problems." Instead, the problem is the code. The code, states Bourdieu (1987, p. 80), is "the basic minimum level of communication." If, in fact, communication was essentially a problem of information, of "getting the message out" in the journalists' ill-considered colloquialism, then there would be little need for study of communication. It is absurd to think that "getting it out there" is the real problem in a technically charged information age.

To the contrary, both Peirce and Korzybski comprehend the importance of communication as an *experience of consciousness*, not as an instrumentality. Their epistemological similarity lies in the awakening of attention to discourse as the *mediation of the between*, Thirdness in Peirce, unconscious Aristotelian linguistic structure in Korzybski. Both are interested in "the fixation of belief" or the "habits of mind" that cause an unwarranted stop in semiosis (sign action) or insufficiently rational thought. Both men are realists, but realists of particular sorts. Yet, they are precursors, each in a distinctive way, of postmodern thought. (I shall return to this point at the end of this journey.)

In a postmodern context, Bourdieu (2004, p. 89) would call the kind of relation of the knower to the known that appears in Peirce and Korzybski "epistemological vigilance." It is a discipline that requires pauses for *reflection* on the *reflexive* condition of our knowledge. Once engaged, it is also, then, a focus on the *reversible* relationship of the knower and the known.

Logic

What is the usual process of reasoning in these paradigms? The critical aspect of General Semantics opposes the Law of Identity and its corollary Law of Non-Contradiction. The classical position is Korzybski's nemesis. For him, the substrate of the universe is not stable substances but, rather, processes. He prefers Heraclitus to Aristotle. Identities are perceivable only as one is linked to another in endless chains. He criticizes the idea of ascribing "properties" or "qualities" to "nature" (Korzybski, 1951, p. 183-185). Korzybski takes the discoveries of science seriously, and there is no reason, on his account, that the *relations* and *structures* obtaining in the physical and natural world should not be analogous to those of the human world. The impediments to living the truth of a process reality lie in the two-fold problem of Aristotelian logic and its vehicle, a statically conceived discourse that would dissociate time and space, obfuscate the abstract and the concrete, and prevent perception of the whole by means of elementalism.

Thus, A is not A, the proverbial "map is not the territory," time and space are inseparable, language construes reality, and a synthesis of the whole is as valuable as the analytic tendency of Western society to interminably break things down into their constituent parts — to the point that the intended object of analysis is actually lost from view. The logics of non-A and non-el better represent the world, as science now understands it. "Modern science," Korzybski suggests, "makes imperative a language structure which is non-elementalistic and does not split artificially what cannot be split empirically" (Korzybski, 1951, p. 187).

In his posthumously published last essay, Korzybski (1951, p. 173) describes the verbal level of perception as four steps removed from the original nonverbal reality. In fact, the first three levels preceding discourse are all silent. They are ineffable. From this non-Aristotelian point of view, thinking may proceed verbally at the risk of bias built into the verbal structure and imposed upon the silent nonverbal realm, making the ineffable tardily speak, but at a cost. Specifically, he says, "we read mostly unconsciously into the world the structure of the language we use" (Korzybski, 1951, p. 177). His critique is of the "subject-predicate form of representation" and its dominance of our thinking (Korzybski, 1951, p. 181). Korzybski argues that we can learn to think without words, using pictures or other visualizations. He states that, "practically all important advances are made this way" (1951, p. 175).

The scientific basis of right thinking is located in a new "psycho-logic" that is to be distinguished from the discipline of psychology, which should be eliminated, presumably to the extent that it relies upon Aristotelian ascription of intrinsic qualities to the mind considered as an elemental entity (Korzybski, 1933, p. 539). The "deductive grounds for a full-fledged 'science of man' [sic], where both deductive and inductive methods are utilized" are founded in the ontological premise that humans are time-binders (Korzybski, 1933, p. 180). As to Korzybski's "psycho-logic," that is revelatory of his value system and will be discussed under axiology.

Peirce criticized Aristotle's logic well in advance of Korzybski, but their direction is quite similar. They presage the postmodern critical turn by noticing that the precise human condition is one of being and not-being at the same time. Humans are dislodged from the Law of Identity by discourse, which, because it is based on *signifying relations*, disallows an object of perception to be identical with its expression. These are two stages of consciousness in Korzybski, *intension* and *extension*, and three in Peirce, who comprehends the mediation of all experience by the sign. (See Lanigan, 2007 for a precise phenomenological analysis of Aristotle's mistake.)

Korzybski employs deduction to argue that scientific induction is superior to a non-scientific, non-fact based response to the world. He argues for reflection to consider the facts, thinking to precede speaking. Peirce might counter that all thinking is already in signs, and, perhaps in agreement with Merleau-Ponty (1962/1945, p. 178), that "speech accomplishes thought." For Peirce, semiotics *is* logic, for the fundamental reason that logic is intrinsically discursive.

Peirce's logic is the application of phenomenology to the problem of knowledge (Deledalle, 2000, p. 8). He differs from Korzybski in a very significant way. Whereas the latter puts an emphasis on induction, Peirce understands that; "A possible First cannot give birth by itself to an existing Second (or any number of Seconds, even an infinity) cannot produce an organizing Third." "This is, by the way" Deledalle (2000, p. 69) continues, "the reason why Peirce proposed to substitute an abductive logic of invention for the inductive logic of discovery." Simply put, induction cannot discover anything. It is constrained because it has no ideas and cannot alone attain any. The logic of the Third is required. The Third is future oriented; whereas, deduction and induction are past and present, they represent hindsight and insight but are incapable of foresight (Catt, 2008). Deduction condemns the future to the past, because its conclusions are already contained within the major premise. Induction seeks a future but has only repressed its history in deduction. Foresight is manifest as *symbolic form*. Deduction and induction presuppose abduction, which subsumes them both. The only new thought that can ever be produced is abductive for the simple reason that thought is always in signs. Every sign is a subspecies of its ideal, the symbol, and toward which all semiosis is intentionally, in the phenomenological sense of the term, directed (Peirce in Buchler, 1955/1940, 150-156).

Axiology

All paradigms presuppose, at some level of consciousness, a set of values that motivates continued identification within a community of thinkers. While fully recognizing that one philosophical assumption readily bleeds into the next, it must be said that Korzybski's psycho-logic is not just logic, but perhaps more importantly, it is his value system. He argues that a change in discourse is a potential revolution. Changes in our linguistic *habits of mind* (the central theme of pragmatism as well) have the potential to re-shape the social map. In this regard, communication could scarcely be more important, regardless of the context of discourse.

Reasoning with Korzybski on the role of language in shaping perceptions, we must conclude that our *evaluations* are judgments that inescapably express values, a point that should be obvious given the etymology of the word. However, this is not a matter of discovering a new value; but, to the contrary, of becoming aware of the values we already impose through an unreflective exercise of language. Evaluation is the veritable essence of human expression; yet if this is so, it is simultaneously a serious problem of conscious communication (see Urban, 1929, 1939).

At issue is sanity. Korzybski (1933, p. 184) observes that: "these problems of 'adjustment' and 'non-adjustment', 'fictitious' or 'actual' worlds, are strictly connected with our s.r. [semantic reactions] toward these problems, and so ultimately with some structural knowledge about them" (brackets mine). However, consistent with his philosophy, he does not pose an either-or logic but, instead, qualifies the question of sanity as a relative issue of the ability to abstract within a proper order and to comprehend space-time relations. The idea of "adjustment" is itself relative. He comments (1933, p. 225) that, "in most cases of 'insanity' and un-sanity, there is a disorientation as to 'space' and 'time' . . . the 'insane' and the un-sane are the unadjusted; the 'sane' are the supposedly adjusted." He clarifies that the adjustment has to do with discourse and reality. Thus, it will not be the task of General Semantics to change the definitional landscape *intensionally*; rather, the discourse is an *extensional* problem and that is where sanity resides, in the person-discourse-world ratio. The point, of course, is that the ratio can be made more intelligent, flexible, and fulfilling of human potentiality.

Reasoning backward, from the world of our practices to their basis in experience, Korzybski (1951, p. 190) realizes that "the way we evaluate" . . . "may affect the way in which we 'perceive'." More will be said about this in regard to methodology and practices. For the moment, it should be clear that the founder of General Semantics sought to make the world a better place to live by contributing to the sanity of our discourse.

Sanity is associated in Pierce as it is in Korzybski with right thinking, and that is constrained by signs, by discourse. Communicology recognizes that from the beginning perception is already codification of reality (Catt, 2001a, 2001b, 2003; 2006, 2008, 2010, 2011, 2012). The explicit semiotic phenomenology of discourse in Cassirer (see Lofts, 2000) and Sini (1993, 2009) concurs. Bourdieu (1993, p. 217) explains that perception slices or frames "reality." Expression is in signs, and every expression is the realization of a perception, its accomplishment. Merleau-Ponty's (2002) last notes for a course recognized this as the "intertwining" of semiotics and phenomenology, where the pre-objective or pre-logical is, by definition, forever wed to the objective and the logical. Peirce (Buchler, 1955/1940, p. 305) states that: "The fact is that it is not necessary to go beyond ordinary observations of common life to find a variety of widely different ways in which perception is interpretative." This is because: "Abductive inference shades into perceptual judgment without any sharp line of demarcation between them" (Peirce in Buchler, 1955/1940, p. 304). Thus, consciousness of reasoning may have the beneficial result of better judgments. Better judgments are ultimately better habits.

THEORY OF COMMUNICATION

Of postmodern relevance is where Korzybski's General Semantics and Peirce's semiotic phenomenology stand regarding the positing of social reality. The modernist assumption that reality is re-presented by language is countered in every postmodern paradigm with the original phenomenological insight that reality is socially constructed, though the paradigms disagree as to *how* reality is constructed (Catt, 2008, p. 98). This question enters theory from the very first concern of meta-theory, because an image of the human belies every theory. Neo-positivists who focus attention on the message in communication are generally committed to the idea that humans are *information processers* (Radford, 2005). In hermeneutic philosophy, the narration paradigm subscribes to *homo narrans* and the performance paradigm to *homo histrio*, structuralism and post-structuralism (semiotics) to *homo culturalis*, phenomenology to *homo loquens*. Semiotic phenomenology is a synthesis of *homo loquens* and *homo culturalis*; speaking (verbally and nonverbally) is *signifying*. A paradigm's ontology fuels its epistemology; which, in turn, feeds into logic and axiology. Altogether, the meta-theoretical assumptions underwrite theory, and eventually all practices, to the extent the philosophy and theory are methodically followed. Therefore, a positivist will say, with Norbert Wiener, that "The world may be understood as a myriad of 'to whom it may concern' messages" (1947, referenced by Watzlawick to justify his mistaken view that communication "*is* behavior, a misinterpretation of Ruesch and Bateson that unfortunately has had considerable impact on communication research and pedagogy; see Ruesch and Bateson, 1987/1951, p. viii). A narratologist will have it that realities are products of stories. A performance theorist will assert that the story is dependent on its performativity. Structuralists will look for underlying codes that are the invisible or unconscious sources of visible messages. Post-structuralists will name these codes imperialistic cultural and technological powers (sometimes unwittingly proffering a new determinism, see Catt, 2001b) and attempt to subvert them (often a new will-to-power in the guise of "resistance," see Porter and Catt, 1993). Semiotic phenomenologists will want to say that social reality is accomplished in and as embodied speech.

Korzybski argues that the linguistic structure filters an otherwise nonverbal reality. This he does not take to be abnormal, admitting, certainly, that we are symbolic creatures. Yet, the language we use should keep up with our scientific findings, specifically with mathematics and physics. Science informs us that the world no longer consists in the "qualities" intrinsic to a static nature. To the contrary, we construe reality through our perceptions of it. These perceptions are already conceptions, because the structure of language structures reality. To reverse this, he argues that reality is capable of being *construed* differently and more in keeping with its structure, with its *relations* and its *processes* that belie every identity and every substance we might wish to notice.

We come then to the issue of truth. Every theory of communication depends on a position regarding "truth." This can be generalized across competing paradigms. Positivists believe in the *correspondence* theory of truth. Narratologists adhere to *coherence* theory. Performance theorists argue for a *performative* theory of truth. Structuralists and post-structuralists subscribe to a *consensus* theory of truth. Semiotic phenomenologists may be said to argue for an ecumenical *pragmatic* theory of truth grounded in embodied experience.

Korzybski's theory of truth is at once an argument for a better correspondence with scientific reality, a more coherent story and performance of relations and process, critique of the prevailing consensus enforced by linguistic structures, and a change of perceptions through pragmatic alteration of linguistic evaluative practices. Thus, it is quite apparent why he sympathized with pragmatism. However, he is to be understood overall as a realist.

Peirce clarifies the pragmatic conception of truth by contrasting it with what it decidedly is not. He is critical of psychology and of metaphysical conceptions of truth; "pragmatism is, in itself, no doctrine of metaphysics, no attempt to determine any truth of things" (Buchler, 1955/1940, p. 271). This is not to say, of course, that truth is not ascertainable. It is to say that pragmatism makes no paradigmatic claim as to what is the truth. It is not-yet; we must await the consequences of our habits of mind and action. Again, however, it is important to note that Peirce, not unlike Korzybski, will judge consequences from within his self-proclaimed version of realism.

MODEL

The function of a model in theory construction is similar to the role of metaphor in literature. It is a shorthand depiction of reality within the constraints of the theory's discourse. While not supplanting the more thorough description afforded a statement of theory and not being mistaken for the theory itself, a model represents the theory in its ideal form. For example, a model of communication focuses us on an image of what happens when or if the phenomenon communication actually occurs. This, no doubt, seems strange to the uncritical positivist who *presupposes the experience of communication*, regarding it as a given fact or premise from which point we are to move on to various consequences of discursive instrumentality.

By contrast, Korzybski does not presume communication as a *fact* of discourse. To the contrary, his project is anti-positivistic to the extent that he shows how discourse may prevent communication. Communication is a *value* for him. It is an experience that is the rational potential of being human. To this end, he proposes what may be called a "lay scientist model" of the self; by contrast, Peirce offers a "lay pragmatist model" (White, 1984, pp. 333-348; for applications of this model see Catt, 1986; 1995). While Korzybski is after practical consequences, he adheres to science as an ideal of proper, rational thought. It is not the case that Peirce is unscientific, but he recognizes the inherent fallibility of reason. Thus, he (Peirce in Buchler, 1955/1940, p. 125) states:

> Plainly, then, I wish to reason in such a way that the facts shall not, and cannot, disappoint the promises of my reasoning. Whether such reasoning is agreeable to my intellectual impulses is a matter of no sort of consequence. I do reason not for the sake of my delight in reasoning, but solely to avoid disappointment and surprise. Consequently, I ought to plan out my reasoning so that I evidently shall avoid those surprises.

Yet, it is important to remember that Peirce is aware that habits are made to be broken. It is no accident that in his science of signs the order of experience commences with the iconic sign object; imagination is important to Peirce. He is quite aware that the system of thought employed, and its specific conceptual tools, affects what we are able to ascertain. For instance, in his discussion of fallibility (Peirce in Buchler, 1955/1940, p. 59) he reminds us that:

> Numbers are merely a system of names devised by men [sic] for the purpose of counting. It is a matter of real fact to say that in a certain room there are two persons. It is a matter of fact to say that each person has two eyes. It is a matter of fact to say that there are four eyes in the room. But to say that *if* there are two persons and each person has two eyes there *will be* four eyes is not a statement of fact, but a statement about the system of numbers which is our creation.

The predictive value of science is limited, not by the facts but by our imaginative capacities, our creative genius, our habits of mind.

METHODOLOGY

The lay scientist of General Semantics is reflective. The Aristotelian language structure has to be the focus of "epistemological vigilance." Given the deduction that structures of the physical and natural universe should be mirrored by our language and made, therefore, to focus on *relations*, techniques then must be developed to make our discourse appropriately respond. The methodology of General Semantics, as a general framework for thinking and theorizing, is language-centered. Conscious communication is the goal. Therapy is required. Korzybski is explicit about this throughout his work. For example, in his last published work, he states, "Changes in *attitudes*, in our ways of evaluating, involve intimately 'perceptual processes' at different levels. Making us *conscious* of our *unconscious assumptions* is essential; it is involved in all psychotherapy and should be a part of education in general" (Korzybski, 1951, p. 195).

This education is not focused on *intensional* learning as much as on *extensional* training. The deductive enterprise gives way to the empirical experience of induction. The hoped-for result, it could optimistically be said, is the *abduction* of the principles of structure and relations discovered by application of the scientific method to human affairs. However, conformity of language in use with the empirical facts of a relative process world is the actual goal. This goal is underwritten by a realist's perspective.

Peirce questions both deduction and induction, as implied earlier in my discussion of logic. His methodology is abduction. As several postmodern authors have done (for example, Ernesto Grassi, 1980), Peirce sought the originary ground for the major premises of any deduction. He found only the conclusion of a previous deduction, *ad infinitum*. Indeed, the *archai* is elusive. Moreover, induction can have no ideas. Abduction is inclusive of both deduction and induction, neither of which is possible except by the grace of abduction.

A way to think about abduction is to consider the master trope, metaphor, which is the ground of language. To abduce is to reason metaphorically. (A metaphor is not a comparison, as many secondary school teachers have erroneously taught.) Time and space are synthesized as one domain that is *dissimilar* to another is adduced, that is made contiguous (space). Alongside each other, the domains are combined to form something new, a new thought and a single domain in time. Yet, this singularity is also elusive, because (as earlier indicated) every sign is triadic and consists of *continuity* (time), *contiguity* (space), and *familiarity* (time-space). The abduction is encompassing: "In brief, abduction suggests hypotheses or general ideas that deduction develops, and that induction, in a sense entirely different from the classical sense, verifies or rather tests" (Deledalle, 2001, p. 143).

In the postmodern context, semiotic phenomenology offers a synthetic methodology of culture (continuity-time), society (contiguity-space), and person (familiarity-conscious experience). Conscious experience is a time-space union in the existential moment and movement of the *Lebenswelt*. It only occurs in communication where subjectivity is perpetually becoming intersubjectivity, and recursively.

PRACTICES

To describe the general framework is insufficient for Korzybski. A specification of the methodology is required in practices. Indeed, these are enumerated in *Science and Sanity* and further elaborated and extended by all the General Semantics scholars who have followed. *Extensional devices*, Korzybski maintained until the end, appear to be simpler than they are. The point is that training is required in order to make them a part of healthier mental habits. A consequence of incorporating the newly acquired linguistic habits is a change in thinking. The logic behind this is to make the mind adhere to the "natural order," which is reversed in pathological experience and behavior. His realism could not possibly be more explicit (1933, p. 317): "For instance, the natural order is 'senses' first, 'mind' next; object first, label next; description first, inference next . . . The reversal of the natural order appears pathological and pathogenic and is found as a symptom in practically all forms of mental ills, as well as most human difficulties and disturbances . . ."

Thus, Korzybski proposes a program for philosophy in action, a human science in which indexing, chain-indexes, dating, use of etc., quotation marks, and hyphens produce a delay in reactions. The momentary delay of s. r. or semantic reactions induces "*neuro-physiological effects*, as it necessitates thinking in terms of 'facts,' or *visualizing processes, before* making generalizations" (1951, p. 193). The eidetic intellectual foundation for General Semantics is empirically and functionally realized in the physical behavior of speaking, which, in turn, has therapeutic mental effects. The ultimate objective is to extend these changes in discourse beyond the personal level to progressively alter communal thought and, thereby, to impact the world. Changes in language use have the potential to induce a proper alignment of humans with the natural order. The *agency* of Korzybski's deductive philosophy (correspondence of linguistic structure with physical-natural structure) is determined by the *efficacy* of inductive action in speech.

For Peirce, if pragmatism is practical, it is also futuristic and grounded in hope. There is no way to know in advance that our conduct will be the best course of action. Only the consequences will tell. However, we are guided by experience. We make best guesses on an experiential foundation, and it is rather remarkable how often we are proven correct; the pragmatic assumption is that truth is simultaneous with "what works." Additionally, and strictly speaking, the lay scientist model is actually *im*practical in everyday practices. At the level of quality, that is, Firstness, life is more like a stream of consciousness than a rational system. At Secondness, the "right message" is a contingency, not a measure of science. The code, say matching language to a preconceived reality (whether static or processual), cannot require perfect obedience of the message. Adherence to the rules is a discipline, not a law of nature. The governing law, at the level of Thirdness, is a qualitative, dynamic, and symbolic rule of participation. Otherwise conceived, where the lay scientist's desire for "natural order" in-forms the practice, we are condemned to come full circle. Assuming the success of extensional devices, the "natural order" is reflected in language. Then, tautology rules: K is K, K is all of K, and this alienated K stands alone in time and space.

Peirce and Korzybski are different when it comes to practical analysis of relations. As a practice and a method, "semiotics is prospective, not retrospective invention; it takes place in time, and cannot be reduced to a simple process of producing each and every day a copy of external forms" (Deledalle, 2001, p. 154). The *form* of things, ideas, and even perception itself, exists in advance of that which is present to mind. These matters, and all conceivable others, are *manifestations* of *form*. In general, practices of Peirce's philosophic system are intended to analyze *the becoming of the sign*. This *becoming* is the activity of semiosis and, thus, the accomplishment of phenomenological intentionality. We understand this now as the correlate of body and sign that defines consciousness. It is the business of phenomenology, Peirce says, "to make the ultimate analysis of all experiences the first task to which philosophy must apply itself" (Buchler, 1955/1940, p. 71).

CONCLUSION

While some scholars have flirted with the notion that General Semantics, semiotics and phenomenology are related, the precise nature of this association has remained largely unexamined (except by Eicher-Catt's phenomenological explication of writing in E-prime, 2010). Here, I have only begun a larger project that may stimulate more thoroughgoing analyses by others. A paradigmatic approach to theory construction has proven useful to provide grounds for a date, if not a marriage, of the two, Korzybski and Peirce. I have pointed to convergences as well as divergences in their projects as I used theory construction terms to compare them. Furthermore, the setting for the discussion has been the question of their contribution to postmodern discourse. It is interesting that Korzybski wanted to separate himself from semiotics, and we can only speculate where his work might have gone, had he been more familiar with Peircean semiotic phenomenology.

By way of a concluding comment, I should like to remind my readers that both Korzybski and Peirce were realists. That is important to note, because neither was, strictly speaking, a postmodern theorist. The problem of this underlying realism is the ultimate desire for some sort of correspondence in the ratio of person to reality to be accomplished by language. Despite the pragmatic intentions of both, and their considerable contributions, it must ultimately be said that the *construal* of reality is not the same as the *construction* of reality. Korzybski has faith in an existing "natural order" that precedes discourse and for which language in particular is inadequate. To make experience more rational, he reasons from factually based behavior, that is, inductive *extensional* devices, back to thought. Peirce took semiosis to be the means by which reality is construed as thought. He reasons from possibility to thought. Their versions of realism are quite different. Peircean realism is based on habits formed in a community by previous and on-going semiosis, not by belief in a scientific foundation outside of communication.

In a sense, they both nevertheless make the postmodern critical turn that we now recognize: the *becoming of the sign* as history. There is, then, much to be gained by careful reading of Korzybski and Peirce, separately and together. My own abduction of them in a postmodern communicological context suggests that their focus on discourse planted seeds for a fundamental break with classical Western thought. They contributed to a theoretical and practical synthesis of body and spirit that we could optimistically imagine for a future not yet named.

We inherit from this history the task to reason from the sign back through the embodied experience of its *becoming*. This is the practical wisdom of Communicology, the science of which is intended to expose the constraints of discourse and create a clearing for human possibility. We move in a reverse order in our analysis of relations, from sign to body (Catt, 2011). Therein, we recognize that communication is a *possibility of discourse*, not a probability.

Peirce showed foresight in this regard. Distinguishing the pragmatic from any "low and sordid" version of the practical, he comments, "Individual action is a means and not our end; we are putting our shoulders to the wheel for an end that none of us can catch more than a glimpse at—that which the generations are working out. But we can see that the development of *embodied ideas* is what it will consist in" (cited in Deledalle, 2000, p. 32; My italics).

This, then, is the semiotic and phenomenological manner by which the conjunction of history and historicity is realized and actualized. Neither consciousness nor its necessary objects may be presupposed, the polarity gives rise to each. In the sufficiency of their difference body and sign are constituted. Korzybski and Peirce are precursors of contemporary philosophy of culture and communication, which I simply call Communicology.

REFERENCES

Alexander, H. (1972/1967). *The language and logic of philosophy*. Albuquerque: University of New Mexico Press.

Anton, C. (2003). Playing with Bateson: denotation, logical types, and analog and digital communication. *The American Journal of Semiotics*, 19(1-4), 127-152.

Anton, C. (2008). The thing is not itself: Artefactual metonymy and the world of antiques. *ETC: A Review of General Semantics,* 65(4), 365-371.

Bateson, G. (1942). Social planning and the concept of deutero-learning. Conference on Science, Philosophy and Religion, Second Symposium. New York: Harper, 81-97.

Bateson, G. (1972). *Steps to an ecology of mind*. New York: Ballantine Books.

Bauman, Z. (1992). *Intimations of postmodernity*. London: Routledge.

Berger, P. and Luckmann. T. (1966). *The social construction of reality*. New York: Doubleday.

Bois, J. S. (1963). Logic and psycho-logics. *ETC: A Review of General Semantics*, 20(3), 261-267.

Bourdieu, P. (1990/1980). *The logic of practice*. R. Nice (Trans.). Stanford: Stanford University Press.

Bourdieu, P. (1990/1987). *In other words*. M. Adamson (Trans.). Stanford: Stanford University Press.

Bourdieu, P. (1993). *The field of cultural production*. New York: Columbia University Press.

Bourdieu, P. (2004/2001). *Science of science and reflexivity*. R. Nice (Trans.). Chicago: University of Chicago Press.

Buchler, J. (1955/1940). *Philosophical writings of Peirce*. New York: Dover.

Cassirer, E. (1953-1957/1925 Vol. I-III; 1996 Vol. IV). *Philosophy of symbolic forms*. R. Manheim (Trans. Vol. I-III), J. M. Krois and D. P. Verene (Trans. Vol. IV). New Haven: Yale University Press.

Cassirer, E. (2000/1942). *The logic of the cultural sciences*. S. G. Lofts (Trans.). New Haven: Yale University Press.

Catt, I. E. (1986). Rhetoric and narcissism: A critique of ideological selfism. *Western Journal of Speech Communication*, 50(3), 242-253.

Catt, I. E. (1995). The 'cash-value' of communication: An interpretation of William James. In A. Smith and L. Langsdorf (Eds.), *Recovering pragmatism's voice* (97-114), Albany: SUNY.

Catt, I. E. (2000). The institution of communitarianism and the Communicology of Pierre Bourdieu. *The American Journal of Semiotics*, 15 and 16(1-4), 187-206.

Catt, I. E. (2001a). Signs of disembodiment in racial profiling: Semiotic determinism versus Carlo Sini's phenomenological semiotics. *The American Journal of Semiotics*, 17(4), 291-317.

Catt, I. E. (2001b). Foreword by Isaac E. Catt. In R. Wendt *The paradox of empowerment* (pp. xv-xvii), Westport, CT: Praeger.

Catt, I. E. (2002). Communicology and narcissism: Disciplines of the heart. *Journal of Applied Psychoanalytic Studies*, 4, 389-411.

Catt, I. E. (2003). Gregory Bateson's 'new science' in the context of Communicology. *The American Journal of Semiotics*, 19(1-4), 153-172.

Catt, I. E. (2006). Pierre Bourdieu's semiotic legacy: A theory of communicative agency. *The American Journal of Semiotics*, 22(1-4), 31-54.

Catt, I. E. (2008). Philosophical grounds for cultural dialogue in Communicology. *International Journal of Communication*, 18(1-2), 97-116.

Catt, I. E. (2010). Communication is not a skill: Critique of communication pedagogy as narcissistic expression. In *Communicology: The new science of embodied discourse* (pp. 131-150), D. Eicher-Catt and I. E. Catt (Eds.), Madison, NJ: Fairleigh Dickinson University Press.

Catt, I. E., & Eicher-Catt, D. (2010). Communicology: A reflexive human science. In *Communicology: The new science of embodied discourse* (pp. 15-29),

D. Eicher-Catt and I. E. Catt (Eds.), Madison, NJ: Fairleigh Dickinson University Press.

Catt, I. E. (2011). The signifying world between ineffability and intelligibility: Body as sign in communicology. *The Review of Communication*, 11, 2, 122-144.

Catt, I. E. (forthcoming 2012). Communicology for an era of precarity: A research paradigm for interrogating the confluence of social structures and human experience. In *Social uncertainty, precarity and inequality,* RolfDieter-Hepp (Ed.), Berlin, Germany: VerlagWestfälischesDampfboot.

Catt, I. E., & Eicher-Catt, D. (forthcoming July 2012). Semiotics in mainstream American communication studies: A review of principal USA journals in the context of Communicology. *The Review of Communication*, *12*(3).

Cole, M. Message from the Dr. Sanford I. Berman Chair in General Semantics, University of California, San Diego, Department of Communication, Retrieved January 26, 2010 from http://communication.ucsd.edu/berman/

Deledalle, G. (2000). *Charles S. Peirce's philosophy of signs*. Bloomington: Indiana University Press.

Eicher-Catt, D., & Catt, I. E. (2008), Editors. Special Issue on Agency and Efficacy in Communicology. *Atlantic Journal of Communication*, 16(3-4).

Eicher-Catt, D., & Catt, I. E. (2010). Editors. *Communicology: The new science of embodied discourse*. Madison, NJ: Fairleigh Dickinson University Press.

Eicher-Catt, D. (2010a). Recovering the voice of embodied dialogue: Edward Sapir's contribution to Communicology. *International Journal of Communication,* 20(1-2), 1-26.

Eicher-Catt, D. (2010b). What e-prime "is not": A semiotic phenomenological reading. *ETC: A Review of General Semantics*, 67(1), 1-18.

Foucault, M. (1970/1966). *The order of things*. New York: Vintage.

Grassi, E. (1980). *Rhetoric as philosophy*. University Park: Pennsylvania State University Press.

Hardy, A. (2006). *Perspective and the construction of consciousness*. Guilderland, NY: James Publications.

Hayakawa, S. I. (1973). *Language in thought and action*. London: George Allen and Unwin.

Hersch, E. L. (2003). *From philosophy to psychotherapy*. Toronto: University of Toronto Press.

Innis, R. (2002). *Pragmatism and the forms of sense*. University Park, PA: Pennsylvania State University Press.

Jakobson, R. (1990/1942). Langue and parole: Code and message. In L. R. Waugh and M. M Burston (Eds.), *On language* (pp. 80-109), Cambridge, Mass: Harvard University Press.

Jakobson, R. (1990/1956). The speech event and the functions of language. In L. R. Waugh and M. M-Burston (Eds.), *On language* (69-79), Cambridge, MA: Harvard University Press.

Johnson, W. (1946). *People in quandaries*. San Francisco, CA: International Society for General Semantics.

Korzybski, A. (1951). The role of language in the perceptual processes. In *Perception: An approach to personality* (pp. 170-205), R. Blake and G. Ramsey (Eds.). New York: The Ronald Press Company.

Korzybski, A. (1994 5th Edition/1933). *Science and sanity*. Fort Worth, TX: Institute of General Semantics.

Korzybski, A. (2008/1921). *Manhood and humanity*. DODO Press.

Kuhn, T. (1962). *The structure of scientific revolutions*. Chicago: University of Chicago Press.

Lanigan, R. L. (1988). *Phenomenology of communication*. Pittsburgh: Duquesne University Press.

Lanigan, R. L. (1992). *The human science of communicology*. Pittsburgh: Duquesne University Press.

Lanigan, R. L. (1994). The postmodern ground of Communicology: Subverting the forgetfulness of rationality in language. *The American Journal of Semiotics*, 11(3-4), 5-21. (Presidential Address to the Semiotic Society of America delivered in Philadelphia, PA in October 1993.)

Lanigan, R. L. (2007). Communicology: The French tradition in human science. In *Perspectives on philosophy of communication* (pp. 168-192), P. Arneson (Ed.), West Lafayette, IN: Purdue University Press.

Lanigan, R. L. (2010). Verbal and nonverbal codes of Communicology: The foundation of interpersonal agency and efficacy. In *Communicology: The new science of embodied discourse* (pp. 102-128), D. Eicher-Catt and I. E. Catt (Eds.), Madison, NJ: Fairleigh Dickinson University Press.

Lévi-Strauss, C. (1983). *Structural anthropology*. Chicago: University of Chicago Press.

Lofts, S. G. (2000). *Ernst Cassirer*. Albany, NY: SUNY.

Macke, F. (2010). Intrapersonal Communicology: Reflection, reflexivity, and relational consciousness in embodied subjectivity. In *Communicology: The new science of embodied discourse* (pp. 33-62), D. Eicher-Catt and I. E. Catt (Eds.), Madison, NJ: Fairleigh Dickinson University Press.

Merleau-Ponty, M. (1962/1945). *Phenomenology of perception*. C. Smith (Trans). London: Routledge and Kegan Paul.

Merleau-Ponty, M. (2002). Husserl at the limits of phenomenology. L. Lawlor and B. Bergo (Eds). Evanston: Northwestern University Press.

Montagu, A. (1953). On time-binding and the concept of culture. Alfred Korzybski Memorial Lecture presented at the Waldorf-Astoria Hotel, New York City, March 5, 1952. *The Scientific Monthly*, LXXVII(3), September 3, 1953. Printed simultaneously in *General Semantics Bulletin*, Numbers 10-13, Spring-Summer, 1953.

National Communication Association. "Spectra Article About the Mission Statement," Retrieved August 14, 2010 at http://www.natcom.org/nca/Template2.asp?bid=531.html

Peirce, C. S. (1958). *The collected papers of Charles Sanders Peirce*. A. Burks (Ed.), Vol.8, Cambridge, MA: Harvard University Press.

Polanyi, M. (1966). *The tacit dimension*. Chicago: University of Chicago Press.

Polanyi, M. (1969). *Knowing and being*. Chicago: University of Chicago Press.

Polkinghorne, D. E. (2004). *Practice and the human sciences*. Albany, NY: SUNY.

Porter, W. M. and Catt, I. E. (1993). The narcissistic reflection of communicative power: Delusions of progress against organizational discrimination. In *Narrative and social control* (pp. 164-185), D. Mumby (Ed.), Newbury Park: Sage.

Radford, G. (2005). *On the philosophy of communication.* Belmont, CA: Wadsworth.

Rappaport, A. (1955). The role of symbols in human behavior. *ETC: A Review of General Semantics,* 12(3), 180-188.

Read, A. W. (1983). The semiotic aspect of Alfred Korzybski's General Semantics. *ETC:* A Review of General Semantics, XX, 16-21.

Ruesch, J. and Bateson, G. (1951). *Communication.* New York: Norton.

Schutz, A. (1967). *The phenomenology of the social world.* Evanston: Northwestern University Press.

Sebeok, T. (1982). Pandora's box: Why and how to communicate 10,000 years into the future. Alfred Korzybski Memorial Lecture presented at the Yale Club, New York City, November 6, 1981 Retrieved June 21, 2010 from <http://www.generalsemantics.org/misc/akml/akmls/49-sebeok.pdf>.

Sini, C. (1993/1985). *Images of truth.* M. Verdicchio (Trans.), New Jersey: Humanities Press.

Sini, C. (2009). *Ethics of writing.* S. Benso and B. Schroeder (Trans.), Albany, NY: SUNY.

Stjernfelt, F. (2007). Categories, diagrams, schemata: The cognitive grouping of ideal objects in Husserl and Peirce. *Diagrammatology,* 336(Part I), 141-159.

Strate, L. (2009). The future of consciousness. Paper delivered at the Envisioning the Emerging Future Colloquium, sponsored by the Institute of General Semantics, New York City, April 23, 2005. Printed from Literature Online, <http://lion.chadwyck.com.ezaccess.libraries.psu.edu on November 18, 2009>.

Urban, W. M. (1929). *The intelligible world.* New York: George Allen and Unwin Ltd.

Urban, W. M. (1939). *Language and reality*. New York: George Allen and Unwin Ltd.

Watzlawick, P. (1987/1951). Preface to the 1987 edition. In Ruesch and Bateson, *Communication*. New York: Norton.

White, P. (1984). A model of the lay person as pragmatist. *Personality and Social Psychology bulletin*, 10, 333-348.

Wilden, A. (1987). *The rules are no game*. London: Routledge & Kegan Paul.

CHAPTER 5: KORZYBSKI AND MARTIN HEIDEGGER

Corey Anton

"The little word 'to be' appears as a very peculiar word and is, perhaps, responsible for many human semantic difficulties."

—Alfred Korzybski, *Selections from Science and Sanity*

INTRODUCTION[1]

ANYONE FAMILIAR WITH the works of both Alfred Korzybski and Martin Heidegger might find it quite surprising how little has been written of their parallel ideas and co-concerns.[2] Now, admittedly, one can find many differences in their outlooks, and some people may have their reasons for refraining from any comparative consideration at all.[3] For my own part, I want to outline and explore some useful paths of intersection. My attention, while not ignoring differences and divergences, turns mostly to common threads and to points of contact for further dialogue.

Both thinkers, for starters, remained dissatisfied with the way that life and humanity had been approached and understood traditionally. Both were heavily influenced by the turn of the century optimism during which they produced their major works. Both also emphasized the centrality of language and time in human affairs. In addition to these and many other surface commonalities, we also can identify deeper and more complex intersections: Korzybski sought to radically problematize the use of the word "is," or at least to promote habits of conscious awareness regarding the processes of abstracting and to help reduce the kinds of "unsanity" that become possible as people identify with their abstractions. He advanced the notion of "non-identification" and offered his now well-known dictum, *"Whatever I say a thing is, it is not."* Heidegger, for his own part, tried to tease out various meanings within the word "is," and ultimately, he tried to show how existence is the ecstatic temporality designating the being that we ourselves are. Now, this particular statement, the idea that, "existence is the ecstatic temporality designating the being that we ourselves are" may make little sense outside of continental philosophy, and may make even less sense within General

Semantics. Someone schooled under Neil Postman might identify it as a species of "crazy talk" or "stupid talk" (1976), and Korzybski himself might have taken such a philosophical expression as a symptom and illustration of what he called "intensional" rather than "extensional" thinking, that is, thinking based in verbal definitions and abstract speculations rather than thinking that opens to and draws from facts of the world. I will try to show, on the contrary, that this expression is neither crazy talk nor stupid talk, and moreover, we should not try to understand it as "intensional." In fact, I will argue that Heidegger's notion of "existence," when directly compared and contrasted to Korzybski's notion of "time-binding," offers an excellent avenue into a dialogue long overdue.[4]

Accordingly, in this brief and mostly heuristic paper, I begin by first reviewing Korzybski and then turning to Heidegger. I try to show how both thinkers, in seeking to delineate the uniquely human situation as well as clarify the meaning of "being," carefully studied the dynamics of perception, directly combated elementalism by bringing about changes in language practices, and sought to more fully reckon with the uniquely human facts of temporality. Both regarded the uniquely human modes of gathering and elongation, finding such varied modes of time-binding to be the most distinguishing characteristic of the human condition. Hopefully, those familiar with both thinkers will see the obvious connections, and those familiar with only one thinker will find a path into the other. At the very least, this initial sketch should help future scholars see the need for further research and interdisciplinary dialogue.

As one final prelude to my comparative consideration and in an attempt to set the right context for the following analysis, I stress the need for serious, genuine questioning. The questions to be raised are so radical that, at first pass, we may find the task simply too much or too thoroughgoing. It seems improbable if not downright impossible to question the very ground that we stand upon, including an interrogation of our feet and legs as well. Culture itself seems *always already* to provide a sustained response, the always already present ground upon which each and every person stands. The question is: Can we recover a genuine questioning of the whole of nature including ourselves? Can we ask about our nature and the nature of the world and not immediately—i.e. spontaneously and effortlessly—find ourselves somehow already within a response? Can we learn how to see with "first-timer eyes" and actually ask about the meaning of all of this? Seriously, how ought we understand all of *this*? And by the word, "*this*," I mean the biggest, most inclusive, absolute THIS to which we can refer by our words and thought. Said quite otherwise, can we even ask such a question, or, to what extent aren't we always already standing within the horizon of our response? How ought we grasp the very meaning of these challenges?

Korzybski and Heidegger, I maintain, both successfully have done precisely this kind of radical questioning. Admittedly, their mode of address and strategies can seem quite different (and there are plenty of other differences too), but their findings and conclusions are not so different as to preclude the possibility of a meaningful dialogue. Each thinker holds a force and rigor of questioning that needs careful study, appraisal, and further engagement, and so, I turn now to my analysis.

KORZYBSKI, "TIME-BINDING," AND "NON-IDENTITY"

In his book, *Manhood of Humanity*, Korzybski suggests that the diverse character of life on this planet, including the nature of humans, has been profoundly misunderstood. What makes matters worse, argues Korzybski, is that we seem unwilling to grasp the depth and significance of the error. People too commonly have understood humans as either supernatural beings, or as animals not that different in kind from other animals. To challenge both of these presuppositions, Korzybski offers various distinctions to help hierarchically organize different "classes of life."

Classes of Life

Briefly reviewed: Korzybski offers a tri-part distinction of "chemistry-binders," "space-binders," and "time-binders." He begins by postulating that, at the most basic level, we should note the differences between the kinds of activities found in "inorganic" and "organic" chemistry. In the former, despite the complexity and variety of interactions, chemical bonds remain without capacities for autonomous activities. In the latter, we find emergent properties, what we formally can designate as *"life."* The first order of *life,* therefore, emerges only by way of organic chemistry, for here we find a binding of chemicals that enables various forms of *autonomous* continuance including forms of individuation and biological cessation (e.g. growth, development, exchange, reproduction, transmission of hereditary characteristics, etc.). More than mere mineral, plants and the vegetative realm engage in new orders of activity, what could be called "behavior" and which embody a whole new dimension, a next level up from the lifeless world of inorganic chemistry.

Now, atop vegetative processes, at a level that incorporates and yet transcends the facts of inorganic chemistry-binding, we can identify another order of life: the wide range of space-binding behaviors across various classes of animals. Animals rove space in order to gather the chemicals they need for survival, and here we can see properties that are unique to that class of life. The space-binding of animals, said otherwise, opens a new dimension of life such as experiences of distance, inchoate desires and appetites as well as resources for stalking prey and fleeing from predators, etc.

Atop this space-binding dimension of life another level emerges: the "time-binding" that Korzybski reserves for designating the uniquely human situation. Accounting for the peculiar characteristic of human life, Korzybski provocatively states that humans "*must act first, in order to be able to live*" (2001, p. 72), by which he means that humans must bind time (symbolically, culturally, socio-historically) in order to bind space to bind chemicals.

This newly emergent class of life, "time-binding," places humans within a unique position in the cosmos, and unfortunately, it has become a main source of unreason and unsanity, perhaps the source of many forms of maladjustment.[5] Summarizing his notion of "time-binding," Korzybski writes:

> … Man is neither an animal nor a miraculous mixture of angel and beast…what is *characteristic* of the human class of life—that which makes us *human*—is the power to create material and spiritual wealth—to beget the light of reasoned understanding—to produce civilization—it is the unique capacity of man for binding time, uniting past, present, and future in a *single growing reality* charged at once with the surviving creations of the dead, with the productive labor of the living, with the rights and hopes of the unborn… (1921, pp. 192-193)

Further clarifying the kinds of differences he had in mind, Korzybski comparatively suggests that just as the geometric properties of point, line, surface, and volume operate along different mathematical dimensions, so too we might imaginatively consider the different classes of life; they operate along different dimensions, or might be understood as each introducing its own additional properties.

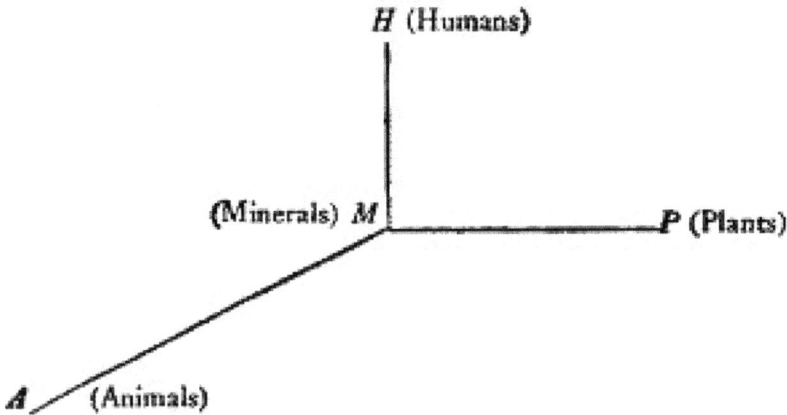

We can identify, then, two classes of chemistry: the inorganic and the organic. The latter—by the combination of Carbon, Hydrogen, and Oxygen— accounts for the emergence of "life" on the planet. Further delineating his suggestive taxonomy, Korzybski states that minerals, as engaging only in inorganic activities, represent a kind of 'Zero point.' The emergence of plant life, as depending upon organic chemistry-binding, would then represent the 'One dimensional line.' Animals, as traversing and incorporating space, represent the 'Two dimensional surface,' and only humans, as in space but as uniquely installed by their time-binding, would represent the 'Three dimensional volume.' I wish to stress that for Korzybski these figurative comparisons help us attentively discriminate some cardinal classes of life and further underscore the kinds of differences found throughout nature. Moreover, the properties at one order include the properties of lower orders and yet the higher orders introduce properties peculiar to that class and give it its own unique character.

Korzybski's tri-part distinction between "chemistry-binders," "space-binders," and "time-binders," does not merely call us to recognize different classes of life. It more importantly stresses that humanity, as the time-binding dimension, poses its own unique kinds of possibilities and challenges, and we easily overlook these unique challenges and possibilities if we fail to see it for what it is. As Korzybski adds, "to treat a human being as an animal—as a mere space-binder—because humans have certain animal propensities, is an error of the same type and grossness as to treat a cube as a surface because it has surface properties" (1950, p. 60). We therefore continue to make category mistakes if we fail to grasp the full implications of time-binding. The unique time-binding class of life encumbers the peculiar vulnerabilities, obstacles, and opportunities of living by *historical action*.

We should focus more on Korzybski's expression "*we must act first, in order to be able to live*" because it addresses the fact that we, trans-generationally, map the world around us and largely substitute our symbolic maps for the world. Such processes of abstracting constitute our historical situation; they offer one more example of our difference from the world of animals. Now, admittedly, all animals abstract according to the selection and omission processes of their nervous system, but other animals seem unaware of this process. They seem not to register the event-level "behind or underneath" the objective-level, and they seem limited in their ability to make second or third order abstractions. Humans not only share physiological abstracting processes in common with animals, they also have come to substitute the world of immediate sensory perception with a conceptual world, a highly abstract set of verbal symbols, maps, models, and other forms of abstract representation.[6] Moreover, their capacity to make inferences atop inferences and to continue on indefinitely in their abstracting separates humanity categorically from the animal kingdom. But on its grimmer side, this means that humans often react by an identification to their own symbols, confusing orders of abstraction and it is to remedy this persistent difficulty that Korzybski offers his dictum, "Whatever I say a thing is, it is not." Humans can apprehend the world around them not only in terms of visible objects (for example, rocks, tables, chairs, and automobiles), but they recognize those objects as composed of events beneath the level of everyday perception, and they can talk about any of those objects at varying levels of abstraction.[7]

The historicity of human experience, therefore, is more than the imbedded and largely hodological memory and physiological installment of animals; human experience and human memory include the possibility of indefinitely more levels of abstraction; they are meta-representational and decontextualizable. We have long ago ceased to *react* to physiological abstractions taken from the immediate world and instead we *act* according to the interposition of semantic [evaluational] reactions and symbolic recollections. And moreover, we can—and mostly do—remain unaware or neglectful of this fact. For the most part, we act intensionally, roughly meaning that we are habitually inattentive to our abstracting and to our semantic [i.e. evaluational] reactions.

Extensional Devices

We should find little surprise then, that, in addition to his tri-part distinction, many of Korzybski's ideas and applications in his *General Semantics Seminar 1937: Olivet College Lectures* attempt to help people become more extensional (i.e. oriented toward facts). He develops models and devices by which semantic reactions can be brought into awareness and put into check; he constructs a system that offers wholly new ways for humans to become consciously aware of how they actually encounter their world. His extensional devices attempt, broadly, to help handle a reversed order of evaluation and offer continual reminders of (or attempts to bring about an on-going awareness of) those specific differences that enable more thoughtful and discerning, more sane, action.[8] Clarifying his extensional devices Korzybski writes, "There are five of them: 1) Indexes, 2) Dates, 3) Etc., 4) Quotes, 5) Hyphens" (2002, p. 65).[9] Further expounding on the nature of the devices, Korzybski noted,

> ... Everything has to be indexed, dated, and whenever you have a statement put an "etc." so you will be conscious you have not stated 'all' or 'everything.' See the premise "*not all.*" This connects directly with the "*is not*" premise. Those first three extensional devices are what I call *working devices* and the fourth and fifth, quotes and hyphens, I call *safety devices* ... (2002, p. 67)

Each of these devices helps people become more self-reflexive, more attuned to their own acts of abstracting and to the fact of semantic [evaluational] reactions, both in themselves and others. Across the lot, Korzybski urged people to become more aware of their own time-binding, their neglect of differences due to over-generalizations and also their failure to recognize how language cuts boundaries and introduces divisions and demarcates discrete entities. The working devices offer ways of attempting to manage the "process-nature" of the world, its endless difference and uniqueness, while the safety devices remind us that humans easily suffer from elementalism. Hence, the safety devices of quotes and hyphens stress that the referent for many terms such as "emotions," "body," or "mind" are to be handled with explicit recognition.[10] The safety devices keep attention on the potentially loaded and/or problematic extra-baggage carried along in our words, and accordingly we can explicitly remind ourselves, by way of the hyphen, that we are dealing with something that has been questionably split off and treated as separated or independent. Korzybski, then, does not deny the relevance of categories but rather suggests that we too often underestimate (or outright ignore) relevant differences. He writes,

> The great mathematician, Sylvester, said, 'Mathematics discovers similarities among differences and differences among similarities'...You have a 'chair,' that is a label only for a definition by similarities. But if you have 'chair$_1$' you have similarities in the 'chair' (definition) and *differences made conscious by the index*...This *consciousness of differences* affects life and affects professions. You get very little out of the standard intensional attitude going by similarities. It does not work, except in the simplest cases. (2002, pp. 118-119)[11]

Because the world is both unique and ever-changing, we often need help in registering its once-occurrence and particularity.[12]

The need for extensional devices runs deep, particularly with regard to the different meanings of the word "is." Regarding the word "is," we often treat it "intensionally," meaning that we act as if it has a meaning. We need, on the contrary, to act more extensionally to all words, but none perhaps more than to the little everyday word "is." Korzybski writes, "For instance, we have four different 'ises': 1) 'Is' an auxiliary verb. 2) 'Is' of existence. 3) 'Is' of predication. 4) 'Is' of identity" (2002, p. 135). He further argues that, "The 'is' of *predication* on the 'sense' level and the 'is' of *identity are always, invariably, false to fact*" (2002, p. 135). His suggestion that the latter two are "false to fact" implies that we need to watch over uses of the word "is" in these latter senses. They mislead and can be trouble, especially if we try to live by them.

In all of these ways, Korzybski provided a thoroughgoing re-consideration of language, being, and human life. These many facets of Korzybski's thought provide easy entrance for a dialogue long overdue: the possible intersections between the ideas of Heidegger and Korzybski. To help ease this transition, I turn to Robert P. Pula's excellent resource for understanding Korzybski's language, *A General Semantics Glossary*, which also holds an interesting passage, perhaps a crucial explanation for making the bridge into phenomenology and Heidegger's philosophy of existence. Pula, citing the introduction to the Second Edition of Korzybski's *Science and Sanity* and explaining the concept of "$^{over}/_{under}$ –defined terms," writes,

> In its most succinct formulation, it reads "...most terms are $^{over}/_{under}$ –defined. They are over-defined (over-limited) by intension, or verbal definition, because of our *belief* in the definition; and they are under-defined by extension or facts, when generalizations become merely hypothetical." Succinct, but densely packed. He then spends $4^4/_5$ pages fleshing out (extensionalizing) his definition—so that *it* not be over-defined by intension. (2000, p. 43)

What makes this passage both problematic yet quite illuminating is how Pula basically maintains that verbal clarification and illustration by further explanation (i.e. text and words) need not be exclusively understood as *intensional*. He spells out a position that appears in various places in Korzybski's writings: the issue resides not simply within "language per se," but with our *attitude* toward language and the *use* we make of it.[13] Here, then, we find an excellent angle of entrance for understanding Heidegger's use of "de-familiarizing language" as a strategy (or device) to reveal the fact that everyday terms are already overpopulated with repressed and unrecognized meaning (i.e. over-defined intensionally and under-defined extensionally).

HEIDEGGER, "DASEIN," AND THE MEANING OF HISTORY

A strategic point of contact between Korzybski and Heidegger comes into focus if we more carefully think about Korzybski's term, "extensional." By the notion of someone becoming more extensional, Korzybski meant that the person comes to rely less upon mere verbalism and relies more upon facts of the world. Commonly contrasting extensional to intensional orientations, Korzybski suggests that too many philosophers have become overly intensional in their approach. Now, about this general problem of speculative verbalism within philosophy, phenomenologists could not agree more. In fact, Edmund

Husserl, Heidegger's predecessor, teacher, and to whom *Being and Time* was dedicated, was a mathematician who sought to locate the origins of geometry in its practical applications.[14]

De-Familiarizing Descriptions of Existence

Husserl's famous dictum was "back to the things themselves," and his program of phenomenology sought to develop a rigorous descriptive science, one that was true to human experience.[15] Phenomenology, then, attempts to move beyond mere theorizing and philosophical speculation and seeks to recover "the things themselves" by careful descriptions, though often through de-familiarizing ones. Such de-familiarizing language, when intentionally employed as a strategy for helping people become more extensional, serves as a constant reminder that everyday terms carry much problematic baggage. It requires of readers increased tolerance for ambiguity as part of the on-going project of meaning, and it helps people recover the sense that language remains forever open and that traditionally used terms all-too-commonly fail to register the fact of the unsaid and unsayable lurking "behind" and "beyond" all that we say and all that we talk about.

Glaring examples of de-familiarizing language can be found throughout *Being and Time*. For example, where Heidegger argues against the "mind-body problems" spelled out by Descartes, he does not use words intensionally; he uses them extensionally to reveal and/or to illustrate, through a kind of phenomenological description, that "mind-body problems" occur only derivatively, and that they, as well as the very "worldhood of the world," remain inseparable from the peculiar nature of our temporality. Heidegger thus attempts a most radical mode of questioning partly by problematizing the assumed transparency of language. He wants to make plain how everyday words such as "mind," "body," "time," or "world," bear highly problematic assumptions, and also that such words, as mostly $^{over}/_{under}$ –defined," cover-over and obscure more than they clarify and illuminate.

The early Heidegger, somewhat similarly to Korzybski, carves out a tri-part delineation for different classes of being, and once again he uses strategies of de-familiarization to illustrate how the word "is" ambiguously signifies at least three different modes of being. To counter any confusion, he first reserves the word "extants" for non-living objects and material substances, things merely present before us and which are wholly in the space 'and' time they occupy. Next, he addresses the being of the living: plants and animals *are* but their being is more than the merely extant. Living beings live through their openness to their environments; they are characterized by and best understood in terms of biological processes of parturition, metabolic exchange, growth and development, aging and cessation. They react to elements around them, and animals experience their movement vis-à-vis their environment and also experience degrees of appetite and distance. The next mode of being, "existence," designates humanity uniquely; only humans "exist" and they exist as "being-in-the-world." This means that the words "existence" and "world" are reserved for understanding the nature of the being we commonly speak of as "the human."[16] So, for example, when Heidegger suggests that tables and chairs do not exist, he is not denying their extant being, but rather, he is using the term "existence" in a very specific, extensional, way. That is, humans *are*, though their mode of being is not reducible to the extant being of things, nor even to the sheer living of animals; *to be human is to exist*.

Heidegger's notion of "existence" thus runs parallel to Korzybski's notion of "time-binding." In fact, each thinker basically offers an entire world-view to challenge the dominant Western orientation and both basically agree that "time-binding," or something akin to what Heidegger called, "ecstatic temporality," has been neglected and most needs our critical attention. To clarify this claim, as well as offer an even more striking example of Heidegger's de-familiarizing language, consider his word choice, "Dasein," which ambiguously means both "being-here" and "being-there" and which refers to the being that we ourselves are. He suggests that Dasein exists as "being-in-the-world," and his extensive use of hyphens throughout *Being and Time* operate very similarly to Korzybski's working devices: to circumvent elementalism. Heidegger's notion of "Dasein" thus stresses how humans, as existing, differ from other classes of life. For example, one of the peculiar features of "existence" is its ecstatical character: Whenever one finds oneself, one finds that one always already has begun. We emerge to self-awareness or self-consciousness only after already having a "thrown past"; no one is "there," as it were, from the bottom up. On the other side, existence is fundamentally characterized by a "not-yet-future," meaning that to exist is always to have something still outstanding: we are that being whose being can be in question, and we exist as a "being-toward-death." More than mere biological cessation, authentic being-toward-death (e.g. 'conscience' and 'anticipatory resoluteness') becomes a possibility for that being who exists. In a word, we can make choices in light of the context of our ultimate demise.

Predication as Emergent Capacity

If we now reconsider the nature of whatever is extant, we can make some needed points of clarification. For the early Heidegger (e.g. of *The History of the Concept of Time, Being and Time* or *The Metaphysical Foundations of Logic*), "extants" sometimes reveal themselves within Dasein's world as merely "present-at-hand" objects whose properties appear objectively present and definable in terms of sheer materiality.[17] One might think of predicating a substance and/or the determination of properties and qualities therein. The history of philosophy runs deep along these lines, for the "is" as copula operates through an analytic disclosure of "properties" released or isolated from their particular (e.g. empirical or sensory) manifestation. Heidegger uses the expression "referential intentionality" (cf. 1984, p. 101) to describe the predicative powers of speech that enable assertions bearing propositional content. For example, consider the following assertion: "My finger is part of my hand and part of my body but is not part of my leg." Or, take some even simpler cases: "The ball is round" or "The ink is black." Predicative uses of "is" such as in the examples just given analytically punctuate boundaries, and then, "the 'is'" takes apart and brings together in just such a way as to reveal the belonging-together of what it took apart (i.e. of what remains only eidetically separable). Hence, we can speak with some specificity regarding my finger separate from my hand and my hand separate from my leg, even though "finger," "hand," and "leg" have always been part of my "body." Likewise, we can speak of the "blackness" as a property of the ink, or the "roundness" as a property of the ball, as if each were separable from their actual sensory material objects. Heidegger nicely (1982) describes this process where he states,

> predication is primarily a disparting of what is given, and in fact an *exhibitive disparting*. This disparting does not have the sense of a factual taking apart of the given thing into thing-pieces but is apophantic: it displays the belonging-together of the manifold determinations of the being which is asserted about. In this disparting, that being is at the same time made visible, exhibited, in the unity of the belonging-together of its self-exhibitive determinations. (p. 209)

Recall that for Korzybski "the is" of predication on the sense level is "invariably false to fact." But by 'false to fact' he seems to imagine, if only surreptitiously, the world as something that could be encountered first perceptually and to which language would then come later on (I address this more in a moment). To help illustrate the point at hand, consider a more sophisticated example of "exhibitive disparting," a case where someone states or writes, "This sentence is in English."[18] Here the predicative "is" eidetically separates out an abstract feature, the code itself known as "English," and which remains forever fused to only particular items at the sensory or empirical level. Nevertheless, if one were to translate the sentence into any other language, it would become false, suggesting that there "is" a proposition which stands abstractly at a level separate from the code, (i.e. "English") by which it was conveyed. Note here that "English" per se is not a direct sensory quality in a way that "black" or even "'a' finger" seems to be, and it is not something that presumably occurs at the 'objective-level.'[19]

Clearly, Korzybski maintains that we are not to confuse the silent objective-level and the verbal-levels, and he admonishes against succumbing to reversing the Natural Order of Evaluation. These are points well taken but the trouble remains: humans do encounter the world though predicative powers and *this fact about existence needs further analysis*. Said quite simply, for Korzybski to maintain that "the is" of predication is false to fact is for him, in actuality even if only surreptitiously, to imagine an objective-level for humans that could be fully freed of any mapping by verbal-levels. But if on the contrary, we suggest that the only world that Dasein has ever known is the world that *always already* includes speech, including predicative speech, then what was called "false to fact" might equally but more positively be called, "an emergent capacity."[20] Let's consider this "emergent capacity" a little bit more carefully.

We need to recall Korzybski's Structural Differential, with its three-part division of the event-level, the objective-level, and the verbal-levels.

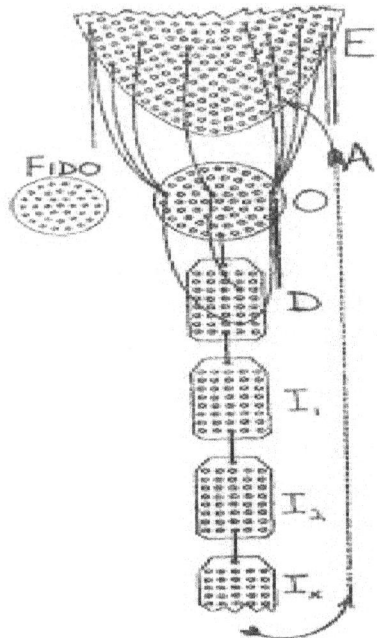

Note that Korzybski identifies two different kinds of objects, one that is off to the left-hand side, signifying the object encountered by animals, and the other, the object known by humans, an object that mediates between verbal-levels and the event-level. Korzybski stresses that science has disclosed the event-level, and that the animal, infant, and primitive remain unaware of it "beneath" or "behind" the objective-level. Hence, the event-level is in one sense 'prior' to the objective level but we must remember that it is the outcome and product, one of the fruits, of the modern scientific world-view.[21]

Part of the difficulty, then, appears when Korzybski talks about people using language in ways that are similar to animal reactions, his point being that people commonly fail to realize that they are identifying with their abstractions. In some of his early writings, Korzybski (1990, p. 69) even playfully suggests that those who remain unaware of their abstracting easily become "*categorists*" and "*dog*matists." But is he intending to imply that the human object, prior to the discoveries of science, was basically similar to the animal object? Unfortunately, his text is not all that clear.

In fact, some of Korzybski's writings somewhat invite people to postulate the parabola, the event-level, as 'below' the level of perception, which would then serve as a kind of solid base upon which perceived objects could be abstractly conceptualized and then talked about within an escalating ladder of abstraction.[22] As helpful as this might be, it easily leads us amiss if we cover-over the dynamic difference between animal space-binding and human time-binding.

Others, Events, and "Beyond"

To learn the name of any object in the world is to imagine how that object enters the consciousness of others. Words, as Bakhtin suggests, partly belong to someone else. This means that when someone learns the name of some object, any object, (e.g. "pencil" or "apple"), unseen others now slide between that person and that kind of object. The object becomes animated through a verbal spirit of otherness. The human word, then, is not merely a conceptual substitute for the object; on the contrary, it is just as much the means by which persons become somewhat substitutable with others who also speak that language. This tension gets revealed in Korzybski's work when we try to determine, exactly, the role played by "the other." Carefully consider the following questions: Are other people, basically, not really 'there' (sheer event-level)? Are they merely objects within *my* world (objective-level)? Are they merely something I talk about, describe, and make inferences about (verbal-levels)? Korzybski's Structural Differential perhaps underestimates the unique kind of sociality that comes into play with time-binding. The meaning of time-binding, I would suggest, can be found to align with something akin to Heidegger's "Mitsein und Mitdasein" (i.e. "Being-with" and "Dasein-with"), meaning that *"others are a condition of existence, not an occasional feature of experience"* (also cf. Anton, 2001; 2010a). To the extent that we are time-binders and to the extent that both language and science are inherently collective enterprises, then, we need to see how others so penetrate into the inner precincts of consciousness that the human object is never just an object *"for me."*

So, I now return to the Structural Differential, first reviewing the animal object on the left and then moving over to the human object on the right. Beginning with the animal object, notice how it has no direct attachment to either the parabola (event-level) or to successive levels of verbal-abstraction, including descriptions and/or inferences. But the question remains: what was the nature of the human object, as opposed to the animal object, prior to the discoveries of modern science?[23] A different way to ask the question and perhaps to force the issue is, "Does not the sheer fact of speech 'and' language always introduce some kind of 'beyond' to any object?"

If we now move our focus to the right, turning to the human object per se, we can postulate that just as 'the word is not the thing,' so too 'the thing' is not 'itself.'[24] Human objects are never merely themselves; they have been transformed and now always already carry an animated sense of attitude, gesture, or unseen spirit.[25] The human object is always saddle-bagged on both sides: a range of levels to speak about it on the one side and the object itself holding invisible possibilities, backsides, and connections to unseen though present forces. An otherness literally haunts the human objective-level, and this is part of what happens to objects for the speaking, time-binding organism. The animal-object is therefore not only not recognized as a product of abstracting, but the human object, even if not scientifically opened to "the event-level," has always already been opened beyond itself. Humans encounter objects through the veil of otherness that language provides; to name an object is to accept that that object, more than merely extant for me, exists in a consciousness other than mine (cf. Royce, 1967).

The animal's encounters with its objects seems limited to its own ego-centricity, whereas for humanity, even pre-scientific humanity, objects are never merely themselves.[26] Consider, for example, how aspects of the world were once thought to be composed of earth, air, fire, water, or even consider something as basic as burial rites whereby an "invisible realm" is petitioned. Here we can see that the human object is always double-posed: we use language on multiple levels of abstraction to talk about an object whose being is more than what we can say or even perceive. To know that what I say about something is fundamentally not that thing, to realize that others may have different words for it, and to know that it can be talked about in furtive code, circumlocution, or simply "in other terms," is not only to have self-reflexive language and consciousness of abstracting, it is to realize that human objects are beyond themselves.

Korzybski's Structural Differential, and his explanation of it, holds the source of the problems as well as the possibilities of re-interpreting his findings. He may have found more than he realized and may not have grasped identification's relation to predication for what it is. He suggests at many points that primitive peoples took "mere similarities and evaluated them as identities" (p. 133).[27] He seems not to recognize that humans transcend any encountered object by both the ability to recognize it as other than it currently appears as well as to talk about it on various levels of abstraction. The animal, on the other hand, seems to do neither.[28] It encounters objects within its world and seems to neither interrogate their composite nature nor to speak *about* them on multiple levels of abstraction. For some of these very reasons Heidegger suggests that animals live in an environment whereas humans exist in the world. Not only do humans have the powers of exhibitive disparting that are given in speech, but, through the copula, they have released essences from any particular installment. Perhaps we would do better, then, to suggest that the idea of "levels of abstraction" makes sense when limited to the verbal "levels" but, when carried over to the relation between the "objective-level" and the "event-level," its coherence starts to break apart. The event-level, it would seem, is the modern scientific account, but humanity has always experienced objects in terms of some kind of otherness, some kind of "beyond," even if not aligned with the contemporary scientific notions of events "beneath."[29]

Part of the residual difficulty encumbered by the Structural Differential is that its graphic representation of the event-level ironically postulates something beyond experienced reality. "Reality" remains, as it were, one step removed and forever beyond human experience. A more phenomenological orientation would suggest that we, in using the Structural Differential, might inadvertently invite a reversing of the Natural Order of Evaluation. In fact, if one wanted to be strict to the facts, humans are historical clearings who open to beings of the world, including themselves, only from within a history that is always already underway. The phenomenological strategy of de-familiarization, which can be both a working device and a safety device, deftly handles the fact that the verbal and nonverbal are not as easily as separable as the Structural Differential would imply. Rather than literally postulating and then vigilantly trying to maintain awareness that "the word is not the thing," one might use the phenomenological strategy of de-familiarization to achieve a highly similar effect but without introducing temptations toward literalist reductions.

This brief and mostly heuristic paper sought to eke out the space for the beginning of a much larger dialogue regarding the interconnection between Korzybski and Heidegger. The more that this project developed the more apparent it became to me that more work on the connections needs to be done. So much could be said of the differences, and these are not to be denied, but a worthwhile project awaits the person who can, perhaps with more space and time, outline and explore all of the significant points of contact and mutual edification.

NOTES

[1] I wish to express thanks to both Bruce I. Kodish and Lance Strate for discussions and assistance that helped to inform the present manuscript.

[2] At the time of writing this paper (October 10, 2010), I "googled" the phrase "Korzybski and Heidegger" and found only two references, both to me.

[3] Heidegger's early alliances with the Nazi party certainly might disincline some students of Korzybski's work to be interested in Heidegger, but Heidegger suffered much remorse in later life. He had much regret and anguish over his youthful arrogance and the revivalist optimism that blinded him to the atrocities soon to leave their indelible mark in Western history. But just as $Heidegger_{1\ (1927)}$ certainly is not $Heidegger_{2\ (1969)}$, so general semanticists of today might now be ready to look for some of the avenues for further discussion.

[4] And scholars of Korzybski would do well to suspect that outside of General Semantics (GS), the expression, "Whatever I say a thing is, it is not" sounds a little less than sane, or at the least, sounds as if it might be a bit of "stupid talk." Also, adherents to *eprime* within GS perhaps ought to note that Korzybski employs the word "is" twice within his now famous and often-quoted statement.

[5] It is the order of evaluation that becomes easily disturbed and misaligned in the human realm. Humans commonly and routinely succumb to extremely intensional orientations and thereby unconsciously project inferences into their observations and experiences.

[6] Korzybski stresses the difference between veterinary science and medicine, and how the latter is made more difficult because the human nervous system does not simply get added onto the prior nervous system. The new cortex is integrated throughout the body. In his book *On Dialogue*, physicist David Bohm writes, "The thing to notice is that the major environment of the old brain is now, not nature, but the new brain, because nature is now filtered through the new brain" (1996, p. 54).

[7] For more on the issue of what is meant by a "level" of abstraction, readers should consult Linda Elson's book *Paradox Lost*.

[8] Korzybski writes, "For sanity's sake, for adjustment's sake, we must reverse the prevalent reversed order of NATURAL ORDER OF EVALUATION…(2002, p. 167).

[9] A fascinating tale could be told regarding Heidegger's use of hyphens throughout Being and Time. In the fairly recently released book, *The History of the Concept of Time*, what amounts to the rough draft of *Being and Time*, Heidegger dedicates the first 100+ pages to Husserlean work on "intentionality," but, for *Being and Time* itself, that particular material is dropped out but its logic and orientation are brought into play through Heidegger's abundant use of hyphens. A rather easy argument to make would be to suggest that Heidegger's early use of hyphens, signifying intentional relations now brought to an existential level, has clear parallels to Korzybski's use of hyphens to facilitate a more extensional orientation.

[10] Worth underscoring here is Holenstein's work on Roman Jakobson. Recall that for Jakobson "context" is the word used to designate the "referential function of language," partly on the ground that no item can be referred to which also does not have a context.

[11] One might imagine the future work to be done on the relations between the ideas of Korzybski and Nietzsche or between Korzybski and Sartre. Robert P. Pula began to explore the first pairing in "The Nietzsche-Korzybski-Sapir-Whorf-Hypothesis? In *ETC.: A Review of General Semantics*, Vol 48. No 4. pp. 462-464. For the former, simply consider that for Nietzsche all ideas, as modes of dissimulation, acts of equating of the unequal, are lies. This is so much the reason why Korzybski stresses, "Whatever I say a thing is, it is not," so much the reason for the use of "etc." as an extensional device. Also relevant is Nietzsche's essay "On the Utility and Liability of History for Life" from his collection *Unfashionable Observations*. It would be not too difficult to draw solid connections between Nietzsche's observations and Korzybski's remarks about classes of life and "time-binding." As one example, consider that Nietzsche writes,

> Observe the herd as it grazes past you: it cannot distinguish yesterday from today, leaps about, eats, sleeps, digests, leaps some more, and carries on like this from morning to night and from day to day, tethered by the short leash of its pleasures and displeasures to the stake of the moment, and this it is neither melancholy nor bored. It is hard on the human being to observe this, because he boasts about the superiority of his humanity over animals and yet looks enviously upon their happiness—for the one and only thing that he desires is to live like an animal, neither bored nor in pain, and yet he desires this in vain, because he does not desire it in the same way as does the animal. The human being might ask the animal: 'Why do you just look at me like that instead of telling me about your happiness?' The animal wanted to answer, 'Because I always immediately forget what I wanted to say'—but it had already forgotten this answer and hence said nothing, so that the human being was left to wonder. (1995, p. 87)

Consider too that Sartre's rich and provocative work on "Bad Faith" from his *Being and Nothingness*, outlines the mistakes that occur if we indiscriminately apply categories to humans which are, in fact, only appropriate only for categorizing things. It would be quite easy to show how Sartre's work on "bad faith" nicely aligns with and gives further support to Korzybski's contentions regarding the "non-identity" rule for the time-binding class of life. This means that both Korzybski and Sartre agree that a major error in Western thought, perhaps inherited from Aristotle's logic, has been to take the logical orientation that A=A, A≠B, and there is no middle between A and B, and then, to apply this logic to the level of human life. Consider, for example, that Sartre writes,

> We have to deal with human reality as a being which is what it is not and which is not what it is…the principle of identity must not represent a constitutive principle of human reality…and yet…he slides surreptitiously towards a different connotation of the word 'being.' He understands 'not being' in the sense of 'not-being-in-itself.' He lays claim to 'not being cowardly' in the sense in which this table is not an inkwell…If I were sad or cowardly in the way in which this inkwell is an inkwell, the possibility of bad faith could not even be conceived…I am not any more courageous than cowardly, if we are to understand this in the mode of being of the-in-itself. (1956, pp. 58-70)

Sartre's notion of bad faith open's wide avenues for commerce with Korzybski's extensional devices.

[12] Future work ought study the relation between Korzybski and Bakhtin, in particular, someone should examine intersections and divergences between Bakhtin's *Towards a Philosophy of the Act* and Korzybski's *General Semantics Seminar 1937*.

[13] In his solid review of Korzybski and General Semantics, Bruce I. Kodish writes, "The goal of general semantics 'is' consciousness of abstracting, not changing the language per se. A given instance of the 'is' of identity or predication is not in itself sure evidence of identification" (2003, p. 165).

[14] Husserl's work locates the origin of geometry not in Plato's Heaven but rather in the practical surveying activities at the Nile. Also note that Husserl is claimed to have suggested, "we are the true positivists," by which he meant that a rigorous science could be built upon the recognition that all objects are "objects as meant," meaning objects for consciousness. The Structural Differential largely addresses this issue where, on the object level, neither the animal object nor the human object refers to the "real object" per se. In both cases, the organisms, deal only with the object as always already abstracted.

[15] By the expression "back to the things themselves," Husserl did not mean something like access to whatever is independent of consciousness. On the contrary, his point is that all objects are objects as meant.

[16] Much could be said, especially in Heidegger's "Letter on Humanism," on why Heidegger would object to the ways the human and humanity are being equated with Dasein.

[17] I am not going to address the later Heidegger, including the revision of his earlier accounts of non-Dasein beings (as either readiness-to-hand or presence-at-hand) that was precipitated by his work on "The Origin of the Work of Art," and his positing four elements, called the fourfold, as being essential to our Being "earth, sky, divinities and mortals." Addressing the later Heidegger is simply beyond the scope of this essay.

[18] See Elson, Wilden, and Anton (2010b) on the issue of levels.

[19] Note here that the 26 letters of the English alphabet do not comprise English per se, though they do help narrow down the possibilities for someone trying to ascertain the particular code through which a written proposition has been expressed.

[20] For an entirely different line of reasoning that comes to nearly the same conclusion see my "Playing with Bateson."

[21] As Korzybski writes, "Without science, we have no event" (2010, p. 130).

[22] *Science and Sanity* certainly holds enough textual evidence to suggest that Hayakawa's "Abstraction Ladder" was not completely off from Korzybski's orientation. But still, other parts of the text make clear that the event-level is an inference postulated as a principle to keep language and scientific research open, not a concrete ground upon which we stand.

[23] Admittedly, the being of many extants is not reducible to mere "predicated substances." The entire world of tools and utensils, as just one example, reveals beings whose being cannot be determined by mere analysis of predicated properties. We find entities, in Heidegger's terms, which are not so much "present-at-hand" as they are "ready-to-hand," meaning that they have been covered over in their being, largely because they remain transparently incorporated in our projects and dealings and their very servisability renders them mostly passed over. Imagine a workman on the job. The tool appears as object only during moment of "break down." The person might, in the course of building something, look down and begin to reach for a hammer and then notice a hairline fracture in the handle. When the person then thinks, "the hammer is broken," this not using the "is" to predicate any substance.

Brokenness is not a property of the hammer; brokenness discloses the being of the hammer as a tool, a being that depends upon Dasein's projection of possibilities. The being of a tool or utensil appears only against the backdrop of a larger "toward-the-ends-of-which" it serves. There is a referential totality, or a hermeneutical implicature, of any such items. It is, therefore, not the properties that can be found in objects merely present-at-hand but the entire equipmental whole that gets called into play. Nails imply hammers and materials that need securing. This is, if only as a nascent sense, the object as "known" by the animal. It is encountered in terms of the properties it assumes in interaction; the animal seems not to predicate. In all candor, I once heard a graduate student describe parts of *Being and Time*, especially the parts on the "readiness-to-hand" of objects, as possible descriptions of animal consciousness. In this way, one might argue that the difference between the animal object and the human object on the Structural Differential is the difference between space-binding and time-binding. The question of how objects relate to other objects, (or to what do they relate and how might they be brought together?), all of these are part of the practical everyday coping, the embodied ways that even humans bind-space. We should remember that although we, as human, are of the time-binding class of life, we are also animals who space-bind. But as soon as we raise questions regarding (and talk about) the nature of something, what makes up its substance or matter, essence or being, even if done so in a wholly an unscientific manner, we move toward the level of time-binding, the more than animal.

[24]Interested readers should see Heidegger's *What is a Thing?* Please also see Anton (2008; 2011).

[25] Kenneth Burke's (1966) masterful essay, "What are the Signs of What?," shows how one can demonstrate that once people are able to speak, they not only have words for a beyond but the things become the signs of words. The things, as Burke suggests, become the visible manifestation of the spirit that infuses them through the words. Also see Susanne Langer (1942) on the "Symbolic Transformation" that lies at the root of both presentational forms (e.g. human artifacts, gesture, and architecture) as well as discursive forms (e.g. language).

[26] See Dewey's (1988) account of the ways we encounter objects in terms of how we imagine those objects operating in others' experiences.

[27]Recall Monty Python's witty example of post hoc ergo propter hoc, "If she weighs as much as a duck, she must be made of wood and therefore is a Witch."

[28] See Anton (2003 & 2011).

[29] It is worth noting in this context that supercomputers today still chug along calculating the next known value in the sequence of "pi."

REFERENCES

Anton, C. (2001). *Selfhood and Authenticity*. Albany, NY: SUNY Press.

Anton, C. (2003). "Playing With Bateson: Denotation, logical types, and analog and digital communication," *The American Journal of Semiotics*, *19*, (1-4), 129-154.

Anton, C. (2008). "The Thing Is Not Itself: Artefactual Metonymy and the World of Antiques," *ETC: A Review of General Semantics*, *64*, (4), 365-371.

Anton, C. (2010a). *Sources of Significance: Worldly Rejuvenation and Neo-Stoic Heroism*. West Lafayette, IN: Purdue University Press

Anton, C. (2010b). "A Levels Orientation to Abstraction, Logical Typing, and Language More Generally," In Linda Elson's *Paradox Lost: A Cross-Contextual Definition of Levels of Abstraction*. Cresskill, NJ: Hampton Press. 183-201.

Anton, C. (2011). *Communication Uncovered: General Semantics and Media Ecology*. Fort Worth, TX: Institute of General Semantics.

Bakhtin, M. M. (1981). *The Dialogic Imagination*. (C. Emerson & M. Holquist, Trans.). Austin, TX: The University of Texas Press.

Bakhtin, M. M. (1993). *Toward a Philosophy of the Act*. (V. Liapuno, Trans.). Austin, TX: University of Texas Press.

Bateson, G. (1972). "A Theory of Play and Fantasy," In *Semiotics: An Introductory Anthology*. (ed.) R. Innis. Bloomington, IN: Indiana University Press.

Bohm, D. (1996). *On Dialogue*. New York, NY: Routledge.

Burke, K. (1966). "What are the Signs of What?," In *Language as Symbolic Action: Essays on life, literature and method*. Berkeley, CA: University of California Press.

Dewey, J. (1988). *The Later Works of John Dewey, 1925-1953. Vol. 1: 1925. Experience and Nature*. Carbondale, IL: Southern Illinois University Press.

Elson, L. (2010). *Paradox Lost: A Cross-Contextual Definition of Levels of Abstraction*. Cresskill, NJ: Hampton Press.

Heidegger, M. (1962). *Being and Time*. (J. Macquarrie & E. Robinson, Trans.). San Francisco, CA: Harper Collins Publishers.

Heidegger, M. (1967). *What is a Thing?* (W. B. Barton & V. Deutsch, Trans.). Chicago, IL: Henry Regnery Company.

Heidegger, M. (1982). *The Basic Problems of Phenomenology*. (A. Hofstadter, Trans.). Bloomington, IN: Indiana University Press.

Heidegger, M. (1984). *The Metaphysical Foundations of Logic*. (M. Heim, Trans.). Bloomington, IN: Indiana University Press.

Heidegger, M. (1985). *The History of the Concept of Time*. (T. Kisiel, Trans.). Bloomington, IN: Indiana University Press.

Heidegger, M. (1993). "Letter on Humanism," In *Basic Writings*. (D. F. Krell, Trans.). San Francisco, CA: Harper Collins Publishers.

Heidegger, M. (1995). *The Fundamental Concepts of Metaphysics*. (W. McNeill & N. Walker, Trans.). Bloomington, IN: Indiana University Press.

Holenstein, E. (1976). *Roman Jakobson's Approach to Language: Phenomenological structuralism*. (C. Schelbert & T. Schelbert, Trans.). Bloomington, IN: Indiana University Press.

Kodish, B. I. (2003). *Dare to Inquire: Sanity and survival for the 21st century and beyond*. Pasadena, CA: Extensional Publishing.

Korzybski, A. (1933). *Science and Sanity: An introduction to non-Aristotelian systems and general semantics*. Lakeville, CN: The International Non-Aristotelian Library Publishing Company.

Korzybski, A. (1990). *Collected Writings 1920-1950*. Englewood, NJ: Institute of General Semantics.

Korzybski, A. (2001). *Manhood of Humanity*. (2nd ed.). Brooklyn, NY: Institute of General Semantics.

Korzybski, A. (2002). *General Semantics Seminar 1937: Olivet College Lectures*. (3rd Ed.). Brooklyn, NY: Institute of General Semantics.

Korzybski, A. (2010). *Selections from Science and Sanity*. (revised Ed.) Fort Worth, TX: Institute of General Semantics.

Langer, S. K. (1942). *Philosophy in a New Key: A study in the symbolism of reason, rite and art*. New York: Mentor Books.

Nietzsche, F. (1964). "On Truth and Falsity in their Ultramoral Sense," In *The Complete Works of Friedrich Nietzsche: Early Greek Philosophy*. New York: Russell & Russell, Inc.

Nietzsche, F. (1999). "On the Utility and Liability of History for Life." In *The Complete Works of Friedrich Nietzsche: Unfashionable Observations*. (R. T. Gray, Trans.). Stanford CA, Stanford University Press.

Pula, R. R. (2000). *A General-Semantics Glossary: Pula's guide for the perplexed*. Concord, CA: International Society for General Semantics.

Royce, J. (1967). "Perception, Conception, and Interpretation," In *The Problem of Christianity*. Hamden, CN: Archon Books.

Sartre, J-P. (1956). *Being and Nothingness*. (H. E. Barnes, Trans.). New Jersey: Gramercy Books.

Wilden, A. (1972). *System and Structure*. London: Tavistock Publications.

CHAPTER 6

KORZYBSKI AND FRENCH STRUCTURALISM

Jean-Yves Heurtebise

INTRODUCTION: PHILOSOPHY AND SCIENCE

"GENERAL SEMANTICS IS not any 'philosophy', 'psychology' or 'logic', in the ordinary sense. It is a new extensional discipline which explains and trains us how use our nervous system most efficiently. It is not a medical science but, like bacteriology, it is indispensable for medicine in general and for psychiatry, mental hygiene, and education in particular. In brief it is the formulation of a new non-aristotelian system of orientation which affects every branch of science and life."[1]

Let us be clear from the very start: we will consider Alfred Korzybski's *Science and Sanity* as a piece of systematic philosophy whose consistency has to be evaluated.[2] That means that regarding the scientific validity of the therapeutic value that general semantics can bring, we will adopt a skeptical approach, i.e. technically we will suspend our judgment. Not because we doubt it can work; actually, a lot of things "work" but only for a small number of them we can know how, when, to what extent and with what frequency they work: they belong then to the domain of "Science." *Science and Sanity* appearing to us as a philosophic, pragmatic and educational text-book, the so-called problem of "the scientificity of general semantics[3]" is not relevant for us, because of the general difference between philosophy and science.

The fact that a philosophy uses precise and scientific tools like mathematical functions or logical connectors to prove its points more or less successfully does not transform this philosophy into a (physical) science. The fact that a philosophy can bring actual relief to his followers regarding the management of their life is not a proof that it is a (medical) science. Actually, using mathematical device to understand universe, prescribe psychological training to cure our soul and promote new kind of psycho-physiological behaviors in sociopolitical organization are features belonging to pure philosophy[4] since its birth in Pythagorean school.[5] Moreover, as well as Aristotelian system was not (an experimental) science (and Aristotle not a "scientist"), Non-Aristotelian system is not (an experimental) science and for the same reason: because it is a system—a system in which Alfred Korzybski's own works are included. Systematic thinking is the mark of philosophy, defined by its intrinsic consistency and its capacity to translate data coming from science, history and art into philosophical concepts.[6]

Perhaps it is contrary to the desire expressed by Alfred Korzybski ("the non-Aristotelian system presented here has turned out to a strictly empirical science, as predicted...[7]") whose ambition was that the introduction of general semantics will mark "the beginning of a new era, the scientific era, in which all human desirable characteristics would be released from the present animalistic, psychophysiological, *A* semantic blockages."[8] However, epistemologically speaking, to assimilate a change of paradigm *in* science (from Aristotelian to Non-Aristotelian) to the birth *of* Science itself seems too emphatic and quite misleading. Moreover, such a transformation of scientific theories into new cultural consciousness is precisely the role of philosophy. Thus "general semantics" is not a non-Aristotelian *science* but a philosophical interpretation stressing the key cultural value of post-Newtonian physics.

So let us forget about the problems of "the scientificity of general semantics" and its aims at providing experimental psychological cure through meta-linguistic analysis; let us only consider Korzybski's general semantics as a reflection about the impact of common "Aristotelian" common logic on ordinary life (semantic behaviorism) and the importance of new scientific discoveries (relativist and quantum physics) whose revolutionary data can help us to propose a new world vision which can become for philosophy what was abstract painting for art, i.e. *an escape outside the ("sameness/allness") realm of representation.*

In this perspective, we will draw some parallels between Alfred Korzybski's *Science and Sanity* and some contemporary French philosophers like Henri Bergson and Gilles Deleuze regarding their conceptions of Time and Difference. Korzybski, Bergson and Deleuze seem to share a common theoretical framework: go beyond the substantialism of classical ontology, towards an ontology of relations and interactions. Moreover, Korzybski's central idea that "the only content of all knowledge is structural [...] structure can be considered as a complex of relations[9]" will lead us to question the conceptual links between Korzybski and Structuralism.

Korzybski and Bergson: Critical Intuition of Time

French philosopher Henri Bergson defined the philosophy of a philosopher by two dialectically related characteristics: a systematic complex construction, an illuminating simple intuition: "He [The philosopher] could not formulate what he had in mind without feeling himself obliged to correct his formula, then to correct his correction: thus, from theory to theory, correcting when he thought he was completing, what he has accomplished, by complication which provoked more complication, by development headed upon development has been to convey with an increasing approximation the simplicity of his original intuition. All the complexity of his doctrine, which could go ad infinitum, is therefore only the incommensurability between his simple intuition and the means at his disposal for expressing it."[10] This philosophical intuition is not a mystical hearing of voices from above, it is a vague but insisting feeling that there is something fundamentally wrong in common and available theories: "What is this intuition? ... a receding and vanishing image, which haunts unperceived perhaps the mind of the philosopher, which follows him like his shadow through the in and outs of his thoughts ...What first of all characterizes this image is the power of *negation* it possesses." The intuition of a philosopher is a kind of psychic scandal: "It cannot be like that! This doesn't match with the world I know, with the age I live in!" Since Plato ascribed to every philosopher the goal to perpetually redefine what is True, Just and Beautiful, this philosophical sense of scandal is at the same time moral, aesthetical and epistemological: "it is not true, it is not good; it is ugly to do/say that." The negative intuition is the sense of scandal that leads us to start to think in a new direction before knowing where we are going, where we want to go.[11]

This philosophical sense of scandal is very perceptible in Korzybski's *Science and Sanity*. Epistemological scandal comes from the fact that Ancient and Medieval European Science dominated by Aristotelian agenda and Modern European Science leaded by Newtonian way of thinking don't match with our "intuition" of *relatedness*: the conception of objects isolated in void space and subjects living in Mind's eternity don't match neither with a natural World made by the interconnection of co-evolutive "objects" nor with a human World made by subjects living in past-and-future perspective and present context. From this epistemological scandal derives a moral scandal since old habits of thinking impede our accommodation to the present living world. In this sense, like every classical philosopher and especially Plato again, Korzybski claims for an ἐπιστροφή, a conversion from an old common way of non-thinking/non-living to a new difficult way of thinking/living: from "Subject-predicate methods" to "Relational methods," from "Symmetrical relations" to

"Asymmetrical relations," from "*Static,* '*objective,*" 'permanent,' 'substance,' 'solid matter' tec. Orientations" to "*Dynamic,* ever-changing etc. electronic *process* orientations," from "Euclidean system" to "Non-Euclidean systems," from "Newtonian system" to "Einsteinian or non-Newtonian systems," from "Elementalistic structure of language and orientations" to "Non-Elementalistic structure of language and orientations," etc. [12]

Moreover, if we can refer to Bergson to give some light to the formal idea of intuition, the content of Bergson's idea of intuition is also relevant to Korzybski's non-Aristotelian intuition. For Bergson, intuition means, first of all, intuition of duration, firstly expressed in *Time and Free Will*: "Pure duration is the form which the succession of our conscious states assumes when our ego lets itself *live,* when it refrains from separating its present state from its former states. For this purpose it need not be entirely absorbed in the passing sensation or idea; for then, on the contrary, it would no longer *endure.* Nor need it forget its former states: it is enough that, in recalling these states, it does not set them alongside its actual state as one point alongside another, but forms both the past and the present states into an organic whole, as happens when we recall the notes of a tune, melting, so to speak, into one another. [...] We can thus conceive of succession without distinction, and think of it as a mutual penetration, an interconnexion and organization of elements, each one of which represents the whole, and cannot be distinguished or isolated from it except by abstract thought."[13] The notion of duration in Bergson's philosophy comes from the idea that the "identity" of a subject must be understood in terms of a subjective *continuity* constructed through the fusion of multiple moments of life into an organic and dynamic mind-and-body whole; it is then evolutionary qualified and cosmologically extended: "There is no doubt that life as a whole is an evolution, that is, an unceasing transformation. But life can progress only by means of the living, which are its depositaries. Innumerable living beings, almost alike, have to repeat each other in space and in time for the novelty they are working out to grow and mature."[14]

Bergson's concept of duration is very close to Korzybski's essential idea of "time-binding". Perhaps it doesn't really matter to know whether it is a direct influence of Bergson's works, an indirect influence coming through Whitehead's philosophy (often quoted in *Science and Sanity*) or a sheer convergence of minds in a philosophical environment globally dedicated to understand variations of Time (from Hegelian historicism and Nietzsche's refined Heracliteism) – before Vienne circle, migrating from Austria and

Germany, imposes again to philosophy, at least in the United-States, the old Cartesian and Newtonian idea of philosophy *sub specie* logical *aeternitas*. Whatever, "duration" and "time-binding" express a similar idea of a capacity to contract times in Time which is essentially "spiritual." The difference being that Korzybski assimilated this synthetic power to unify a multiplicity in a consistent whole not so much to the property of an individual but to the property of humanity in general: "the present writer introduced the term 'Time-binding' to cover all the factors 'as-a-whole' which made man, a man. We may agree that man differs somehow from animals by the capacity for building this accumulative affair called civilization."[15] "The energy of the human intellect is a time-binding energy, for it is able to direct, to use, to transform other energies. This time-binding energy is of higher rank — of higher dimensionality – than the other natural energies which it directs, controls, uses, and transforms. This higher energy – which is commonly called the mental or spiritual power of man – *is* time-binding because it makes past achievements live in the present and present activities in time-to-come."[16]

Korzybski and Deleuze: Philosophy of Difference

Korzybski's "negative" "intuition" directed against the union between Aristotelian principles and Newtonian physics (précised later by his positive "intuition" of the multiordinality of time process) can find an interesting support in Antonio Drago's essay about the Newtonian paradigm of differential mathematics: "To my knowledge, no criticism of the Aristotelian organization of Newton's *Principia* has ever been published [...] Let us inspect Newton's mechanics. Its first principle postulates a situation (the equivalence between rest and uniform, rectilinear motion) which could be realized only if one were able to exclude all the effects of friction – a very idealized situation which may be compared with the petition of dx as a non-zero infinitesimal. However, in the subsequent development of mechanics, the equation of motion of any real body takes into account friction by means of a macroscopic force. This is a second mistake because, as a theory of isolated mass-points, mechanics could not be applicable to a macroscopic, collective phenomenon. Yet, in a curious way, it can both account for the real facts and yield the correct results. [...] The double fault is actually the main feature of an Aristotelian theory. Its self-evident principles cannot represent a real process but only an idealized fiction: the second fault which is usually the second principle then redresses the first one in order to obtain correct results [...] The "Newtonian paradigm" stood unrecognized for several centuries while the Aristotelian option was so deeply ingrained in the scientific community of physicists that they substantiated it in the form of a physical magnitude, viz. space. It can be shown that, in the work of the founders of physical theories, there exists a sharp correlation between the choice of the Aristotelian model of organization and their use of the concept of absolute space (Descartes, Newton, Euler, Maxwell, Hertz, Boltzmann) and between the choice of the problematic model of organization and the use of relational space (Lagrange, L. Carnot, S. Carnot, the chemists, Faraday, Einstein)."[17]

In the classical conception of knowledge, abstract principles come first and then empirical corrections follow: reality is not included in principles; it is left to marginal corrections, boringly accommodating theory with reality. Reality is assimilated to a bad boy who doesn't want to obey the rules but from whom we accept turbulent behavior since it is in "youngster nature." Reality is the imperfect thing we have to take in account since "nothing is perfect in this world." However, in non-standard conception of knowledge, principles must incorporate reality in the first place: instead of theorematic hierarchy and absolute space-and-time, principles will reflect problematic processes and relational space-and-time. Similarly, when social organization succeeds in embodying real-life, youngsters' turbulent behavior are no more destructively opposing rules but creatively overcoming them.

Korzybski's philosophy seems to stem from this "intuition" of an asymmetric relational/differential/temporal dynamism governing Nature and Mind. In this respect, the very idea of a logic based on interactions, of an ontology of relativity (that has nothing to do with skeptical relativism) creates another convergence between Korzybski and Gilles Deleuze. They seem to share the core non-standard idea that the very substance of something is nothing but its actual process of variation, of continuous infinitesimal self-differentiation: "the intensional verbal definition of 'man' or 'chair' etc., brings to our consciousness *similarities*, and, so to say, drives the *differences* into the 'unconscious.' In a world of processes and non-identity, it follows that no individual, object, event, etc., can be the 'same' from one moment to the next. And so individualizing (indexes) and temporal devices (dates), etc., should be used *conjointly*. Thus obviously, $chair_1^{1600}$ and $chair_1^{1940}$, nor is $Smith_1^{Monday}$ the same as $Smith_1^{Tuesday}$. Orientations in such extensional terms bring to our consciousness not only similarities but also differences."[18] "The tree imposes the verb "to be," but the fabric of the rhizome is the conjunction "and... and... and." This conjunction carries enough force to shake and uproot the verb "to be."[19] "... starting from a basic "field" I, successive adjunctions to this field (R', R'', R''') allow a progressively more precise distinction of the roots of an equation, by the progressive limitations of possible substitutions." "Every phenomenon refers to an inequality by which it is conditioned. Every diversity and every change refers to a difference which is its sufficient reason. Everything which happens and everything which appears is correlated with orders of differences: difference of level, temperature, pressure, tension, potential, *difference of intensity* [...] every intensity is differential, by itself a difference. Every intensity is E-E', where E itself refers to an e-e' and e to ε-ε', etc..."[20]

In classical philosophy, Identity comes first and then empirical differences are taken into account to allow the down-the-line/approximate accommodation of sameness/allness principles to incorrect/misleading/culprit reality. In non-standard philosophy, Difference comes first (Difference is internal) and then empirical similarities are taken into account to understand analogies between things and convergences between forms. Time and place are not accidental/empirical/secondary factors but essential/endogen /virtual forces.

Ontology of Structures

Of course, it will be a complete misunderstanding to assimilate Time Differential process to a so-called "Heraclitean" flow of indistinct and destructive becoming.[21] On the contrary, the idea is that Time Creative Process can be precisely qualified as a process of differentiation in which every moment, with its virtual singularity, marks an order of intensity, structuring the topology of time's differentiating field.[22] It is the composition between these virtual differences and their interactions that gives an order and a *structure* to Time's "flow."

This is why the relation between Korzybski and French contemporary philosophy lies not only in the fact that they share *in some way* the concepts of Time as producer of Difference and of Variation as producer of Time. Actually, more important is the connection between Becoming and Structure with its fundamental semiotic consequences – as Deleuze shown in *Difference and Repetition*: "There is no more opposition between event and structure or sense and structure than there is between structure and genesis. [...] Those systems of differential elements and relations which we call structures are also sense from a genetic point of view, with regard to the actual terms and relations in which they are incarnated. The true opposition lies elsewhere between Idea (structure-event-sense) and representation. [...] Multiplicity tolerates no dependence on the identical in the subject or in the subject. The events and singularities of the Idea do not allow any positing of the essence as "what the thing is" [...] It is not surprising that, among many of the authors who promote it, *structuralism* is so often accompanied by calls for a new theatre or a new (non-Aristotelitian) interpretation of the theatre: a theatre of multiplicities opposed in every aspects to the theatre of representation, which [...] through the vicissitudes of the play, can become the object of a production of knowledge or final recognition. Instead a theatre of problems and always open question which draws spectator, setting and characters into the real movement of an apprenticeship of the entire unconscious, the final elements of which remain the problems themselves."[23]

There is no opposition between Structure and Becoming (structural order implies a diagram of singularities that Time forces will actualize) but between Structure and Representation: the essence of a thing is not given by the correspondence of an image in our Mind to what the thing IS in "reality"; the essence of a thing is nothing but the process through which we get acquainted to it and learn how to manipulate it while "this" "thing" *becomes* through a process of continuous intra-differentiation and inter-actions.

Structuralism means to go beyond the correspondence between idea, image and reality as explained by Michel Foucault in its opuscule *This is not a pipe* dedicated to René Magritte's famous painting *The Treachery of Images* (1928). For Foucault, contemporary painting subverts the categories of classical representation: "Two principles, I believe, ruled Western painting from the fifteenth to the twentieth century. The first asserts the separation between plastic representation (which implies resemblance) and linguistic reference (which excludes it) [...] The second principle that long ruled over painting posits an equivalence between the fact of resemblance and the affirmation of a representative bond. [...] With a sovereign and unique gesture, Kandinsky dismissed the old equivalence between resemblance and affirmation, freeing painting from both. Magritte proceeds by dissociating the two: disrupting their bonds, establishing their inequality, bringing one into play without the other, maintaining what stems from painting, and excluding that what is closest to discourse – pursuing as closely as possible the indefinite continuation of the similar, but excising it from any affirmation that would attempt to say what is resembled. An art of the "Same" liberated from the "as if."[24] Contemporary painting thus went into two directions: abolition of Representation and assumption of the Difference for itself (non-figurative art), perversion of Representation and assumption of the Repetition for itself (pop-art). Kandinsky revealed what is behind the representation, the deepness of things: Nature and forces, movements and intensities. Magritte displayed what is at the surface of representation, the shallowness of words: Mind and auto-referential concepts.

In this perspective, Foucault stresses the importance of Magritte's *The Treachery of Images* where a (representation of a) pipe is accompanied by a legend: "*Ceci n'est pas une pipe*".

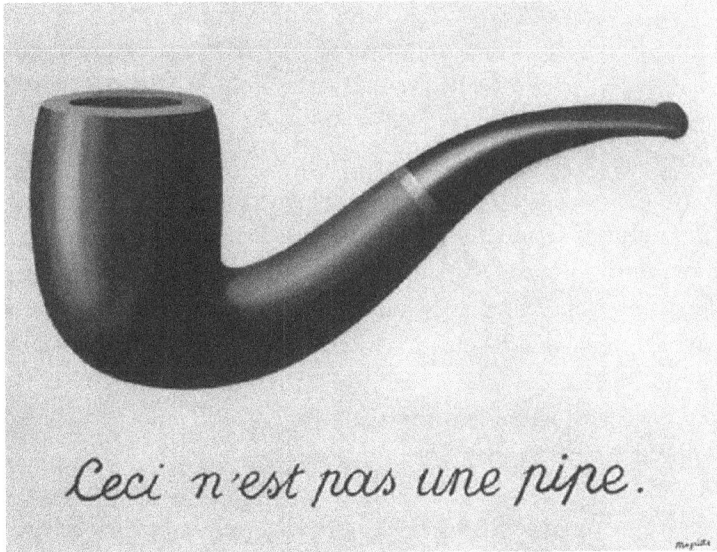

Foucault expresses the semiotic complexity of Magritte's painting by a succession of sentences, differentially exposing, continually correcting and increasingly complicating its "meaning": "'This is a pipe' [...] 'This is not a pipe, but the drawing of a pipe.'" "This is not a pipe but a sentence saying that this is not a pipe." "The sentence 'this is not a pipe' is not a pipe." "In the sentence 'this is not a pipe,' *this* is not a pipe: the painting, written sentence, drawing of a pipe – all this is not a pipe."[25]

If we go back now to "general semantics," we could notice that deconstruction of identity, disjunction between words and things, relativity (not relativism) of reality, correlation between process and structure, all these things seem present in Korzybski's *Science and Sanity*: "the use of the 'is' of identity [...] must be entirely abandoned. Whatever we may *say* a happening 'is', *it is not* [...] Words are not the things they represent."[26] "Let us repeat once more time the two crucial negative premises as established firmly by all human experience: (1) Words *are not* the things we are speaking about; and (2) There is no such thing as an object in absolute isolation."[27] "We start with the negative $\bar{A}$ premise that words are not the unspeakable objective level, such as actual objects outside of our skin and our personal feelings inside our skin. It follows that the only link between the objective and the subjective level is exclusively structural, necessitating the conclusion that the only content of all "knowledge" is structural. Now structure can be considered as a complex of relations, and ultimately as multidimensional order."[28]

These ideas are conceptually connected: if difference is the first principle, difference appears only in the relations between two "things" constituted by their interactions; if relation (not identity) defines "things," to qualify the "identity" of something will reveal only our perception of it, our relation to it; if there is no natural, foundational link between us and the world, the link is "arbitrary" or, more precisely, structural: "If words are not things, or maps are not the actual territory, then, obviously, the only possible link between the objective world and the linguistic world can be found in structure and structure alone."[29]

So could we be justified to say that Korzybski's general semantics is an unknown "precursor" of French Structuralism?

How Do We Recognize Structuralism?

Gilles Deleuze's essay "How to recognize structuralism?"[1] give some clues to answer this question. Deleuze defines seven criterion of structuralism: 1. Symbolic: "the positing of a symbolic order, irreducible to the orders of the real and the imaginary, and deeper than they are"; 2. Topologic: "The scientific ambition of structuralism is not quantitative, but topological and relational"; 3. Differential: "Singularities correspond with the symbolic elements and their relations, but do not resemble them"; 4. Virtual: "Structures are necessarily unconscious, by virtue of the elements, relations and points that compose them [...] In a certain way, they are not actual."; 5. Serial: "the terms of each series are in themselves inseparable from the slippages or displacements that they undergo in relation to the terms of the other. They are thus inseparable from the variation of differential relations."; 6. Distributive: "Distributing the differences through the entire structure, making the differential relations vary with its displacements, the object $=x$ constitutes the differenciating element of difference itself."; 7. Functional: *"As a general rule, the real, the imaginary and their relations are always engendered secondarily by the functioning of the structure, which starts with having its primary effects in itself."*

The first criterion is perhaps the most important. For Deleuze, the merit of Structuralism was to identify an order of reality named symbolic different from real and imaginary orders of reality. In order to explain that point Deleuze makes a comparison with the meaning of Real and Imaginary in Mathematical sciences: "We can distinguish three types of relation. A first type is established between elements which enjoy independence or autonomy: for example, $3 + 2$, or even $2/3$. The elements are real, and these relations must themselves be said to be real. A second type of relationship, for example, $x2 + y2 — R2 = 0$, is established between terms for which the value is not specified, but which in each case, however, must have a determined value. Such relations can be called imaginary. But the third type is established between elements which have no determined value themselves, and which nevertheless determine each other reciprocally in the relation: thus $ydy + xdx = 0$, or $dy-/ dx = - x/y$. Such relationships are symbolic, and the corresponding elements are held in a differential relationship. Dy is totally undetermined in relation to y, and dx is totally undetermined in relation to x: each one has neither existence, nor value, nor signification. And yet the relation dy/dx is totally determined, the two elements determining each other reciprocally in the relation."[31]

Perhaps it will be useful to remind the reader some elementary notions conveyed here. In mathematics, Real numbers ($\mathbb{R}$) include rational (whose decimal representation is infinite periodic $13/7=1.85714285714285714$) and irrationals ((whose decimal representation is infinite aperiodic like π $=3.14159265358979323846...$, e and $\sqrt{2}$); Imaginary numbers ($i\mathbb{R}$ or $\mathbb{I}$) includes numbers that give a negative result when squared. Real numbers and Imaginary numbers compose together Complex numbers ($\mathbb{C}$): a complex number z is the sum of $a + bi$ where a and b are Real numbers and i the standard imaginary unit satisfying $i^2 = -1$; in Cartesian coordinate, z is the vector of a diagram with b belonging to ($\mathbb{I}$) in ordinate and a belonging to ($\mathbb{R}$) in abscissa. The particularity of Complex numbers is that they form an algebraically closed field, where any polynomial equation has a root, i.e. whose complexity can be resolve in polynomial time (P). In this sense, if the Symbolic is of a higher order, its characteristic is to belong to non-polynomial problems (NP) whose resolution is whether undecidable whether exponential: growing with N. To give an inexact metaphor: the problems of humanity are NP problems because they are growing with humanity; humanity will never know the whole truth about the universe because universe complexity is growing in time (and humanity is one of the factors of this growing complexity).

But it is not exactly the way Deleuze presents the difference between imaginary and symbolic: Deleuze opposes x2 + y2 — R2 = 0 (algebraic equation of a circle) and a differential equation: ydy + xdx = 0 "which signifies 'the universal of the circle or of the corresponding function.'"[32] The difference is that in the algebraic equation, the value of x and y can be determined by other algebraic terms whereas in the differential equation the value of dx is nothing but its relation to dy.[33] To understand this point, one must remind that there exist three interpretations of differential in mathematics: "... the three kinds of mathematics involved, viz. non-standard analysis, 'rigorous' calculus, and constructive analysis, present three different conceptions of the concept of point. A point in non-standard analysis in general is an infinitesimal, in 'rigorous' analysis it is a classical real point [...] and in constructive analysis one is restricted to the use of intervals only [...] The three kinds of mathematics differ with regard to any differential equation, but the differences are particularly striking in the case of the problem of the exact differential. The non-standard analysis allows for infinitesimals and differentials [...] 'Rigorous' mathematics, on the hand, bans all infinitesimals and differentials [...]. Finally, constructive mathematics gives no meaning at all to differentials. Here the problem of exact differential is changed into the problem of studying when an integral over any closed path is equal to zero."[34] Deleuze's interpretation consists in rejecting both the realism of 'rigorous' calculus (defining point as something real and differential as something non-real) and the imaginary of non-standard analysis (defining point and differential as an infinitesimal via Hyperreal numbers *R: 1<w, 1+1<w, 1+1+1<w...) while adopting the constructive definition of

(symbolic) differential as a series converging to a limit ($\lim\limits_{x \to c} f(x) = L$)—which forms the basic of metric topology.

Let us take another way to explain it *via* semiotics and more especially Peirce's Trichotomy. We think that Deleuze's definition of real, imaginary and symbolic can be approached by Peirce's definition of icon, index and symbol—since Deleuze was particularly aware of Peirce's semiotic and used it as a grid for his classification of images in his books on Cinema. Peirce distinguishes three levels of reality, three kinds of ideas: "Firstness is the mode of being of that which is such as it is, positively and without reference to anything else. Secondness is the mode of being of that which is such as it is, with respect to a second but regardless of any third. Thirdness of that which is such as it is, in bringing a second and a third into relation to each other."[35] To these three orders of relations correspond three kinds of signs that express them: "In respect to their relations to dynamic objects, I divide signs into Icons, Indices and Symbols. I define an Icon as a Sign which is determined by its dynamic object by virtue of its own internal nature. Such is any qualisign, like a vision, - or the sentiment excited by a piece of music considered as representing what the composer intended. Such may be a sinsign, like an individual diagram; say a curve and its distribution of errors. I define an Index as a sign determined by its dynamic object by virtue of being in relation to it. Such is a Proper Name (a legisgn); such is the occurrence of a symptom of a disease. I define a Symbol as a Sign which is determined by its dynamic object only in the sense that it will be so interpreted. It thus depends upon a convention, a habit or a natural disposition of its interpretant or the field of its interpretant."[36] Icons have a physical resemblance between the signal and the meaning (a picture is an icon of the person represented); Indices have a correlation in space and time with its meaning (a grey cloud announces probable rains and a red light means stop); Symbols are words whose associations with other words create mental associations in correlation to a categogical context (Tiger is related to Strength, Wilderness, Jungle, a poem of Thomas Blake,…; it belongs to the group of Feline, Mammal, Animal, Organic, Existing,…; it has Stripes, Eyes, Fur, Fangs,…).

This tripartite order is followed by Deleuze in his definition of the symbolic nature of structure in Structuralism: "structure is at least triadic, without which it would not 'circulate'—a a third at once unreal, and yet not imaginable" (the symbolic is differential, it contains Difference, it is defined by internal differences: relations between differences create structure, relations of signs to another signs create meaning). For example, in Jacques Lacan's structuralist psychoanalysis a psychoanalytic problem is neither a problem with a Real father, nor a problem with an Imaginary Father but a problem with the Symbol of Father — whoever embodies this symbol in reality and whatever actualizes this symbol in our imagination. Thus psychological problems are problems of symbolization. But isn't it precisely the claim that Korzybski intended to put forth through general semantics?

CONCLUSION: KORZYBSKI AND THE SYMBOLIC

Now, in conclusion, we can go back to Korzybski and try to answer the question entitling our paper "is Korzybski's general semantics an unknown precursor of French structuralism?" Our first answer will be "no" — not because of Korzybski but because of the nature of this question that we need now to transform. Because the notion of "precursor" is a misleading concept; it indulges us to think that novelty was already present in the past whereas it is nothing but the creative product of the future — an illusion named by Bergson "the retrograde movement of truth."[37] French structuralism didn't exist before French structuralists give birth to it in the field of Mind. So the question must be modified and should take the following form: "is French structuralism an appropriate frame to evaluate the pertinence of Korzybski's *Science and Sanity?*" More precisely our question can be transformed in: "Can we find in Korzybski's *Science and Sanity* an articulation of the concept of symbolic rightly supporting his notion of structure?" Let us examine Korzybski's text: "If words are not things, or maps are not the actual territory, then, obviously, the only possible link between the objective world and the linguistic world can be found in structure and structure alone. The only usefulness of a map or a language depends on the similarity of structure between the empirical world and the map-languages."[38] The problem lies in the use of the notion of "similarity."

This notion of similarity seems to identify Korzybski's conception of Structure with the indexical notion of Order in Classical representative thinking.[39] Classical representative thinking dismissed the Aristotelian idea of an identity between reality and sensibility[40]: ideas coming from the senses are not representative of reality objectively but only subjectively. Ideas "resemble" to "reality" when they come from Mind and the unity of knowledge is possible due to the universality of human mind (whatever the source of such an universality: innate reason for rationalist, divine principles for idealist, human conventions for empiricist). But an epistemological problem appeared here: if we think that truth comes from Mind, how it comes that Mind matches with the world? In Classical, Cartesian and Newtonian philosophy, this correspondence was "supported" by the belief that, since the book of Nature was written by God in mathematical language, so the knowledge of mathematics will give to human the key to understand nature. In Modern, Kantian philosophy, this correspondence is justified by the theory upon which the world we see and feel is actually our representation: if the world matches with our mind, it is because it is in itself an "image," a phenomenon, and because sensible data are eventually indexed on mind categories.

Korzybski affirms: "If the structure is not similar, then the traveler or speaker is led astray, which, in serious human life-problems, must become eminently harmful. If the structures *are similar*, then the empirical world becomes 'rational' to a potentially rational being, which means no more than that verbal or map-predicted characteristics, which follows up the linguistic or map structure, are applicable to empirical world."[41] But the problem is: for what reason the fact that our Mind structure is *rational* will necessarily help us to reach a better accommodation with the *empirical* world? It is only because we *believe* that the World is rational that we can make this assumption. But how the world could be rational before reason is applied to it? The only possible answers will then come from philosophical variants of two theological conceptions: 1. Monotheism: we can understand the World because a Supra-Intelligence made it; 2. Buddhism/Taoism: we can understand the World because this world is nothing but an image of our Mind (therefore, the only important thing is learn how to deal and conveniently manage with human conventions: Pragmatism/Confucianism). Here are we trapped into the dialectic of real and imaginary without succeeding to reach the symbolic level of Mind. Actually, Korzybski's immediate answer doesn't help: "In fact, in structure we find the mystery of rationality, adjustment, and we find that the whole content of knowledge is exclusively structural."[42] The oxymoron "mystery of rationality" is very unsatisfying to explain this adjustment, especially for a promoter of positivism, science and rationality.

However a more convincing structuralist sense of the notion of structure appears in Korzybski's often obscure idea of "Structural Differential." The first principle of Korzybski's Structural Differential is evenementiality and therefore non-representationality: "Whitehead points out the fundamental difference between an event and an object in terms of recognition: namely, that an event cannot be recognized, and that an object can be recognized."[43] The second principle of Korzybski's differential structure is multiordinality: "In the language of the present general semantics a statement about a statement is not the same statement, but represents, by structural and neurological necessity, a higher order of abstraction and should not be confused with the original statement."[44] Therefore, the reason of a structure doesn't lie in its mimetic capacity to *imaginary* represent in Mind the *real* Order of the world "outside." The real reason of structure lies in its power of "*symbolization,*" i.e. in Mind faculty to create orders of generality[45] whose consistency does not depend on empirical organization of things "as they are." Because things ARE *not*, they **become**: how could we make a map "similar to" the world when the world itself is dissimilar, defined by probabilistic positions at the quantum level and by cosmologic expansion at the relativist level? Any similarity between structure and representation, between Idea and object will be only occasional.

This is why it is not similarity but creativity that symbolizes a Structure: "under such structural condition, the freedom of the writer or speaker becomes very much accentuated: his vocabulary consists potentially of infinite numbers of words, and psychological, semantic blockages are eliminated."[46] The freer Mind is in its operation, the most void is the center of the Structure, the most congruent will be the convergence between the series of Mind Differences and the series of Nature Differences. *It is only when our Mind is creative that we can catch the creativity of the World we live in: explaining reality means give to our Mind enough liberty to assimilate the creativity of Nature and enough differential precision for inner structure and outer order to slowly converge* (if mathematics can have an application in physics, perhaps it is because mathematics having no other constraints than Mind's rules can match with the level of liberty of the World only determined by Nature's rules).

Perhaps, some precepts for mind's sanity can be extracted from that: don't impose to your Mind the representation of what a rational thinking "must" be (imagination), don't impose to your representation the perception of what the things "are" (reality), be confident in Mind's power of symbolization, train and extend this power to actualize your potential of creativity. Stop to generalize and interpret (imagination), stop to isolate and identify (perception); serialize (chair$_1^{1600}$ > chair$_1^{1940}$), contextualize (Smith$_1^{\text{Monday}}$ > Smith$_1^{\text{Tuesday}}$) and symbolize (ydy + xdx = 0).

NOTES

[1] Alfred Korzybski, *Science and Sanity*, "Introduction to the second edition", New York: Institute of General Semantics, 2000, p. xxxix.

[2] According to Martín Gardner, Facts and fallacies in the name of science, Mineola: Dover Publications, 1957, p. 281: "[Science and Sanity] is a poorly organized, verbose, philosophically naïve, repetitive mish-mash of sound ideas borrowed from abler scientists and philosophers, mixed with neologisms, confused ideas, unconscious metaphysics, and highly dubious speculations about neurology and psychiatric therapy." About Korzybski's style it is perhaps not so false but our purpose will be to evaluate the resonance of some of its most sounding ideas with Structuralist theory.

[3] In Martín Gardner's Facts and fallacies in the name of science, Korzybski's general semantics is, with many others therapeutic practices, rejected as non-scientific. But the problem is that science is evolving and practices that appeared non-scientific at one moment can receive scientific accreditation later, like osteopathy whose efficiency seem to have been certified by various scientific studies: J.C. Licciardone, A.K. Brimhall, L.N. King, "Osteopathic manipulative treatment for low back pain: a systematic review and meta-analysis of randomized controlled trials", BMC Musculoskelet Disord, 2004, 6: 43; Gunnar B.J. Andersson, Tracy Lucente, Andrew M. Davis, Robert E. Kappler et al., "A Comparison of Osteopathic Spinal Manipulation with Standard Care for Patients with Low Back Pain", *The New England Journal of Medicine*, 1999 341: 1426-1431; R. A. Deyo, J. N. Weinstein, "Low back pain", *The New England Journal of Medicine*, 2001, 344: 363-370.

[4] Pierre Hadot, Qu'est-ce que la philosophie antique?, Gallimard, 1995.

[5] Alexey Stakhov & Scott Olsen, *The Mathematics of Harmony: from Euclid to Contemporary Mathematics and Computer Sciences*, Singapore: World Scientific Publishing, 2009, p. 37: ""Pythagorean School," or "Pythagorean Union," was simultaneously a philosophical school, a political party, and a religious brotherhood". Georgia Lynette Irby-Massie & Paul Turquand Keyser, *Greek Science of the Hellenistic Era: a sourcebook*, London: Routledge, 2002, p. 9: "Pythagoras himself never published anything, and the evidence that he founded any sort of self-perpetuating school is very dubious. (He did run a secret political society in his own lifetime). [...] The evidence of Aristotle and Aristoxenos, who wrote books on the Pythagoreans, suggests that it was in the mid-fourth century that the movement was reorganized as a formal school [...]

It is at this time that the characteristics Pythagorean doctrines of medical import are first attested: advocacy of vegetarianism, and denial of surgery and abortion [...] The neo-Pythagoreans emphasized the fundamental roles of number in the kosmos, and focused their thought especially on astronomy and music."

[6] Myron A. Penner, "Normativity in Deleuze and Guattari's concept of philosophy", *Continental Philosophy Review*, March 2003, 36 (1): 45-59: "An interlocutor might think that by criticizing a concept she is pointing out mistakes in a truth-functional way. However, according to [Deleuze and Guattari] what her criticism reveals is simply that concepts cannot transcend their plane of creation and their sphere of operation. And that revelation is of little philosophical worth unless it is accompanied by new concepts on new planes." Reidar Due, *Deleuze*, Polity Press, 2007, p. 150: "Deleuze does not characterize philosophy as knowledge or the search for truth. He does not characterize philosophical thought by its relation to an outside about which it would purport to produce knowledge. His conception of philosophy is thus radically constructivist: philosophy is a practice of immanent invention which is not answerable to any external instance of truth – such as God, experience or scientific theories [...] The task faced by any philosopher as a result of this radical immanence is to produce a system of concepts and problems that has sufficient internal consistency and specificity in order not to collapse into mere opinion. Philosophy derives this consistency from the internal systematicity of is construction."

[7] Alfred Korzybski, *Science and Sanity*, "Introduction to the second edition", New York: Institute of General Semantics, 2000, p. xxxviii.

[8] Alfred Korzybski, *Science and Sanity*, New York: Institute of General Semantics, 2000, p. 18.

[9] Alfred Korzybski, *Science and Sanity*, New York: Institute of General Semantics, 2000, p. 20.

[10] Henri Bergson, *The Creative Mind*, "Philosophical intuition", in *Key Writings*, transl. Keith Ansell-Pearson & John Mullarkey, New York: Continuum, 2005, p. 234.

[11] Maurice Merleau-Ponty, *In Praise of Philosophy and Other Essays*, Evanston: Northwestern University Press, 1988, transl. John Wild & James Edie, p. 18: "What precisely is intuitive in intuition? Bergson admits that most of the time it is present to the philosopher only in the form of a certain "power of negation" that excludes theses which are insufficient. Should we suppose a

positive and already made view which underlies these negative appearances and sustains them? This would be to give way to the retrospective illusion, precisely criticized by Bergson. The global view which he calls intuition orients the whole efforts of the philosopher, but it does not contain it in abridged form."

[12] Alfred Korzybski, *Science and Sanity*, "Introduction to the second edition", New York: Institute of General Semantics, 2000, p. liii.

[13] Henri Bergson, *Time and Free Will: An Essay on the Immediate Data of Consciousness*, translated by F.L. Pogson, London: George Allen and Unwin, 1910, p. 100-1.

[14] Henri Bergson, *Creative Evolution*, translated by Arthur Mitchel, New York: Random House, 1944, p. 252.

[15] Alfred Korzybski, "Time-Binding: the General Theory: First Paper", Presented in abstract before the International Mathematical Congress, August, 1924. Toronto, Canada.

[16] Alfred Korzybski, *Manhood Of Humanity The Science and Art of Human Engineering*, New York: E. P. Dutton & Company, 1921, p. 89.

[17] Antonio Drago, "A characterization of the Newtonian Paradigm" in *Newton's Scientific and Philosophical Legacy*, ed. Paul B. Scheurer, G. Debrock, Dordrecht: Kluwer Academic Publishers, 1988, pp. 239-252.

[18] Alfred Korzybski, *Science and Sanity*, "Introduction to the second edition", New York: Institute of General Semantics, 2000, p. lxiii.

[19] Gilles Deleuze, *A Thousand Plateaus*, "Introduction: Rhizome", London: Continnum, transl. Brian Massumi, 2004, p. 27.

[20] Gilles Deleuze, *Difference and Repetition*, London: Continnum, transl. Paul Paton, Massumi, 2004, p. 227-228, p. 280-281.

[21] It is Plato's interpretation Heraclitus' philosophy in *Cratylus*, 402 a: "λέγει που Ἡράκλειτος ὅτι "πάντα χωρεῖ καὶ οὐδὲν μένει," καὶ ποταμοῦ ῥοῆἀπεικάζων τὰ ὄντα λέγει ὡς "δὶς ἐς τὸν αὐτὸν ποταμὸν οὐκ ἂν ἐμβαίης." Translated by Harold N. Fowler, Cambridge: Harvard University Press, 1921: "Heraclitus says, you know, that all things move and nothing remains still, and he likens the universe to the current of a river, saying that you cannot step twice into the same stream." But Heraclitus' philosophy itself on the contrary stress the continuity of becoming through cyclic renewing: Heraclitus B VI: ὁ ἥλιος νέος ἐφ' ἡμέρῃ ἐστίν/ the sun is renewing in every moment.

[22] Mary Jane West-Eberhard, *Developmental Plasticity and Evolution*, Oxford University Press, 2003.

[23] Gilles Deleuze, *Difference and Repetition*, London: Continnum, transl. Paul Paton, Massumi, 2004, p. 240-1.

[24] Michel Foucault, *This is not a Pipe*, ed. And transl. James Harkness, Berkeley: University of California Press, 1983, p. 32, p. 34, p. 43.

[25] Michel Foucault, *This is not a Pipe*, ed. And transl. James Harkness, Berkeley: University of California Press, 1983, p. 30.

[26] Alfred Korzybski, *Science and Sanity*, New York: Institute of General Semantics, 2000, p. 751.

[27] Alfred Korzybski, *Science and Sanity*, New York: Institute of General Semantics, 2000, p. 60-1.

[28] Alfred Korzybski, *Science and Sanity*, New York: Institute of General Semantics, 2000, p. 20.

[29] Alfred Korzybski, *Science and Sanity*, New York: Institute of General Semantics, 2000, p. 61.

[30] Gilles Deleuze, *Desert Islands and Other Texts* (1953-1974), Semiotext(e), ed. David Lapoujade, transl. Michael Taormina, 2004, p. 170-192.

[31] Gilles Deleuze, *Desert Islands and Other Texts* (1953-1974), Semiotext(e), ed. David Lapoujade, transl. Michael Taormina, 2004, p. 176.

[32] Gilles Deleuze, *Difference and Repetition*, London: Continnum, transl. Paul Paton, Massumi, 2004, p. 218.

[33] Henry Somers-Hall, "Hegel and Deleuze on the metaphysical interpretation of the calculus", *Continental Philosophy Review*, 42 (4): 555-572: "the calculus cannot be conceived of as operating with algebraic terms, since in this case ''there must always be a particular value charged with representing the others and with standing in for them.'' Thus, the equation of the circle, $x2 + y2 — R2 = 0$, is opposed to its differential, $ydy + xdx = 0$, in which such a substitution of arbitrary values cannot be made."

[34] Antonio Drago, "A characterization of the Newtonian Paradigm" in *Newton's Scientific and Philosophical Legacy*, ed. Paul B. Scheurer & G. Debrock, Dordrecht: Kluwer Academic Publishers, 1988, pp. 239-252.

[35] Charles Sanders Peirce, *Collected Papers of Charles Sanders Peirce: Reviews, Correspondence and Bibliography*, Volume 8, "To Lady Welby: On signs and the Categories", London: Oxford University Press, ed. Arthur W. Burks, 1957, p. 220-230.

[36] Charles Sanders Peirce, *Collected Papers of Charles Sanders Peirce: Reviews, Correspondence and Bibliography*, Volume 8, "To Lady Welby: On signs and the Categories", London: Oxford University Press, ed. Arthur W. Burks, 1957, p. 220-230.

[37] Henri Bergson, *The Creative Mind*, "Introduction I: Retrograde Movement of the True Growth of Truth," translated by Mabelle L. Andison, Philosophical Library, New York, 1946, 13.

[38] Alfred Korzybski, *Science and Sanity*, New York: Institute of General Semantics, 2000, p. 61.

[39] Descartes, *Méditations Métaphysiques in Descartes*, Œuvres philosophiques, Tome II, édition Alquié, Garnier-Flammarion, 1980 p. 433[2] : « Entre mes pensées, quelques-unes sont comme les images des choses, et c'est à celles-là seules que convient proprement le nom d'idée : comme lorsque je me représente un homme, ou une chimère, ou le ciel, ou un ange, ou Dieu même ». « Quaedam ex his tanquam rerum imagines sunt, quibus solis proprie conventi ideae nomen : ut cum hominem, vel Chimaeram, vel Coelum, vel Angelum, vel Deum cogito. »

[40] Aristotle, *On Interpretation*, §1: "Spoken words are the symbols of mental experience and written words are the symbols of spoken words. Just as all men have not the same writing, so all men have not the same speech sounds, but the mental experiences, which these directly symbolize, are the same for all, as also are those things of which our experiences are the images"

[41] Alfred Korzybski, *Science and Sanity*, New York: Institute of General Semantics, 2000, p. 61.

[42] Alfred Korzybski, *Science and Sanity*, New York: Institute of General Semantics, 2000, p. 61.

[43] Alfred Korzybski, *Science and Sanity*, New York: Institute of General Semantics, 2000, p. 390.

[44] Alfred Korzybski, *Science and Sanity*, New York: Institute of General Semantics, 2000, p. 432.

[45] Alfred Korzybski, *Science and Sanity*, New York: Institute of General Semantics, 2000, p. 439: "structurally and potentially, man can abstract in indefinitely many orders, and no one can say legitimately that he has reached the 'final' order of abstraction beyond which no one can go."

[46] Alfred Korzybski, *Science and Sanity*, New York: Institute of General Semantics, 2000, p. 437.

REFERENCES

Aristotle's De interpretatione, translated by David A. Blank, Oxford: Clarendon Press, 1996.

Bergson, H. *Creative evolution*, translated by Arthur Mitchel, New York: Random House, 1944.

Bergson, H. *The Creative Mind*, translated by Mabelle L. Andison, Philosophical Library, New York, 1946.

Bergson, H. *Time and Free Will: An Essay on the Immediate Data of Consciousness*, translated by F.L. Pogson, London: George Allen and Unwin, 1910.

Deleuze, G. *Desert Islands and Other Texts (1953-1974)*, ed. David Lapoujade, transl. Michael Taormina, Los Angeles: Semiotext(e), 2004.

Deleuze, G. *Difference and Repetition*, London: Continnum, transl. Paul Paton, Massumi, 2004.

Deleuze, G. *Thousand Plateaus*, London: Continnum, transl. Brian Massumi, 2004.

Descartes, R. *Méditations métaphysiques* in Descartes, *Œuvres philosophiques*, Tome II, édition Alquié, Garnier-Flammarion, 1980.

Deyo, R. A. & Weinstein, J. N. "Low back pain", *The New England Journal of Medicine*, 2001, 344: 363-370.

Drago, A. "A characterization of the Newtonian Paradigm" in *Newton's Scientific and Philosophical Legacy*, ed. Paul B. Scheurer & G. Debrock, Dordrecht: Kluwer Academic Publishers, 1988, pp. 239-252.

Due, R. *Deleuze*, Polity Press, 2007.

Foucault, M. *This is not a pipe*, ed. And transl. James Harkness, Berkeley: University of California Press, 1983.

Gardner, M. *Fads and Fallacies in the Name of Science*, Mineola: Dover Publications, 1957

Hadot, P. *Qu'est-ce que la philosophie antique ?* Gallimard, 1995.

Irby-Massie, G. L. & Turquand, Keyser P. *Greek Science of the Hellenistic Era: A Sourcebook*, London: Routledge, 2002.

Kappler, R.E. & al. "A Comparison of Osteopathic Spinal Manipulation with Standard Care for Patients with Low Back Pain", *The New England Journal of Medicine*, 1999 341: 1426-1431.

Korzybski, A. "Time-Binding: the General Theory: First Paper", Presented in abstract before the International Mathematical Congress, August, 1924. Toronto, Canada.

Korzybski, A. *Manhood Of Humanity The Science and Art of Human Engineering*, New York: E. P. Dutton & Company, 1921.

Korzybski, A. *Science and Sanity*, New York: Institute of General Semantics, 2000.

Licciardone, J.C. & al. "Osteopathic Manipulative Treatment for Low Back Pain: A Systematic Review and Meta-Analysis of Randomized Controlled Trials." *BMC Musculoskelet Disord*, 2004, 6: 43.

Merleau-Ponty, M. *In Praise of Philosophy and Other Essays*. (Trans. John Wild & James Edie Myron). Evanston: Northwestern University Press, 1988.

Peirce, C. S. *Collected Papers of Charles Sanders Peirce: Reviews, Correspondence and Bibliography*, Volume 8. (Ed. Arthur W. Burks). London: Oxford University Press, 1957.

Penner, A. "Normativity in Deleuze and Guattari's concept of philosophy." *Continental Philosophy Review*, March 2003, 36 (1): 45-59.

Plato. *Cratylus*, translated by David Sedley, Cambridge: Cambridge University Press, 2003.

Somers-Hall, H. "Hegel and Deleuze on the Metaphysical Interpretation of the Calculus." *Continental Philosophy Review*, 42 (4): 555-572.

Stakhov, A. & Olsen, S. *The Mathematics of Harmony: From Euclid to Contemporary Mathematics and Computer Sciences*. Singapore: World Scientific Publishing, 2009.

West-Eberhard, M. J. *Developmental Plasticity and Evolution*, Oxford University Press, 2003.

William Henry Sharp

THE COURSE OF SOCIAL MOVEMENTS is often shaped by men and women who join them, bringing their own considerable creative talents. The field of general semantics, founded by Alfred Korzybski, was especially gifted in terms of its followers. Indeed, Korzybski went to great lengths to speak to and attract the best minds of his time. But such gifted followers can be a mixed blessing.

In the preparation of my book *Alfred Korzybski: Time Binder*, I read the entire body of Korzybski's writings, as well as at least some the works of other contributors to the field of general semantics. Like many, I was first attracted to general semantics through the works of those who wrote about it, particularly the novels of A.E. van Vogt[1] and several books by J. S. Bois and S. I. Hayakawa.

The term "general semantics" has its own history, and, as in all things, Korzybski's choice of the term was deliberate. From *Manhood of Humanity* (1921), it took him a dozen years to come up with a name for his mission that would distinguish it from other subjects. As I read the *Collected Writings*, a compilation of articles, talks, letters and other documents by Korzybski, I noticed that towards the end of his life Korzybski began to dwell on what he found to be a profoundly aggravating problem with the interpretation of his work, that was, the perversion of "general semantics" into "semantics." When I read the heated exchange between Korzybski and Hayakawa in the *Collected Writings*[2] I came to understand Korzybski's difficulty.

One of the questions I asked when I undertook a systematic study of Korzybski's life and work was its relevance to the 21st century. Korzybski died 60 years ago. In July of 2010 I visited the house at Lime Rock, Connecticut, where he lived the last few years of his life. That house remained the center of the general semantics movement for some years under the stewardship of Marjorie Kendig and Charlotte Schuchardt Read. I don't hear about people visiting that house or Korzybski's grave. The physical places associated with Korzybski have, perhaps, been forgotten. But, thankfully, Kendig, Read and a handful of others scrupulously preserved his work.

As important as preservation of the body of work of a thought leader is, the interpretation and use of those works after their death can define their presence in the history of ideas. Korzybski's works are hard to read, so it is natural that we turn to interpretations. However, having read Korzybski's own works, not once, but several times, as he suggested, I have learned that no one has even begun to make an adequate interpretation of his work. And, worse than inadequate interpretation, I believe we would all agree, is misinterpretation. In attempting to understand Korzybski's distress with the term "semantics," I found two of his "followers" at the root of the issue: Stuart Chase and S. I. Hayakawa. In this article I will write about Stuart Chase and his relationship to Korzybski. In a following article I will cover Hayakawa.

While offering this critique of these two men, I must apologize in advance for the feelings it will undoubtedly invoke. As I learned at a meeting of general semanticist a few years ago, there are still some sensitive feelings about the Hayakawa-Korzybski dispute. Given that the Institute of General Semantics recently established the S. I. Hayakawa Book Prize for the best works in the field of general semantics, I am also aware that these articles will likely evoke disputation. Still, I believe it is time to have this conversation.

Korzybski Goes Public

The year 1938 was important in the life of Alfred Korzybski. Two events in the history of general semantics that year were, first, the founding of the Institute of General Semantics in Chicago in June 1938, and, second, the publication of Stuart Chase's *The Tyranny of Words* which introduced Korzybski and his work to a large audience.

Stuart Chase (1888-1985) was one of the best-known popular economists during the American Depression era. By the end of a long life (97 years), he had published 35 books. He wrote hundreds of articles and pamphlets and was in demand as a speaker. He was the first major writer to introduce Korzybski and general semantics to a wider reading audience. Three of his books touched on the topic of general semantics.

Chase studied engineering and economics at MIT and business, banking and economics at Harvard, graduating *cum laude* in 1910. He then went to work for his father's accounting firm in Boston, qualified as a CPA and became a partner in the firm his grandfather had founded. He became a recognized expert in cost accounting. In 1917 he joined the Federal Trade Commission (FTC) and was sent to Chicago to study the meatpacking industry to help determine fair, wartime profits. After an extensive cost accounting of the industry, his findings, "Profits of the Packers," were published by the FTC and redefined fair and reasonable profits. Warren G. Harding, then Republican Senator and future President of the U.S., successfully pressured to have Chase fired in 1920.

The following year Chase moved to New York City where he established himself as a radical and vocal economic critic. He had served at the Jane Addams Hull House while in Chicago and been a member of the Boston Fabian (socialist) Society. He served as a pro bono volunteer for the Labor Bureau and was influenced by the radical British artist and social critic John Ruskin (1819-1900). He collaborated closely with arguably the nation's most outspoken, radical economist and sociologist, Thorstein Veblen, and became involved with a group that called itself the "Technical Alliance," an association of engineers working under Veblen's guidance to improve American industry. From his research into the inefficiencies he found prevalent in many businesses[3] he published *The Tragedy of Waste* in 1925. As a pioneering consumer advocate, he published a bestseller, *Your Money's Worth,* in 1927 and in 1929, with F.J. Schlink, set up the non-profit Consumer Advocacy Agency, the forerunner of today's *Consumer Reports*. In 1927 he traveled to Russia on an economic mission and met with Joseph Stalin, which in later years resulted in allegations that he was a Bolshevik.

His greatest fame came from his book, *The New Deal* (1932); the title of this bestseller was adopted by Franklin D. Roosevelt for his great social revitalization program that helped bring the U.S. out of the Great Depression. Chase had apparently met Franklin Roosevelt, then governor of New York, in 1931, the year before he published *The New Deal*. Roosevelt first used the "New Deal" theme in his acceptance of the Democratic nomination for president in 1932. Chase became actively involved in a variety of Roosevelt's New Deal programs, mostly as a consultant, and FDR later included Chase in his kitchen cabinet. Roosevelt once called Chase one of the most important economists and the most effective public teacher of economics in the country, indeed, the equal of all the others combined.

A Shade of Red

Predictability, Korzybski repeatedly stressed, is the essence of the scientific method. Predictability is perhaps the central purpose of scientific enquiry. Social philosophers, since the Enlightenment, and social scientists at least since the days of Comte and Spencer, sought a positivistic, law-based, science of humanity. The most mathematical, by far, of the social sciences, is economics. In a world of economically focused enterprise and in the pursuit of political ambition, a close study of economics is fundamental. From national budgets to business plans of small startup companies, the principles and basic assumptions of economics must be closely attended to. A long line of Nobel prizes has been awarded to economists.[4] The vast graduate business school system that feeds world commerce is dominated by economists.

Hand-in-glove with economics is the field of politics. Stuart Chase was a "political economist." In his early days Chase identified with the radical left; however, I would sum up the drift of Chase's work as not only radical but at times violently revolutionary. Never an avowed communist, as far as I know, Chase was nonetheless extremely sympathetic to the Russian Communist Revolution. In some of his writings, he even advocated measures as extreme as the use of firing squads to rid society of recalcitrant businessmen and bring about social change.

Chase was an avowed Keynesian. Keynes, Einstein and Korzybski, he later said, were the three greatest revolutionary figures in his life. He opened chapter one of *The New Deal* with the sentence "John Maynard Keynes tells us" (and this is the first of his questionable predictions) "that in one hundred years there will be no economic problems." Chase affirmed that, "He is probably right." How that will come about, Chase explained, is through advancing means of production that, in the U.S. and Russia, will leave economic scarcity behind. It is not so much a matter of productive power, which he saw as already in place, but a problem of distribution. This problem, he pointed out, had been seriously aggravated by the Depression but it is also deeply rooted in our political system.

Chase outlined three forms of political development in the U.S, the most likely, he stated, was "the drastic and progressive revision of the economic structure." This required a collective will and would be aided by a dictator. He believed the Depression would provide the means for mobilization of an intelligent minority of workers, fortified by scientific knowledge, who would be opposed by the "stupid," entrenched power brokers (stupid because they must inevitably fail). Taylor[5], he said, was a forerunner of scientific organization and change. Close to Scientific Management are the engineers, technicians and operating managers who man the switches of industry and have a realistic perception of cause and effect. Indeed, "They must have." Such a class, he added, existed in Russia.

The bottom line for Chase is economic planning and control from the top. "The foundation of economic planning is science supervising people's housekeeping:" economically engineered working in the kitchen. It is a coordination of science and finance. Chase used as an illustration the American troops fighting in Europe during World War I: "In return for their service, soldiers were provided with food, clothing, shelter, tobacco and a fabulous tonnage of lethal weapons and explosive." They were readily given what they needed to do their job. A general staff insured the flow of these materials and services. Thus, he reasoned, a general staff, or National Planning Board, was required for the economic recovery — "a group which sees the whole picture, and how each segment dovetails with the next; a group which has access to a steady flow of facts and statistics covering all significant aspects of the country's economic life; a group which knows the past, can give capable advices as to the present, and sees into the future, especially the technological future." Under it would be Regional Boards manned by engineers, physical scientists, statisticians, economists, accountants, and lawyers; the real work would be done by "clearheaded" technicians. The Planning Board must carefully study conditions and devise a workable plan and then set up appropriate programs. Chase listed a number of public works projects to be undertaken and added that his list was supported by one of the American Engineering Societies.[6]

The Wrong Map

Chase was a public educator and a lifelong advocate of adult and continuing education to insure that the public understood important civil issues and could better resist the insidious influence of mass-market advertising. He was considered a charismatic and passionate lecturer. He had a reputation for having a gift for presenting complex ideas in simple terms, in both speech and print. He constantly challenged waste and adopted Ruskin's term "illith" for economic and social activities that produced no social good. He found waste in poor cost accounting, in inefficient plant and business management, and in dependence on the market to define demand, etc.

In 1932 Chase began to look at his own methods of communications. In his search for a better means to express himself, Chase "found certain men who had penetrated boldly into the heart of the subject." *The Tyranny of Words* was the result of this investigation. He wrote: "Three human beings to my knowledge have observed and reflected upon the nature of meaning and communication for any considerable period. By considerable I mean years and years of intensive effort." Korzybski was at the top of his list. Chase gave him the first of his chapters on "Pioneers." While warning his readers that his book was "not pure Korzybski," he set out to explain some of Korzybski's key ideas. For example, Chase related how our remote ancestors, like children, objectified their feelings and treated them like objects. To this very day those concepts, he noted, are rooted in the structure of our language, "To plague us." Primitive languages, he continued, have given us "the subject-predicate form with the 'is' of identity." They also gave us one-valued and two-valued appraisal, he added. He wrote that we too often "become" the label casually attached to us. Korzybski's cardinal point, Chase said, is that "If we wish to understand the world and ourselves, it follows that we should use a language whose structure corresponds to physical structure." Chase illustrated this point with the map-territory metaphor.

Chase elaborated on the contamination of human language, which was full of the waste products of past ages, such as habits of identification and the confusion of abstract symbols with actual objects of experience. There are also subject-predicate forms with the "is" of identity, two-valued reasoning, myth, metaphysics, creeds and outworn beliefs. Our representation of the world is dissimilar to the world itself—indeed "false to facts." He also explained the meaning of the term "Non-Aristotelian." He agreed with Korzybski that mathematics provides a model for language. Chase described the structural differential, talked about extensional devices, summarized the process of consciousness of abstraction, and noted that reputable psychiatrists reported success using Korzybski's methods.

Chase did an admirable job of conveying the basic principles of general semantics in twenty pages and in other scattered comments. His presentation was clear and well illustrated with attractive examples and stories. In another part of the book he provided a more detailed list of the principles of Korzybski's system and on several occasions, used some of those principles to illustrate and clarify his own thinking about economics and social change.

Chase did add some critical comments, however. For one, he said he had read *Science and Sanity* three times "completely through," and certain portions up to a dozen times, and found it ironic that a book on the clarification of meaning should be so hard to read. He noted that the book does, in fact, include a lot of scientific explanation and that Korzybski had "entangled this study with an earlier concept called 'time binding.'" "But," he added, "I am confident that the material with which he has so exhaustively dealt is of the first importance, and that many of his findings will survive to do him lasting honor. To one who reads and reflects patiently upon this book, the world can never look as it did before. It seemingly moves nearer. Many things which were once blurred and misty come into focus."

In his last chapter, "Facing the World," Chase attempted to summarize his own semantic insights. He said he had become an advocate of continuing education in order to prepare the public for democratic participation and to help people better understand the state of the world and potential remedies for its ills. Yet, while he was a best-selling author, in demand as a speaker and favored by FDR, he somehow found it difficult to communicate his ideas to a public in whose best interest he was working. He felt challenged to overcome social inertia to new ideas. Something was obviously not going right in his life.

His research involved a closer look at the social conditions of the United States of the time. He observed a nation which had undergone a period of incredible change with the settlement of the frontier, the bloody experience of the First World War, was then deeply mired in the Depression, and would likely soon, with Hitler already on the rampage in Europe, have to face another imminent horrific war. We are a troubled and unsettled people, he concluded.

In this last chapter he framed his concerns in personal terms. "Confusions," he wrote, "persist and increase because we have no true picture of the world outside[7], and so cannot talk to one another about how to stop them. We are a talking species but our constant chatter causes us great difficulty. There is a lot of emotion in public discourse, from pulpits and public platforms. We are constantly contradicting each other and that leads to hatreds and violence." He asked a lot of Why questions which "have haunted me for years."

Though he doesn't use Korzybski's name again we find him indexing, working on his undefined terms, and distinguishing man from animal. He wrote: "We desperately need a language structure for the clear communication of observations, deductions and ideas concerning the environment in which we live," a semantic discipline, a "separate mental machinery from tangible events; [which] makes us conscious of abstracting."

He said he kept coming back to the idea of the "map." Like Korzybski he was looking for a foundation for agreement, not forced or coerced, but more like that found in science. We have to learn to "see the things behind the names," he concluded. As an appendix Chase provided 22 "HORRIBLE EXAMPLES" of high-order abstractions; he started and ended each point with examples from his own writings.

Faint Praise

I want to again draw attention to the frequent occasions when Korzybski stressed the difference between "semantics" and "general semantics" during the last years of his life. Korzybski was obviously deeply troubled by the confusion which the use of the term "semantics" by his students was causing. "Semantics' was a popular and widely studied topic at the time. There were several popular works on sale about semantics, but none of those was authored by Korzybski. Korzybski made it clear that the field of semantics was considerably inferior to the formulations of his own work. He obviously believed that confusing the two fields by those who were among his leading students was detrimental to the progress of general semantics.

In fairness, I must point out that Chase said he was not trying to be a general semanticist, but trying to develop his own system, a synthesis of general semantics and other fields, including semantics. He devoted considerable space to Ogden and Richards. Their book, *The Meaning of Meaning,* was an extremely popular text on semantics at the time. None of his three books 'about' general semantics were, in fact, about general semantics. That becomes clear in his comments in the last of these books, *Power of Words* (1953).

Power of Words devotes two chapters to Korzybski, yet it is not until page ten that Chase first mentions Korzybski's name, and then only in passing. Up to that point he has already introduced the "uniqueness of men," and the emotional content of words as significant parts of his system—ideas he had drawn from but without citation to Korzybski. In the section following page ten we find a list of "Twelve kinds of communication failures." While Chase does not name his sources, most of them are clearly from Korzybski. After a long ramble through the sciences, engineering (including computers) and philosophy (including the latest revolution in the philosophy of quantum science), he comes back to Korzybski on page 124 with these words "If science attempts to find out how the universe works, semantics attempts to give ordinary talk some of the benefits of the new talk in science. It is the core of Korzybski's work. How far has this attempt succeeded?" Even here, Chase, while obviously chaffing from Korzybski's criticism of the use of the term, continued his habitual use of "semantics."

Chase's last words, an epitaph, on Korzybski came with this book.[8] He recalled Korzybski:

> As I knew him in his later years—he was 70 when he died—he had the general aspect of an amiable Buddha, bald as a newel post, with kindly, intelligent eyes behind vast, round spectacles, and with a rich Polish accent. He wore as a kind of uniform a khaki shirt, open at the throat, which sometimes kept him out of hotel dining rooms. He was rude, formidable, over-verbalized and strongly appealing—for all I know, an authentic genius. Poland has produced more than her share of mathematical philosophers.

He went on to say:

> I shall never cease to be grateful for the wholesome shock my nervous system received when I first read Korzybski's magnum opus, *Science and Sanity*. It forced me to realize some of the unconscious assumptions imbedded in the language, which I as a writer had been calmly accepting. He published two books and a score of papers, all hard to read. It took me two years of reasonably steady application to bulldoze my way through *Science and Sanity*, and I do not think this sluggish pace was altogether my fault. By a curious paradox, Korzybski, who had dedicated his life to clearing communication lines, had the utmost difficulty in clearing his own —at lest in English prose. When he conducted an oral seminar, with a full display of kinesics and his extraordinary accent, the line was far more open. I can see him now, reaching stout, muscular arms into the air and wiggling two fingers of each hand to make the 'quote' sign, somewhat the way Churchill made the 'V' sign. In semantics the quote sign around a word usually means: 'Beware, it's loaded!'"

Chase outlined the history of Korzybski's research, and summarized: "The question he set himself to answer was how the structure of language could be brought closer to the structure of the space-time world." For that he employed the methods of the then recent revolution in relativity and quantum physics; Chase then outlined the goals of general semantics as three in number:

- To help the individual evaluate his world. As our environment grows more and more complex, greater precision is needed to interpret it.

- To improve communication between A and B, also within and between groups of all sizes.

- To aid in clearing up mental illness. "In Chapter 24 we will describe the brilliant work of Dr. Douglas Kelley with battle shock cases during the last war."

Chase described how Korzybski came to call his system 'non-Aristotelian." Aristotle, in Chase's words, "sometimes mistook the peculiar structure of his own Greek for the universal laws of thought, a most natural error." Aristotle's formal logic was an important contribution "but today it is hardly more useful than the medicine of Galen." Medicine continued to evolve but, today, "Aristotle's logic continues to distort our use of reason." Galileo and the pioneers of science begin to break free from Aristotle. Today "a number of first-rate minds were questioning the validity of verbal processes."[9] He cited particularly Ogden and Richards whose 1921 *The Meaning of Meaning* was soundly critiqued by Korzybski. Chase gave several pages to Ogden and Richards but concluded that section by noting: "I believe the two schools were not in the closest harmony."

In earlier works, Chase had taken exception to Korzybski's term "time-binding." He didn't understand why Korzybski mixed general semantics with time-binding, "an earlier formulation." Chase by now seemed reconciled to time-binding, which likely came about with the then recent re-publication of *Manhood of Humanity*.

Chase devoted a chapter to an overview of Korzybski's principles. They include the map-territory "simile." He explained each of the extensional devices briefly. He included the "Abstraction Ladder" a controversial idea formulated by Hayakawa but without giving credit to him.[10] He listed the twenty-one statements Korzybski used to summarize the principles of general semantics in the introduction to the second edition of *Science and Sanity*.

Twelve of these statements Chase attributed to Korzybski's forerunners and nine he judged "uniquely Korzybski's." Chase gave himself credit for increasing the circle of interest in general semantics with *The Tyranny of Words,* published in 1938, of which he said, "It was the first attempt to interpret both semantics and Korzybski's General Semantics for the layman." While he took the time to relate Korzybski's own careful delineation of the two topics, especially during the last few years of his life, he continued to use the term "semantics" when referring, rather unclearly at times, to "general semantics."

In closing this chapter Chase offered a "critical evaluation," which was, for the most part, a personal criticism of Korzybski. First he noted "that while General Semantics has made important contributions to the study of communication it has not seized the leadership," and "it is more a point of view than a rigorous scientific discipline." Chase claimed that Korzybski "inaugurated no clinic for practicing his methods, no controlled experiments to validate them. There are few reliable case studies of effects on individual persons or groups, in the sense that clinical psychologists have case studies."[11] He then related that he considered that "Korzybski was something of a prima donna, and he had a few unfortunate prejudices. He was overcritical of the work of others in his field. I felt the sting of this criticism from time to time, though I had done my best to make his work more widely known. At one point the whole movement seemed to be heading toward a cult with disciples who knew the lingo, but little else. This danger I believe has been safely passed."

Chase wasn't done with Korzybski. He went on: "Sometimes it seemed as if the originator of General Semantics were trying to set up a one-man philosophy in the great tradition, which would supersede the system of Aristotle, Aquinas, or Hegel. Yet the scientific method, upon which he constantly relied, is incompatible with one-man philosophies. ... If he had been more of a scientist he would have written a shorter and better structured book and given himself more time to inaugurate the research which Professor Lee calls for. He would thus have allayed a good deal of frustration in persons like myself who were trying to understand him."

Then Chase closed with these words of reconciliation:

> Despite the frustration, some of us kept at it, and rich was our reward. Doors which had been closed began to open; the world took on a new dimension. Among the semanticists who have been

carrying on since his death are objective scholars, shy of cults and revelations. They will succeed, I believe, in steering General Semantics into the moving front of the social sciences, where it belongs. Korzybski included in his approach both the natural sciences, represented by physics, and the social sciences, represented by psychology. One of his favorite phrases was 'organism-as-a-whole.' ... He did not station himself behind any of the verbal partitions.

Twenty years of General Semantics have demonstrated that one's evaluation of men and events can be sharpened by its use, that certain mental blocks can be remedied, that one's speaking and writing can be clarified.

Students of General Semantics report a better ability to listen, a reduction in the terrors of stage fright, help in cases of stuttering.

This is no small contribution for one person to make. We owe Korzybski a good deal, not only for what he discovered or highlighted, but for the furor created by his personality. He lit fires, started controversies, caused people to look to their terms, and so gave a much-needed impetus to the whole subject of communication.

What is the difference, Count Korzybski, between man and other living creatures?' he was sometimes asked. His eyes would gleam behind the great round spectacles and his deep voice with its rolling accent would replay: 'A quar-rter-r of an inch of cor-rtex.'

Following his discussion of Korzybski, Chase passed on to new topics, talking first about Kurt Lewin's group dynamics. Chase also included reference to Graicunas, which he perhaps drew, unacknowledged, from Korzybski's work. Chase wrote at length about cybernetics, the mass media, the art of listening, propaganda and various forms of "gobbledygook" after which he added a chapter on "Medical talk" and a critical review of "Schoolroom talk.

"Medical talk" was mostly about Dr. Kelley's use of general semantics to treat combat trauma. Kelley had set up a group therapy program, in January 1944, first founded at Stafford England, from which it derived a name, and then at a 1,000-bed hospital in Ciney, Belgium. "The results were spectacular, both in the higher percentage of cures and the greatly reduced cost per patient." Two specific sets of tools were reportedly employed: "semantic group dynamics,' the work of Alfred Korzybski, and group analysis, by which Kelley "helped restore thousands of men to sanity." Kelley's program treated 7,000 men for shell shock, combat exhaustion and battle fatigue. Chase noted that 96% of Kelley's patients were restored to duty, and no more returned than proportional to the number coming from the general population of combat troops. This discussion clearly belies Chase's earlier claim that there was little evidence about the clinical effectiveness of Korzybski's methods.

In a long list of "Feedback" comments at the end of the book, Chase made a short reference to the foundation of general semantics by Korzybski, which, he noted was "almost single-handed, and was chiefly founded on the new talk in physics." Chase also referenced "the unused potential," an idea (which he likely knew Korzybski had talked about) that was beginning to gain a growing popular and professional interest and evolved a decade later into the human potential movement.

It is not my style to criticize the works of writers I review, but I find in Chase an attitude that, despite his evident closeness to Korzybski, could seriously impede the progress of general semantics as a subject. I have to ask just how well did he understand Korzybski? Chase repeatedly complained about the difficulty he had reading Korzybski. For a man of his intelligence and education, this is indeed puzzling. He accused Korzybski of lacking clarity. I find something especially insightful in his explanation of how he painfully restudied calculus to study Korzybski's Book III and particularly Einstein's relativity theory. Reading those sections of *Science and Sanity*, it is clear to me, a non-mathematician, that Korzybski provided all the background needed to understand his dissertation on calculus and relativity. Ironically, there is, in fact, very little mathematics in his treatment of Einstein.

Chase's reference to the Korzybski cult is equally interesting since his wife served as a member of the Institute Board of Directors for a number of years and was close to Korzybski at the end of his life. Most telling, however, is his reaction to Korzybski's "criticisms." Korzybski never publicly mentioned Chase's use of the term "semantics," yet it is clear that Chase felt the criticism personally. His own writings indicated that he had at a least a verbal understanding of the distinction between "general semantics" and "semantics," but right up to the end he stubbornly persisted in using the term "semantics."

It is evident to me that Chase, first of all, never clearly understood general semantics, and second, that his intent was to develop his own system, despite a lack of the requisite genius. True, Chase was a popularizer, but his thinking in his many books appears superficial and unsystematic. Why, I have to ask, did he feel the need to improve his power to communicate his work? His books continued to sell well to popular audiences, and his demand as a speaker continued until World War II directed public attention to new arenas. Very likely the shadow that hung over him was not his skill as a writer and speaker as much as the taint of communism that came out of his outspoken advocacy of communist principles, including violence.[12] With the reaction against "anti-Americanism" of the '50s, as the Cold War settled in, his leftist leanings were very likely costing him popularity.

After extensive study of Chase's life and work, I find no solid reasonable clue to his unfortunate estrangement with Korzybski. While I would not attempt to psychoanalyze him, there seems, however, to be a displacement of a certain frustration he expressed. But perhaps there is more to their relationship than the record provides. Perhaps that will become clearer in the Korzybski biography.[13] And perhaps it is time that some able scholar undertook a biography of Stuart Chase, a man who history has largely forgotten.

NOTES

[1] William Henry Sharp, "A.E. van Vogt and the World of Null-A," *ETC: A Review of General Semantics*, January 2006

[2] S.I. Hayakawa is the subject of the second article in this series and there I reference and describe the exchange mentioned.

[3] Chase parallels Korzybski's interest in the Scientific Management movement.

[4] Notably and recently including John Nash (of *A Beautiful Mind*).

[5] Frederick Taylor, founder of Scientific Management.

[6] This model is not unlike that proposed by Korzybski in *Manhood of Humanity* in 1921.

[7] Korzybski's map and territory.

[8] By then Korzybski had been dead three years.

[9] His list included some dedicated neo-Aristotelian minds as well as some of the more progressive, but according to Korzybski, unsuccessful pioneers. It is in this broad, salad-bowl, mix of ideas, however, that Chase frequently loses his sight of general semantics.

[10] With the implication that it originated with Korzybski.

[11] Despite having discussed Dr. Kelley's work in detailed in the book. See below.

[12] Referencing specifically his suggested use of the firing squad as an appropriate means to chasten difficult business managers.

[13] Bruce I. Kodish, *Korzybski: A Biography*, Pasadena, CA: Extensional Publishing, 2011.

CHAPTER 8: KORZYBSKI AND S. I. HAYAKAWA

William Henry Sharp

THIS IS THE SECOND of a pair of articles about leading figures of thought who were associated with Alfred Korzybski and general semantics. The thesis of these two pieces is that some "followers" have a mind of their own which can be inimitable to the movement's central message. In the first article, Stuart Chase was highlighted. Chase was a luminary in American literature at the time Korzybski finished *Science and Sanity* and gave general semantics its first popular boost. In this article I will discuss S. I. Hayakawa, who had far more influence on the course of general semantics.

S. I. Hayakawa was a rising star in the 1930s and went on to achieve considerable fame (or notoriety) during the Counterculture days of the Sixties and then serve a term in the US Senate. Hayakawa wrote his first book "about" general semantics in 1941 and became editor of the movement's journal, *ETC*. He was at one time considered by some the heir apparent to Alfred Korzybski but they became estranged, bitterly so. The quarrel was not only not resolved by Korzybski's death, but, to a degree far greater than the case with Chase, the controversy, albeit one-side, continued, and does so to this day.

During the 1960s one of Hayakawa's books became arguably the primary text on "general semantics." Selling a million copies it was phenomenally influential. That book, however, was built upon interpretations of general semantics that gave Korzybski no end of distress. This article will summarize that conflict between these two great men of thought.

The Law and Order of "Semanticists"

Samuel Ichiye Hayakawa was born in 1906 in Vancouver, British Columbia, completed high school in Winnipeg and received his B. A. degree from the University of Manitoba, his M. A. in English literature from McGill and his Ph.D. in 1935 from the University of Wisconsin where he worked as an instructor of English from 1936 to 1939. In 1938 Stuart Chase introduced him to Korzybski and he became closely associated with Korzybski and general semantics in Chicago. In 1939 he became an instructor in English at the Armour Institute of Technology in Chicago. In 1941 he published a Book-of-the-Month selection entitled *Language in Action: A Guide to Accurate Thinking,* "which he used as an official text for Freshman Courses at the University of Wisconsin and the Armour Institute." He was the founder (in 1943) and for many years editor of the general semantics journal *ETC.,* published by the newly formed International Society for General Semantics.[1] In 1949 he enlarged the text of his book, brought out as *Language in Thought and Action,* and used it as a text for lectures in 'semantics' at the University College of the University of Chicago from 1950 to 1955.

A biographical sketch of Hayakawa called him "a pioneer in the development of general semantics," and that he "relied heavily on the work of Alfred Korzybski," whose "main idea, popularized by Hayakawa, holds that words are not identical with reality, but can either disguise it or help in understanding it."

In 1959 Hayakawa moved to San Francisco State College where he became a highly popular lecturer. In 1968 student protestors were rocking college campuses across the country and that year they targeted the SFSC campus. Following the resignation of the college president, Hayakawa stood up to a group of 500 striking students, and under the eye of national television cameras pulled the wires out of their sound equipment. He stated publicly that this small group did not have the right to interfere with the studies of 17,500 other students who were not on strike. The strike was ultimately broken and the militant students agreed to return to class. Then California governor Ronald Reagan supported Hayakawa's promotion to acting president of the college. Hayakawa became known as an advocate for law and order. In 1973 he transferred his affiliation from the Democratic to the Republican Party and in 1976 was encouraged to run for the U. S. Senate, a seat he won by a solid majority.

Hayakawa was a charismatic individual. He stood five foot three inches, dressed colorfully, and often wore a Scottish Tam O'Shanter. He liked to fish, practiced fencing and Japanese cooking, collected oriental and African art and loved Jazz. He at one time served as a director of the Consumers Union (with Chase). He was an advocate of racial equality. He was, however, a promoter of cultural integration of foreign residents. He sparked the ire of the Japanese-American community when he said that the Japanese interment during World War II had the positive effect of accelerating Japanese integration into American society. He advocated English as the official, and constitutional mandated, language of the United States. His single term in the U. S. Senate was undistinguished; indeed he was reputed to nap during speeches and debates. He lived a long and full life, passing in 1992. The AP obituary said he was "a soft-spoken semanticist," "former U. S. Senator" and "an internationally known semanticists for nearly three decades."

Standing Korzybski on His Head

Reviewing the 1940 edition of *Language in Action*, Hayakawa's "introduction to general semantics," I find, curiously, that 'general semantics' does not appear in the index and that Korzybski is cited only four times, beginning with page 126 where Hayakawa's introduced his "abstraction ladder," which represents a version of Korzybski's Structural Differential (SD) turned upside down.[2] Here Korzybski was acknowledged for allowing "kind permission" to adapt the diagram. Hayakawa used the "map and territory" metaphor, talked about 'abstraction,' and others of Korzybski's principles without citation. Korzybski never played more than a bit part despite the liberal use of his ideas.

A few years later a well-documented break occurred between Korzybski and Hayakawa. In a long letter dated March 1947 to the editor (Hayakawa) of *ETC.*,[3] Korzybski unequivocally laid his indictment against Hayakawa, and I quote:

> "To the Editor of *ETC.: A Review of General Semantics*" The Chicago Society for *General* Semantics has published a circular about six lecturers, the writings of four of whom deal with my work (a copy of that circular was included in the letter). This circular and certain statements in recent issues of *ETC.*, involved misinformations and distortions of my work such as are practically unprecedented and not tolerated in scientific circles. I therefore am compelled to make a public protest and ask you to publish this in the next issue of *ETC.*, the official organ of the Society.

Korzybski started the second paragraph of his letter with this line: "There are many ways to misinform or deceive the public." He went on to explain acts of commission and omission and pointed out that both were involved in the Society's statements. Korzybski's then addressed the motives behind these "sins[4]," that may "range from ignorance, stupidity, etc., or self-seeking, to even perfidy, and what not." In the next paragraph he talked about "publicity stunts."

There were two acts of omission and two of commission. The most significant issues appear to be the acts of commission. Those were two statements highlighted by a box. Korzybski wrote: "The following box is a 'masterpiece'. Whether it is due to incompetence, or whether more perfidious factors enter, I do not know." That box contained two definitions: "SEMANTICS: ... The Study of how people act, with and under the influence of words and other symbols." And, "GENERAL SEMANTICS: ... A system for applying the findings of semantics to every-day life." Korzybski also noted the sentence: "General Semantics will be the subject behind the subject in each of these widely varied lectures."

After a page of relevant history and facts about the field of 'semantics,' Korzybski concluded: "From what was said here it is obvious that my work in General Semantics has nothing to do with the above-mentioned disciplines..." He added: "I selected the term 'General Semantics' for an empirical natural science of non-elementalistic *evaluation*, a theory of *values*." He emphasized that he had never even used the word 'semantics,' except as an adjective. He stated that the difference between 'semantics' and 'General Semantics' was on the order of the difference between the Cartesian system and modern calculus.

Korzybski clarified that 'semantics,' 'pragmatics,' and 'logic' apply only to the inner, philosophical, life "and so eliminates the *possibility of evaluation* as a living issue with a living individual, which is the main aim of *General Semantics*." He noted that the word 'semantics' does not even appear in the index of *Science and Sanity*. He added: "I coined the term '*General Semantics*,' on the assumption that intelligent laymen will be able to discriminate between 'semantics' and 'general semantics'..." Even those involved in the fields of 'semantics,' etc., are careful to point out, when they are familiar with general semantics, the distinction between the two subjects. Whether done consciously or unconsciously, "by commission or omission, of equal virulence; or a cheapening advertising stunt, hardly less harmful," works representing serious misrepresentations of general semantics had been published in *ETC.*, "*without consulting with me*." Consultation, Korzybski added, was customary among scientific men.

"Semantics," Korzybski explained, is popularly used to designate a science of meaning, to which he added: "I have shown many years ago that theories of 'meaning' are humanly impossible, as they do not take into consideration undefined terms, which label non-verbal, silent levels and verbal levels, due to lack of consciousness of abstraction, ..."

Korzybski complained that these statements "misinform or deceive the public." They are "false-to-facts," and deliberate acts of commission, rather than error. He went on with a strong indictment: "Cheap advertising treatment of theoretical discoveries is one of the worst things popularizers can do, unless they want to paralyze the future of humans."

Korzybski explained in detail that:

> 'Science' is an ambiguous term, generally misused, because unindexed and undated. So far, the highest standards of science and scientific method, as judged by results, are to be found in the exact sciences. Theoretical discoveries often guide empirical researches, prodding nature, so to say, combining both induction and deduction, where constructive theories most of the time lead to search for new data. Accidental discoveries are not fruitful in a broader sense if they are not understood theoretically. The greatest discoveries in mathematics, physics, chemistry, etc., involved some theory of knowledge and proper evaluations of previous discoveries. For instance, the work of Einstein was, and is, strictly theoretical, out of which, however, the new empirical quantum mechanics and even the liberation of nuclear energy followed.

Korzybski then attacked a five-page glossary that appeared in *ETC.*, (Volume III, No. 4) and asserted that: "Practically every 'definition' misses the main point and trend of my life work." He then provided examples.

Korzybski continued: "Unfamiliarity with a new discipline might be historically forgivable, but what is unprecedented among serious individuals is that the authors should undertake such misevaluations in my lifetime without ever consulting with me, although they lived then only a few blocks away from the Institute." He also protested against editorials which he saw as jeopardizing the future work of the Institute, even after he had frequently asked to be consulted on them. He pointed out: "The Society was founded to help the Institute, not to destroy it." He found particularly egregious the request by the Society for funding for work in 'various institutions' without even mentioning the name of the Institute of General Semantics, unnamed yet given as dedicated to "linguistic, epistemological, scientific and education" research and education. This was done at a time when the Institute was virtually paralyzed for lack of funds; indeed, Korzybski said he was paid no salary for over six months. And the function of the Institute, he added, is neither research nor education.

The Society, Korzybski pointed out, was organized in 1942 "with a most precious asset of the Institute, the international mailing list" built up since *Manhood of Humanity*, and containing the names of many personal friends and friends of the Institute. He said he had urged people to join the Society but now regretted that, "least those who are interested in my work become monopolized, not only financially, but with harmful incompetent dilutions of the discipline which amount to misinformations and misrepresentations of its fundamentals, by *commission* or *omission*." He protested against managerial policy that subverted the by-laws of the Institute and added a list of other issues.

Korzybski gave as an example of the seriousness of the misrepresentations, that if he had misquoted Whitehead or Einstein, or others, harm could be done to the readers understanding of the cited works. Yet such liberties have been taken in reference to his own work. He then protested against the inclusion of articles in *ETC.,* which had nothing to do with general semantics, degenerating the journal into 'just another magazine.' Further, the implication is made that he is a consulting editor and that "Harm is thus done to the Institute and my own work when it *appears as if* I approved the Society managerial and editorial policies which are decided *without consulting with me.*" He thus tendered his resignation as consulting editor. He then said: "I want to do more creative work, of which I am capable, if the attrition imposed on my work by some students will not continue to paralyze it."

Korzybski concluded with these words: "Let us also not forget the great Pavlov's bequest: 'Never attempt to screen an insufficiency of knowledge even by the most audacious surmise and hypothesis. However this soap bubble will rejoice your eyes by its play, it inevitably will burst and you will have nothing except shame.'"

An attempt was made to heal the rift. Following Korzybski's letter, O. R. Bontrager, representing Korzybski, met with Irving Lee, representing The Society. F. P. Chisholm, M. Kendig and Robin Skinner also attended. Bontrager reported (published in the *Collected Writings*) the results of several specific topics that were discussed, which included: The *Encyclopedia Britannica* article on general semantics written by Hayakawa: *Encyclopedia Britannica* had turned down Korzybski's paper on the topic and had attempted to reach Lee for the article. Failing that they contacted Hayakawa who wrote the article without consulting or notifying Korzybski. Korzybski learned of it only after copies of it were distributed to members of the Society.

Lee suggested that part of the protest letter might be published but was reluctant to publish it entirely. Some discussion as to how relations between the Society and Institute could be improved was undertaken. Kendig stressed that the break between the Society and Institute was not due to 'personal feelings." "Kendig, Bontrager and Skinner repeatedly emphasized the necessity for rigor in editing of ETC., which is widely recognized as the official G. S. publication."

Regarding membership, it was pointed out that all but some 200 names appeared on both the Institute and Society mailing lists. Lee was concerned that Korzybski's letter would affect membership. Kendig pointed out that the Institute had suffered serious loss in revenue drawn away from it by the Society. Lee used the excuse of rising production cost.

Lee added he believed the protest letter misrepresented 'fact.' He also said he feared the present situation would result in conflict between the Society and Institute, and that he was considering writing his own rebuttal. Bontrager pointed out that such a rebuttal would surely create conflict. Lee suggested that he could resign as a Trustee but was advised not to. Bontrager concluded that Lee was aloof and defensive, more concerned with academic credibility than resolving the conflict. He found little willingness on Lee's part to resolve the difficulties.

On November 17, 1947, Lee did write a letter to Korzybski, on behalf of the Board of the Society for General Semantics, "earnestly requesting you to withdraw your resignation as a Consulting Editor of ETC." Lee emphasized that changes had been made in the Society since March. Korzybski continued to appear as Consulting Editor until his death.

On July 8, 1949, Korzybski sent Hayakawa another letter of protest. Hayakawa had asked him for permission to print his 'abstraction ladder' in his new book rather than Korzybski's structural differential. Korzybski responded, first, that Hayakawa's representation of the structural differential did not follow the normal convention of reading from top to bottom, and second, that as he, and a psychiatrist, had repeatedly pointed out "the main ills of our different civilizations can be found in the reversal of the natural order of evaluation." The structural differential, Korzybski pointed out, was designed specially "To undo the prevalent 'non-objective', non-factual way of thinking, to counteract … neurotic tendencies …"

Korzybski then reflected that Hayakawa had known for years that he was unhappy with "your reversal of the natural order of my original Structural Differential"—a misrepresentation of his work, and now that Hayakawa was becoming better known, a serious difficulty. He pointed out Hayakawa's "growing confusion of 'semantics' with 'general semantics', and misuse of terminologies" and that "I believe that the reversal *as an orientation*, the persistent visualization of that reversal, has a great deal to do with your confusion." He also pointed out that the growing circulation of Hayakawa's books can serve only to confuse more people.[5]

Korzybski further critiqued Hayakawa's "unnatural construct," the 'abstraction ladder,' which he said fails to represent much of the function of the Structural Differential. Korzybski stressed the need to prevent Hayakawa from harming both his own scientific reputation and further misleading the public. Korzybski additionally emphasized that his disapproval of the 'abstraction ladder' included that it violated the map-territory relationship. Korzybski enclosed a copy of his writings regarding the term 'semantics.' He also sent a copy of his letter to Hayakawa's publisher.

Language in Thought and Action appeared without the Structural Differential diagram. It retained the Abstraction Ladder. Korzybski was cited fifteen times in the index, 'general semantics' not at all, and 'semantics' was defined in the text "as a non-Aristotelian system." In the Preface Hayakawa did say: "My deepest debt in this book is to the General Semantics (Non-Aristotelian System) of Alfred Korzybski." He then listed a sizable group of other acknowledgements.[6]

Hayakawa took the International Society with him to California where it continued on its own more or less independent track for half a century. Hayakawa announced his retirement as president of the Society in late 1950 but retained editorship of *ETC.,* until 1970. By 1952, Lee reported, the two organizations had a total of 4,000 members.[7] In the summer of that year Hayakawa published an article in *ETC.,* in defense of "Semantics." But his greatest influence was still some years away.

In 1964 *Science and Sanity* was listed by *Saturday Review* as one of the most influential books of the previous quarter century. It achieved that status by nomination from a panel who were asked to submit their list of candidates.

Also that year the Esalen Institute, which played a pivotal role in the emerging Human Potential Movement, was launched in California. A number of the leaders in the movement made favorable references to general semantics. Several notable figures of the movement, including Abraham Maslow and Bucky Fuller, both honorary trustees of the Institute, gave annual Korzybski lectures. Also that year, the latest edition of Hayakawa's of *Language in Thought and Action* was published in paperback.[8]

Hayakawa had frequently presented his version of general semantics at Esalen and in the San Francisco Bay area. The version of 'general semantics' he was teaching at the Esalen Institute starting in 1964, was adapted, according to Walter Truett Anderson, to Zen and gestalt therapy (Fritz Perls), two of the most popular Esalen topics.[9] Anderson said that "His seminars were always well prepared, always very intellectual, but he was no dusty pedant. He liked to play the piano for songfests in the lodge, and one visitor to Esalen remembers seeing the future United States Senator lead a group of seminarians in a snake dance across the lawn." Joan Baez was then resident at Esalen, just beginning her singing and protest career. Anderson noted the irony of the vastly different directions these two took in the political turmoil of the coming years.

Misdirection

Among the ills of the world, noted Korzybski, is politics. History is the story of the rise and inevitable fall of civilizations and the road is drenched in blood. Chase began and ended his career in politics. Hayakawa began in academia and ended in politics. Chase never abandoned his agenda: General semantics was a passing fancy and one that never worked for him. Hayakawa claimed leadership of general semantics. He too had a personal agenda and a strong ego to feed. Both were brilliant and neither can be faulted for lack of making an effort to improve the world.

Chase and Hayakawa had a mixed influence on the general semantics movement; they, in turn, collaborated personally with and undermined Korzybski. In the final analysis, their systems deviate so far from the core principles of general semantics that they cannot be used, I believe, even as an introduction to general semantics. I have to conclude, simply, that neither of them 'got it.' The effect of their views, particularly Hayakawa's[10], on a lay reader developing an interest in general semantics can be no less detrimental now than it was then over 60 years ago. Readers would, as did I, at best derive a highly distorted view of Korzybski's work.

Korzybski's *Science and Sanity* is a difficult book. It has to be read repeatedly and given very careful attention. Each reading, I find, provides profound new insights into both the field of general semantics and into Korzybski's thinking. My objective in *Alfred Korzybski: Time Binder*, was precisely to try to capture a better understanding of the thinking that went into Korzybski's work. In that book I attempted to capture, in sequence, Korzybski's ideas. Many ideas appear again and again, each time with a little different interpretation which I find gives the principle a broader perspective.

Plumbing the depths of Korzybski's development is an even more daunting task. He did his best to lay out the foundations of his work and to cite works he found congruent with general semantics. He listed 55 individuals who had a profound influence on his work. He provided an extensive bibliography for *Science and Sanity*, adding much to it in the second edition. He lived an interesting and involved life. The *Collected Writings* help serious students to better understand the genesis of general semantics and particularly his work during the last seventeen years of his life, the period in which he engaged his students in seminars, spoke and wrote extensively, and worked to build a permanent Institute to carry on his work. Unfortunately an intellectual heir did not appear and his work, now sixty years later, is largely as he left it. As I have attempted to point out, the major interpreters of his work, men with agendas of their own, not only failed to do justice to general semantics but, in fact, quite the opposite.

My intent in these two articles is to pose the argument that we need to reevaluate the state and condition of the general semantics movement as it currently stands. A map, to be useful, must represent some territory. I believe it is safe to say that Chase mapped Chase and Hayakawa mapped Hayakawa with only passing reference to a marginal feature called "Korzybski." We need a reorientation—a more reliable map of general semantics. I believe we need to encourage a new generation of bright young men and women to undertake a thorough study of Alfred Korzybski and resume the work of building a science of human evaluation for a world that is, as he predicted, not getting any better. In order to do that they are going to have to study what Korzybski wrote, explore the sources that influence him, and update the Non-Aristotelian library to include important works that have been written during the last sixty years that would have probably found a place on Korzybski's shelves were he still alive. Without a map of Korzybski and his work that will not be possible, and perhaps, the reason we have not gone forward is that we are using the wrong map.

NOTES

[1] An organization separate from and often at odds with the Institute of General Semantics until they merged in 2004.

[2] I, like many others who read Hayakawa before Korzybski, took the abstraction ladder as the genuine article for years.

[3] Included in *Collected Writings* (p. 815)

[4] Authors play on words, not Korzybski's.

[5] Little did either realize that an updated version of Hayakawa's book would become one of the major text of the sixties human potential movement.

[6] My edition of this book is a paperback edition; probably the most widely read text on "general semantics" during the heyday of the Human Potential Movement, and used by me at that time as a cornerstone of my theoretical formulations in the social science which occurred several years before I read *Science and Sanity*.

[7] Membership would grow to some 10,000 a decade or so later.

[8] The 1964 edition of his *Language in Thought and Action* sold as many as one million copies. The book is still in print.

[9] Walter Truett Anderson, *The Upstart Spring: Esalen and the American Awakening*, 1983

[10] Chase has been largely forgotten.

CHAPTER 9: KORZYBSKI AND ALBERT ELLIS

Martin H. Levinson

RATIONAL EMOTIVE BEHAVIOR THERAPY (REBT), formerly called Rational Therapy (RT) and Rational Emotive Therapy (RET), is an active-directive, philosophically and empirically based psychotherapy that focuses on resolving thinking, emotional, and behavioral disturbances and enhancing people's lives. It was originated in 1955 by psychologist Albert Ellis, who was inspired by various teachings of ancient Asian, Greek, and Roman philosophies. When he later learned of general semantics (GS), a non-Aristotelian educational discipline originated by Alfred Korzybski in 1933, he drew on that body of thought, as well.

Ellis referred to general semantics in many of his writings and lectures as an important influence on his thinking and practice. For example, in a speech titled *General Semantics and Rational-Emotive Therapy* that he presented at the Harvard Club in 1991, Ellis gave credit to Korzybski for antedating him in observing that people act as "organisms-as-wholes-in-environments."[1] Ellis also acknowledged that Korzybski first formulated the REBT concept of secondary symptoms (such as anxiety about anxiety and anger about anger) through his description of second-order reactions.[2]

Ellis found Korzybski's view of human functioning similar to the ABC theory of REBT: in the ABC theory an activating event (A) leads to a belief or cognition (B) that produces a feeling or consequence (C). As some evidence for this he noted that Korzybski states when individuals "perceive" a happening or an event they "silently" or "nonverbally" react with evaluations about it and their "emotions" and "evaluations" are organismically together and react with their verbalizations, which quickly follow their silent-thinking level.[3] Ellis also observed that Korzybski was a supporter of George Santayana's notion that humans are much better at believing than seeing.

Science and Sanity

Ellis was impressed with the "revolutionary" title of Korzybski's magnum opus *Science and Sanity,* as Ellis also believed that the scientific method was a beneficial approach for realizing sound mental health since it is (a) pragmatic and tries to make its theory consistent with the "facts" of "reality"; (b) uses logic to check its hypotheses and rules out magic and casual jumping to conclusions; (c) is open-minded and non-dogmatic; and (d) is alternative seeking and non-absolutist.[4]

Unlike science, emotional disturbance (particularly severe neurosis) tends to be replete with thinking that is unrealistic, illogical, dogmatic, devout, and rigid. Korzybski labeled such reasoning "unsane." Ellis termed it "psychologically dysfunctional." Given their similar conclusions on this subject and their mutual admiration for the efficacy of the scientific method in diminishing unsound thinking, Ellis and Korzybski appear to be on the same page in concluding that the scientific method and non-neurotic sanity are related.

Ellis and Korzybski also share the opinion that human beings are not born and reared to defeat themselves. If that were the case then individuals and the human race would quickly disappear. Rather, REBT and GS have as a basic premise the notion that people can, if they choose to, use scientific thinking to reduce their misperceptions, overgeneralizations, and poor judgments to more accurately perceive, accept, and live more contentedly with "reality."

REBT and GS likewise agree that the use of the scientific method to solve everyday problems can help individuals to become less disturbed and more functional, which can lead them to more fully employ their human potential for psychological and mental growth. From a general semantics perspective, one might say such people are also in a better position to more fully employ their time-binding potential to pass along constructive information to future generations.

The "Is of Identity" and "Is of Predication"

GS warns against the use of the "is of identity" (e.g., "I am an American," "I am a lawyer," "I am a Christian") as such usage can fool people into thinking that they have completely described a person when there is always more that can be said about any individual. Ellis agrees with this thesis and further contends that identification with any group or concept implies loss of oneself, what Helmuth Kaiser has labeled "neurotic fusion." Ellis specifically observes that while identifying with a group may give one a sense of belonging and security it can also lead a person to become over conforming and reduce a sense of personal identity.[5] To avoid such problems, REBT tries to get individuals to understand that they *choose* to be in particular groups and do not have to be solely defined by those groups.

Korzybski would probably go along with this sort of reasoning by noting that people are neither only themselves nor only identified with a group. People tend to be both/and rather than either/or when it comes to such matters. More specifically, people are individuals in their own right but once they opt to become part of a group they are no longer responsible only to themselves but also to the group they choose to remain affiliated with.

GS also cautions against the use of the "is of predication" (he is good, she is bad, etc.), as such practice can lead people into erroneously believing that they are capturing the total essence of a person or thing through descriptive adjectives. By being aware of the "is of predication," Ellis maintains he was able to have his clients stop using several kinds of overgeneralizations and instead tell themselves things like, "I am an individual who does good things (e.g., helps others in trouble) but who also does many 'neutral' and 'bad' things (e.g., harms others). I am never really entirely 'good,' 'bad,' or 'neutral.' Because I am, a human, much too complex and many-sided to perform only 'good' or 'bad' or 'neutral' behaviors."[6]

Since humans are complex and multi-faceted, REBT advises that it is not sensible for individuals to rate themselves; as such ratings, like "I am good" or "I am bad," cannot be true in every instance of behavior. Instead, Ellis suggests that people only evaluate what they do or what they don't do. Those evaluations can then be used to improve one's performance. (A general semantics argument against global self-ratings can be made on the grounds that they are "allness statements" and so are incomplete, as there is always more that can be added to such reports. Thinking oneself a "good person, etc." or a "bad person, etc." is more in line with GS philosophy.)

REBT uses various kinds of disputing to counter people's irrational beliefs. For example, Ellis notes in instances when his clients would say, "Because I do many bad things, I am a bad person," he would reply "When you say you are a bad person for doing bad things, you are engaging in what Bertrand Russell called a category error. For the bad things you are doing are in one category and you, the doer of these things, are in a quite different category. You do all kinds of things, good, bad and indifferent. So if you categorize these things as 'good' or 'bad,' you jump to a different category when you call yourself, the doer, 'good' or 'bad.' You are not what you do. So you'd better rate only the things you do and not identify them with your youness, which is quite a different category."[7]

Ellis got the idea for this kind of disputing from the twentieth-century philosopher and social critic Bertrand Russell, who devised a "theory of types" to make distinctions among categories. Korzybski was also aware of Russell's theory of types and explicitly acknowledged Russell for his "epoch making work in his analysis of subject-predicate relations."[8] Both Ellis and Korzybski owe much to Russell's hypothesis concerning category differences in helping them to examine and illuminate the limitations of the "is of predication."

The Use of E-Prime

To encourage people to refrain from using the "is of identity" and "is of predication," David Bourland, a disciple of GS who studied with Korzybski, advocated and used what he labeled "E-Prime," the English language without any inclusion of various forms of the word "to be" or its various tenses.[9] Ellis supported the idea of using E-Prime, and though writing in E-Prime can be difficult and does not fully lead a writer and reader to avoid all semantic and linguistic errors, he composed some of REBT's most important works employing it.[10] REBT is the only form of therapy that has utilized E-Prime in some of its principal manuscripts.

Precise Thinking and Language

Korzybski was a pioneer in appreciating the importance of linguistic behavior in the formation of a person's thoughts, feelings, and actions. He observed that if the words we tell ourselves more or less describe "what is going on in the world" then we have a better chance to adjust to real life conditions than if those words contradict the facts of a situation. Ellis had a like view, noting that his clients often habituated themselves to using inaccurate language, which then interfered with them accepting that they were largely responsible for their own dysfunctional thoughts, feelings, and actions. If they changed their erroneous language to statements that corresponded with what was actually happening in the world, Ellis argued they would be able to think, feel, and behave more effectively.[11] He labeled the technique of getting clients to focus on using more precise language to accurately describe their situations, *semantic precision*.

The following example, in which Ellis is the therapist, shows the importance of using precise language to mitigate psychological dysfunction:

> ...when my clients say, 'Joe lied to me and that made me furious,' I interrupt, 'How could that, or Joe, get into your gut to make you furious?' 'Oh, I see,' they often reply. 'Yes, Joe lied to me, and I chose to infuriate myself about his lying.' 'Yes,' I say. 'Isn't that a much more accurate description of what happened and how you chose to create your fury?'[12]

REBT emphasizes the importance of precise language to distinguish between *preferences* and *demands*. For example, an REBT client might tell his or her therapist, "I'm not getting the love I want Sally to give me, and that makes me feel like a loser." The therapist, differentiating between preferences and demands, might then reply, "Do you only *want* Sally's love, or are you telling yourself that you *need* it? Does not getting Sally's love make you feel like a loser or is it what you are telling yourself about not getting that love that is causing you to feel this way? Why don't you tell yourself: I would *prefer* that Sally love me but if she doesn't it's not the biggest disaster in the world, it doesn't make me into a loser. The only person who can make me into a loser is me if I describe myself that way."

By showing people how to stop inserting overgeneralizations, "demandingness," improper labeling, and other unscientific verbalizations into their thinking and behaving, REBT is one of the few psychotherapeutic schools of thought that puts Korzybski's theory of language into actual practice.

Constructive Change

REBT maintains that human beings are active constructivists who can think about their thinking, realistically assess their unrealistic attitudes, dispute their irrational beliefs, and work hard to reconstruct their disordered thoughts, feelings, and behaviors. It further maintains that if people consistently work at reformulating their disturbed ideas and feelings they have a good chance of bringing about increased levels of happiness and involvement.

GS contains analogous notions. It stresses that individuals who use GS formulations can learn to think and communicate more clearly with themselves and with each other and thereby help themselves to effect positive change. GS and REBT both share as a major goal helping humans to improve their intrapersonal and interpersonal relationships.

Multi-valued Orientation

The general semantics term "multi-valued orientation" describes an orientation that takes into account the complex multidimensional verbal and non-verbal processes involved in human interacting. It is an orientation that stresses a "both-and" approach rather than an "either-or" method of solving problems. It is an orientation that REBT makes use of in helping individuals to overcome their psychological difficulties.

REBT posits that thinking, feeling, and behaving are not separate, but that they significantly influence and affect each other. Because of such overlap, REBT holistically favors strong and direct cognitive, emotive, and behavioral methods of showing people what they are doing to unnecessarily disturb themselves and what they can do to actively minimize their self-disturbance. In consonance with Korzybski's disavowal of either/or solutions to human problems, REBT does not endorse *either* thinking *or* emotive *or* behavioral methods of therapy. It employs all three kinds of therapy and, in line with the GS notion of "etcetera," REBT sometimes recommends combining psychotherapy and pharmacological treatment, environmental change, and other sorts of psychophysical techniques and strategies that may help clients.

Accurate Abstracting

Korzybski notes that general semantics "necessitates (for its users) 'thinking' in terms of 'facts,' or *visualizing processes, before* making generalizations."[13] He also observes that while Aristotelian either-or language fosters our evaluating "by definition" or "intension," the GS "non-Aristotelian or physico-mathematical orientation" involves evaluation by "extension," taking into consideration the actual "facts" in the particular situation confronting us.[14]

REBT also advocates evaluating by extension (weighing facts first), though that particular term is not used. For instance, an REBT therapist might tell a therapy client who claims he or she is a failure the following: When you say you are a failure what you are saying is that you fall short in *everything* you do. Is that really the case? Is there no activity or action in which you are successful? Let's explore that hypothesis and if we discover something you do well at, you can't by definition be a failure.

REBT, like general semantics, tries to get people to examine the conscious underlying assumptions about the inferences they make. For example: Jack asks Jill to marry him. Jill refuses. Jack concludes: (a) "I made a mistake in asking," (b) "Jill must not like me," (c) "I'm just no good." An REBT therapist would attempt to get Jack to look at these assumptions to have him see that he was coming up with dubious high-level abstractions because (a) By asking Jill to marry him, Jack gained useful information about her feelings for him, (b) There is no evidence that Jill hates him, only an indication that she does not want to marry him, and (c) Jill's refusal to marry Jack does not prove he is no good, only that he will not be heading to the altar with Jill for the nonce.

REBT, like general semantics, also tries to get people to explore their *unconscious* underlying assumptions in the inferences they make. (For Korzybski, "making us *conscious* of our *unconscious assumptions* is essential.")[15] In the preceding example, the unconscious underlying assumption that Jack probably holds is the following "*mus*turbatory" overgeneralization: When I ask a woman to marry me she *must* absolutely grant my request—or else (a) I made a mistake in asking, (b) she must hate me, and (c) I am a bad person. An REBT therapist would try to get Jack to change this "must" assumption into an "I would prefer" assumption, to wit: "When I ask a woman to marry me *I would prefer* she grant my request," as one way to relieve his psychological distress.

In the Friday evening demonstrations of REBT that Ellis regularly conducted for the public at his institute in New York, Ellis used to jocularly caution that the practice of "musturbation" is not good for one's mental health. He sometimes labeled "must assumptions" as "should assumptions" and counseled that it is highly unhelpful for individuals to "should on themselves." The purpose of this advice was to have people examine their premises and if they were holding "must" or "should" assumptions to reflect on the notion that such philosophic core beliefs were largely responsible for the anti-factual inferences they were making.

CONCLUSION

The theoretical underpinnings of REBT were influenced by GS formulations. Ellis said that, "This is hardly a coincidence, because I read Stuart Chase's *The Tyranny of Words* (New York: Harcourt Brace, 1938) and S. I. Hayakawa's *Language in Action* (New York: Harcourt Brace, 1943) in the 1940's. In the 1950's, I finally read Korzybski's *Science and Sanity* (Englewood, NJ: International Non-Aristotelian Publishing Company, 1933, 1958) and his essay, "The Role of Language in the Perceptual Processes" in Robert R. Blake and Glenn V. Ramsey, *Perception: An Approach to Personality* (New York: Ronald, 1951)..."[16] Ellis also asserted that, "REBT and general semantics particularly go together because both disclose and actively dispute people's absolutist, one-sided, rigid, musturbatory thinking."[17]

Would Korzybski endorse REBT and place it above all other psychotherapies if he were alive today? In his 1991 talk on general semantics and rational emotive behavior therapy, Ellis answered that question this way, "Perhaps he would—and, quite likely, for one reason or another, he wouldn't. In keeping with his own extensional thinking, I guess he would agree with some of REBT's theory and practice some of the time and under some conditions."[18]

Ellis went on to say, "Rational-emotive practice works quite well some of the time under some conditions with some people. It is not, and will never be, a panacea for all of all people's cognitive-emotive-behavioral problems.... As Korzybski would probably have recommended and as I have previously noted, REBT had better be integrated with the most useful of other therapies so that it becomes and remains effective with many (not all) people much (not all) of the time."[19]

NOTES

[1] Albert Ellis, "General Semantics and Rational-Emotive Therapy," *General Semantics Bulletin* 58, (1991), 14.

[2] Ibid., 15.

[3] Alfred Korzybski, *Science and Sanity: An Introduction to Non-Aristotelian Systems and General Semantics.* (Lakeville, CT: The International Non-Aristotelian Publishing Co., 4th edition, 1933, 1958), 172.

[4] Ellis, "General Semantics and Rational-Emotive Therapy," 15.

[5] Ibid., 20.

[6] Ibid., 18.

[7] Ibid., 19.

[8] Korzybski, *Science and Sanity*, 181.

[9] Bourland coined the term E-Prime in a 1965 essay entitled "A Linguistic Note: Writing in E-Prime" that was originally published in the *General Semantics Bulletin* 32-33 (1965/1966), 111-114.

[10] Important REBT books written in E-Prime include *How to Live With a Neurotic.* (North Hollywood, CA: Wilshire Book Publishing Co., 1975) by Albert Ellis, and *A New Guide to Rational Living.* (North Hollywood, CA: Wilshire Book Publishing Co., 1975) by Albert Ellis and Robert A. Harper.

[11] Ellis, "General Semantics and Rational-Emotive Therapy," 22.

[12] Ibid., 22.

[13] Korzybski, *Science and Sanity,* 193.

[14] Ibid., 194.

[15] Ibid., 195.

[16] Kodish, Presby Susan and Bruce Kodish. *Drive Yourself Sane: Using the Uncommon Sense of General Semantics.* (Pasadena, CA: Extensional Publishing, Revised 2nd edition, 2001), 13.

[17] Ibid., 14.

[18] Ellis, "General Semantics and Rational-Emotive Therapy," 25. A purely Korzybskian analysis of people's cognitive-emotional-behavioral problems can be found in Wendell Johnson's GS classic *People in Quandaries* (New York: Harper and Row, 1946).

[19] Ibid., 25.

CHAPTER 10: KORZYBSKI AND NEW TRENDS IN PSYCHOTHERAPY
Ramiro J. Álvarez

IT IS TRUE: MAPS PROVE very handy as we step out into our uncertain walk through life, giving us confidence that paths we open indeed are the ones we have wanted to mark with our own footsteps. And in the adventure along life's paths, there is no doubt that Psychology—"the psychologies" would better conform to Korzybskian phrasing—tries to provide the 21st century human being with "scientific maps" — maps that are accurate, reliable, and useful.

Especially interesting for those whose work is centered in human concerns—for the psychologist, counselor or teacher—is to consider in light of Korzybskian General Semantics some of the psychological maps that over the course of the last century have greatly influenced how we view ourselves and the context in which we live.

At its start, Psychology, in constituting itself as an autonomous science detached from Philosophy, proceeded not unlike the blind men in the proverb, each one of whom explored a single part of the elephant's anatomy and then announced his findings as a description of the whole animal. The new science of Psychology sought and found individual parcels of territory unclaimed by other sciences, declaring these would yield a comprehensive understanding of "human reality."

Thus, Psychology's futile initial objective of understanding the "soul" was replaced, first, by an attempt to study the "mind"—an entity no less elusive than "soul"—and, later, by a focus on human "behavior"—a field that, while inseparable from the fellow who behaves, offered the advantage of some possible objectivity in observations. In this progression, Psychology became officially the "Science of Human Behavior," and within "behavior" it included not only external performance but also the inner events such as the emotions, thoughts and cognition that occur within every human being.

To a certain extent, if viewed from a humorous perspective, those responsible for the psychological science, in their approach to the subject of their study, acted like that drunkard who was looking for his house key not in the dark corner of pavement where the key had fallen but in an area well lit by a street lamp at the opposite end of the square. The key was not there, to be sure, but the light made the task of searching a lot easier.

All humor aside, what is most interesting about Psychology is not its claim to encompass the whole of human complexity, but rather its applications as "Psychotherapy,"—as "maps" elaborated to orient and to guide human beings in their behaviors as they encounter the many vicissitudes of life in their personal journeys. Consideration of this mapping function brings to mind the following:

Like all maps, Psychology does not cover the entirety of its territory, human behavior. Furthermore, Psychotherapy, as a specialized field within Psychology, offers an especially problematic map: delineating the "normal" and the "pathological" within human behavior.

Additionally, from the inevitable character of self-reflexivity in any map, comes the fact that Psychotherapy has built itself up not as a unitary system, but rather as a discontinuous succession of propositions deriving from multiple points of view, from the personal theories about "normal" and "pathological" advanced by different authors.

Thus, Sigmund Freud eliminated the personhood of the patient by plunging him into the depths of the divan and by then teasing out with word associations, the *lapsus linguae* or the plots of dreams that the patient retrieved during the fifty minutes of their session the theoretical keys to the patient's traumas and repressions that—supposedly—were stifling the patient's psychic energy, causing all kinds of neurotic and psychosomatic symptoms.

The problem with this psychoanalytical approach lies not only in the Freudian theory—the map—that disregards the real "territory" who lies on the divan, stitching together a ramble of ideas and feelings, but in the fact that the true agent, the real source for the psychopathological symptoms, is supposed to be that "psychic energy" named "libido," a kind of "energy" inferred — not directly observed. The fellow on the divan never escapes the status of mere "patient" and helpless victim to the whirlwind of unconscious forces that are operating in some dark corner of his "mind."

The creators of the psychoanalytic map merely changed the coordinates that defined the dogma "soul" with other references, not less dogmatic, about "subconscious." Such a map could hardly point the way toward understanding human "essences."

Predictably, the reaction to those first psychoanalysts' complicated scaffolding of tangled theory about unobservable forces consisted in the urgent search for some points of reference that were objective and directly verifiable. And so, the individual who was looking for psychotherapy was rescued from the depths of the divan and raised up to the level of his therapist, face to face, in such a way that the psychologist might apprehend his client more directly, less filtered through the scaffolding of so much theory.

The new behavioral maps were defined by two objective coordinates: environmental stimuli and observable responses. The day had come for behavioral therapies that focused on observable actions, on the precedents and the outcomes of specific behaviors, on the constellation of stimuli that make up the whole behavioral chain, the physical environment and the physiological observables of the person who acts.

It was time for a "strong" behaviorism—Pavlov's and Watson's theories—interested only in what is obvious, detectable and could be agreed to by different observers: specific behaviors definable as a function of the individual's organismal and environmental conditions. It was time for the paradigm of conditioning: behavior was considered the result of its antecedent stimuli (Pavlov) or as a necessary factor to get some wanted consequences (Watson's "law of effect"), and "thought" was considered a kind of sub-vocal speech associated to overt behavior.

Even though free from the dark labyrinth of his "mind," the human being remained subject to the vicissitudes of his environment. The new traveler's guide did not promise any fascinating adventure either. Although rescued from the divan, the human being remained a kind of victim of his own environmental conditions and his own physiological conditionings.

Moreover, the mechanisms of human conditioning proved much more complex than what seemed to be operating in the animal kingdom. Stimuli and responses seemed to be coordinates too simple for such a complex "reality." It was necessary to come back to consider a new factor that was specifically human, neither so subtle a factor such as "soul" nor so gross a one as "environment:" a factor that could account for the enormous variability of possible human responses in reaction to similar configurations of stimuli.

On that point, some followers of behaviorism turned back towards humans' "inner behavior," and so, patterns of thought, beliefs—"rational" or "irrational"—and their link with feelings and emotions became the new aim of study for an important trend in Psychology. The revolution of behaviorism gave birth to a still more revolutionary offspring: Cognitivism.

The new maps included the cognitive factor and, in this way, they restored to the individual his status as agent, the main character in his own performance. Human behavior was no longer considered as, only, the final product of inner tendencies or environmental forces, but rather was seen as involving the individual's own mental elaborations of the various conditions that impinged upon him.

Albert Ellis and Aaron Beck, the most distinguished representatives of "Cognitive Therapies," placed the origin of human behavior and emotions, whether adjusted or maladjusted, at the mental level: "automatic thoughts" or personal philosophy more or less oriented towards "catastrophism" would constitute the land to explore with the new maps drawn by Beck or Ellis.

And it was Albert Ellis, precisely, who became the first world-famous psychologist to note parallels between his own Rational Emotive Behavior Therapy (REBT) and Korzybski's General Semantics. Ellis enriched his own system of REBT with contributions from GS, which he explicitly acknowledged as contributing to the theoretical basis for his own psychotherapy.[1]

Of course, in the linear account that we are giving, we must not suggest cause-effect connections among different theories. The fact is that, for each period of time, ideas seem to float in the air so that nobody can be considered exactly the only craftsman of his work. Rather, many influences — ideological, cultural, etc. — seem to contribute to interweave the spirit for each time, and thus any theory is always tributary of that vague and diffuse atmosphere of latent ideas.

In this way, when Psychology understood that the description of the elephant—the description of "reality" it was trying to elaborate—depended more on individual perspectives than on the "true" anatomy of the "reality" to be examined, it opened its approach to new considerations about the human being as a builder of subjectivities. In this way, new models came on stage. Five years after Korzybski's death, George Kelly[2] elaborated his Personal Construct Psychology. There are no explicit references to GS in his books, but Kelly's idea of the human being as a "scientist drawing up his personal theory of universe," and the role of psychotherapy as a tool to help formulate the best theory — this correlates well with Korzybski's propositions.

A new cornerstone in the construction of contemporary Psychotherapy was laid a few years later, in 1959, with the founding in Palo Alto (CA) of the Mental Research Institute, one of whose most famous members, Paul Watzlawick, a prolific writer, became a well-known author for his considerations about "the reality of real."[3] Several representative books explicating the "strategic focus" of the Institute directly cite Korzybski, and the design of the Institute's intervention strategies[4] — shocking and seemingly paradoxical at times, positioning therapists behind a one-way mirror — make sense only in the context of accepting basic GS principles about the human process of abstraction.

In this way, the map for psychotherapy takes a "verbal" turn. Its aim becomes less to channel energies supposedly pouring from the unconscious, and more to execute a kind of negotiation between therapist and client in which the former provides the latter with new options for reinterpreting (re-labeling) perceptions of his situation, whether by giving the client "rational" guides (REBT) for examination, interpretation and appraisal, or by suggesting to him dress rehearsals for new behaviors (Kelly's role therapy) in order to test personal reconstructions, or, simply by suggesting to the client new performance strategies different from the ones habitually employed ("brief strategic therapy") as a way to experience new possibilities and get new results within the client's socio-systemic networks.

Still more interesting, when it comes to understanding the "elephant" of human behavior "reality," is that now, at the beginning of the 21st century, we are witnessing a true paradigmatic change in the postulates of Psychology. Post-rationalist thought, based on the ideas of writers like Humberto Maturana,[5] go beyond the old determinist S-O-R (stimulus-organism-response) schemes to consider the unity, the wholeness and the complex net of relations that occur inside that elusive "reality." The human being, as an autopoietic system, is considered the agent builder of "reality," which is no longer considered as "objective" but as "built."

And the practical consequences of this ideological revolution have been quickly evident within the field of Psychotherapy. New points of view more global and ecological are applied in order to understand emotional disturbances: from Virginia Satir's or Salvador Minuchin's Family Therapy to the Narrative Therapy derived from the constructivist views and pioneered by the Australians Epston and White,[6] the Englishman Martin Payne and so many others, as well as Martin Seligman's[7] stimulating Positive Psychology, which opens a way to new approaches for a "proactive constructivism." Maps of human behavior begin to consider the network of relations among persons; drawing the new maps takes into account the individual's social coordinates.

Two psychological techniques seem especially interesting in connection with Korzybski's propositions: Eugene Gendlin's[8] Focusing and Ira Progoff's[9] Intensive Journal.

Focusing can be considered a technique between psychotherapy and phenomenological philosophy. It is based on the activation of a subtle feeling, the "felt sense" that is directly experienced into the body, related with some specific content of the mind that is being explored in the moment, and to which a verbal label is applied in order to define its "quality." A new "felt sense" can arise from comparing the directly experienced feeling with the attempt to verbalize it, a sense of the accuracy or inaccuracy of the labeling, and, in this way, the process consists in going to and fro from what is directly experienced—at the silent level—to what is stated with words, the end result being a possible re-examination of one's own inner life experiences.

Intensive Journal, in a similar way, consists in re-writing one's own history from that imprecise no man's land that lies between the verbal and the non-verbal. It is a kind of writing from the "twilight" of the "mind."

The most interesting consideration in both proposals rests, precisely, on the attention's ebb and flow from direct experiences — non-verbal — and the assignment of verbal labels to such experiences. The affinity with Korzybski seems clear in Gendlin's words:

"We think more than we can say.
We feel more than we can think.
We live more than we can feel.
And there is much more still."

Whether by conscious direction or as a result of inertial forces in the flow of thought over time, Psychology's current seems to be seeking a channel consistent with Korzybski's model, the Structural Differential: from the postulation of a highly complex unconscious or "mental" machinery that brings into being the wholeness of feelings-thoughts-emotions, etc., Psychology — and its applied field, Psychotherapy — has evolved various fragmentary theories to explain the origin and operations of "human behavior;" and different psychological schools seem to have "discovered" and mapped the particular "elephant's limb" each has decided to explore. But psychologists realize, at every new advance, that something important is always left out. As in the blind men's tale, focusing only on a limb of the animal, one never comprehends its totality.

Would a different approach be possible? Might a "new" psychological school arise, undertaking the task of examining the total human "reality," the complex wholeness of human behavior instead of studying the individual parts?

Psychology remains a brave young science, eager to engage new challenges — even to take on a whole "elephant." Historically, the starting point had been to explore the depths of unconscious mind, and so, psychoanalysis can be considered the first wave of psychotherapy; the second wave's aim became the control of environment (behaviorism) as well as of the inner thoughts (cognitivism). Today's psychological schools — the third wave — are offering new proposals bringing together the human being, his behavior and his relation with the environmental factors. Acceptance and Commitment Therapy (ACT), Dialectical Behavior Therapy (DBT), Cognitive Behavioral Analysis System of Psychotherapy (CBASP), Functional Analytic Psychotherapy (FAP), and Integrative Behavioral Couple Therapy (IBCT) are some of the brand names for these new approaches to the elephant.

All these new schools of psychotherapy share a sense of relativism, the awareness of being but a construct, and many adopt other concepts quite close to Korzybski's teachings. For instance, Steven Hayes' ACT[10] emphasizes a need to "deactivate" language as a key toward overcoming emotional suffering. The motto for ACT — *live your life such as the life is, not as your mind says it is* — sounds very close to Korzybski's *Whatever you may say something is, it is not.*

Another concept in the "new" psychologies that seems to derive from General Semantics is that of "*dis-identifying* with thoughts." Hayes uses chess as a metaphor to explain this proposal of "dis-identification." In chess, we tend to consider the positive thoughts — the white pieces — as our allies while seeing the negative thoughts — black pieces — as our enemies. But we "are" neither white nor black pieces; we are the chessboard, so it is no use fighting against ourselves; we must proceed through life carrying in our rucksack thoughts, feelings, fears and hopes — both the white and the black pieces of our personal game.

In sum, we can see a good deal of General Semantics spread into many of the new trends in psychotherapy. Psychology, as an atlas for human "reality," must deal with human complexity rather than simplify it. As the subject of study chosen by this new science remains the vague and uncertain field we call "human behavior," we can expect psychological approaches to human reality to improve their methodology and results as their maps continue to incorporate considerations from General Semantics.

Of course, Korzybski was—necessarily—a creature of his own time and circumstances, and Korzybski$_{1933}$ is not the Korzybski I reconstruct through my reading of his writings and under my personal assumptions in 2010. Thus, some of Korzybski$_{1933}$'s ideas on functions and developments of Psychology may be debatable nowadays under the light of the "new" theories about human knowledge. Nevertheless, as I see it, GS's core assumptions keep a matchless freshness and validity as a system of coordinates useful in drawing the new maps depicting "human reality."

First of all, the idea of "wholeness:" No psychological system, no psychotherapeutic practice should ignore the fact that the main character in any psychotherapy is a human being—complex by definition—and not merely a more or less pathological behavior that it is necessary to "heal," however good the intentions of the practitioner.

Moreover, the concept of "dis-identification" becomes essential in order to avoid negative constructions arising from the use of restrictively pathological diagnostic labels. Any psychopathological diagnostic is but an attempt to describe a restricted vital lot—the "problematic lot"—whose shape and extent will vary depending on every person's individual circumstances and attitudes. In the course of a well-oriented therapy, a person will increase the degree to which this lot can be brought under his or her personal control—expanding the "controlled lot." In life, all humans—diagnosed or not—will cultivate both "problematic plots" and "controlled orchards."

Of course, the main tools for cultivating suitable vital orchards consist of well-organized habits of thought. Applying extensional tools, realistic and suitable to the specific land to cultivate, a person will work toward a harvest of balance and realism.

Finally, the Korzybskian view of human nature as "colloidal" provides an interesting metaphor to explain some of the complexities of human living. Humans not only have the capacity to absorb and develop in our "psychic protoplasm" the several experiences we shape to create our personal history, but we also are able to reverberate in tune with our fellow humans, to be enriched by others' presence, because sociability is a feature of human essence.

This view, applied to the field of psychotherapy, indicates that the sense of psychotherapeutic relation is much more than the application of an aseptic technology or to officiate a "magic" ritual. Psychotherapy must become a meeting between two persons where both, and not only one of them, establish a mutual stream of acceptance, empathy and coherence, such as Carl Rogers taught.

The future? First of all, Psychology and Psychotherapies should increase their consciousness of "subject" of the action: it is not possible to conceive any "human behavior" without a "human-who-is-behaving-in-this-specific-context-with-his-specific-rucksack." Besides, understanding that any psychological theory is but a provisional map—referring to its cartographer's beliefs as well as to the evasive land it claims to represent—would avoid the risk of falling into the kind of "psycho-religion" most of the classic schools eventually became. The aim of any useful psychological map is to provide people with resources to enlarge—not to limit—the vision of their own reality.

Finally, the label "therapy" should not be separated from "living"—the most certain and fundamental activity that humans perform. So, the most effective "therapy" any psychological system could suggest is a sort of "life-therapy" that would consist—as the quoted Hayes says—in *living our life such as the life is, not as our mind says it is.*

NOTES

[1] Ellis, Albert. 1991. "Alfred Korzybski Memorial Lecture: General Semantics and Rational Emotive Therapy." *General Semantic Bulletin.* <http://www.generalsemantics.org/wp-content/uploads/2011/04/gsb-58-ellis.pdf>.

[2] George Kelly. 1955. *The psychology of personal constructs.* Vol. I, II. New York. . Norton.

[3] Paul Watzlawick. 1976. *How Real is Real.* New York. Random House.

[4] Jean Jacques Wittezaele & Luisa Medrano 1992. *À la Recherche de l'École de Palo Alto.* Paris, Editions du Seuil.

[5] Humberto Maturana & Francisco Varela 1987. *The Tree of Knowledge: The Biological Roots of Human Understanding.* Boston. Shambhala.

[6] White, M. & Epston, D. 1990. *Narrative means to therapeutic ends.* New York: WW Norton.

[7] Martin Seligman. 2002. *Authentic Happiness.* New York: New Press.

[8] Eugene Gendlin 1978. *Focusing.* New York. Bantam Books.

[9] Ira Progoff 1992. *At a Journal Workshop.* New York. Jeremy P. Tarcher/Putnam.

[10] Steven Hayes with Spencer Smith. 2005. *Get Out of Your Mind and Into Your Life: The New Acceptance and Commitment Therapy*. Oakland, CA: New Harbinger Publications.

CHAPTER 11: KORZYBSKI AND MARSHALL MCLUHAN

Lance Strate

I

ALFRED KORZYBSKI (1879-1950) wanted to move past the limitations of Aristotelian logic, with its focus on deductive reasoning and dismissal of induction, as well as its two-valued orientation, assumption of a static, unchanging world, and its emphasis on identity relationships. To this end, he developed his general semantics which, following the lead of Albert Einstein, he characterized as a non-Aristotelian system, one that would complement the non-Newtonian physics and non-Euclidean geometries that had resulted in a paradigm shift in science and mathematics. In 1933, he presented his ideas to the world in the form of his magnum opus, *Science and Sanity* (see Korzybski, 1993). At that time, Marshall McLuhan (1911-1980) was a young graduate student studying English literature; a decade later, he completed his PhD at Cambridge University. McLuhan's PhD thesis (published as a book in 2006) was a study of the Elizabethan playwright and poet, Thomas Nashe, but in the course of writing it, McLuhan reviewed the history of ideas in western culture, and developed a novel thesis, that our intellectual history could be understood as an ongoing conflict concerning the trivium, the educational curriculum that originated in antiquity and formed the basis of the medieval university. As the term *trivium* indicates, the curriculum was divided into three subjects, rhetoric, which focused on the means of expression; grammar, which included the study of language and literature, including the reading and interpretation of texts; and dialectics or logic. Of the three, rhetoricians and grammarians were typically allied, and in conflict with the champions of dialectics and logic, including Socrates, Plato, and yes, Aristotle.

McLuhan identified with the ancient and medieval grammarians, and noted that they were the ones who forged the path to modern science, and not the logicians, as many would assume. The grammarians opened the door to empiricism by arguing that God communicated to humanity through the environment as well as through the Bible, that God gave us two books to read and interpret, the book of scripture and the book of nature, the book of words and the book of works. Encountering Korzybski's arguments about the need

199

for a scientific, non-Aristotelian orientation, McLuhan (2006) immediately recognized a fellow grammarian, stating, "In our own time the methods of anthropology and psychology have re-established grammar as, at least, a valid mode of science. Full justification for this statement is found in Count Korzybski's *Science and Sanity*, which makes claims for linguistic study (grammar in the old sense)" (p. 17).

As McLuhan pursued his investigations, he began to place great emphasis on sense perception as well (see, for example, McLuhan, 1962, 2003), and he referred to himself as a Thomist, following Thomas Aquinas who said that, "the senses are a kind of reason. Taste, touch and smell, hearing and seeing, are not merely a means to sensation, enjoyable or otherwise, but they are also a means to knowledge—and are, indeed, your only actual means to knowledge." Coincidentally, in 1962, the year McLuhan published *The Gutenberg Galaxy*, his first major work that emphasized the primacy of sense perception, Margaret Gorman published *General Semantics and Contemporary Thomism*, based on her own doctoral dissertation. There is a common ground in that sense perception is fundamental to the empirical method, but of course, Thomism, as a philosophical tradition rooted in the Roman Catholic religion differs in significant ways from modern science and the scientific method, and Korzybski, raised a Catholic, was a scientist first and foremost. McLuhan, a Catholic convert, personally favored the religious orientation, and was quite fervent in his practice and beliefs, but publicly recognized the pre-eminence of science, and insisted on maintaining an objective, nonjudgmental position in regard to his scholarship. He too maintained a sense of connection to the early, grammarian-based concept of science, as reflected in his posthumously published *Laws of Media: The New Science* (McLuhan & McLuhan, 1988), and he was also consistently interested in the relationship between cause and effects, reaching back to Aristotle's views on causality, as can be seen in the recently published work, *Media and Formal Cause* (McLuhan & McLuhan, 2011).

As McLuhan's focus shifted away from literature and the trivium, he did not discuss or cite Korzybski further; he did, however, build upon the related notion of linguistic relativism associated with Edward Sapir (1921), Benjamin Lee Whorf (1956), and Dorothy Lee (1959) as he came to emphasize the study of media (which he characterized as languages in their own right, see, for example, McLuhan, 2003). Moreover, McLuhan's famous aphorism, *the medium is the message*, resonates with Korzybksi's favorite saying, *the map is not the territory*. For Korzybski, the map is a depiction of the territory, and is distinct and different (and necessarily incomplete and inaccurate) from the territory. For McLuhan, the map is a medium, and the depiction of the territory is the content of the medium, and subject to the biases and limitations of the medium (which is why the medium "is" the message). Neil Postman and Charles Weingartner (1969) recognized the common concern of Korzybski and McLuhan, along with others who pointed to the need to study structure and relationships, in broadening what had come to be known as the Sapir-Whorf Hypothesis, and in general semantics circles as the Sapir Whorf-Korzybski Hypothesis, to the "Sapir-Whorf-Korzybski-Ames-Einstein-Heisenberg-Wittgenstein-McLuhan-Et Al. Hypothesis" (p. 101). Postman (1974) also argued that if Korzybski had been alive during the sixties and seventies, his attention would naturally have turned to media, just as McLuhan's did.

Korzybski's insistence on a non-Aristotelian approach is certainly consistent with McLuhan's argument that the electronic media have brought an end to the dominance of alphabetic literacy that distinguished western culture. Indeed, Aristotle's logic, and for that matter Plato's ideal forms, and Socrates' search for definitions, would, from McLuhan's (1962, 2003) perspective, obviously be a product of the new kind of mindset made possible by alphabetic literacy, with its biases towards decontextualization, high level abstractions, and abstract thinking, towards analysis and atomism or elementalism, and towards linear and sequential modes of expression and thought (see also the extension of McLuhan's work by his former collaborator Robert K. Logan in *The Alphabet Effect*, 2004). By way of contrast, the electronic media favor more concrete forms of expression (often iconic and pictoral), along with synthesis, and simultaneity. McLuhan argued that Einstein's eradication of Newtonian space and time in the early 20th century follows and is made possible by the introduction of telegraphy, the first form of electronic communications, in the mid-19th century, and it would follow that Korzybski's general semantics represents a new approach to thought and reason that reflects the new media environment associated with electronic technology, and more recently with digital, computer-based technologies. No doubt, this is why Postman made both Korzybski and McLuhan required reading in his media ecology curriculum (see Strate, 2006, 2011).

II

Korzybski and McLuhan both were highly independent, interdisciplinary, original, and unorthodox thinkers, and the approach that they hold in common, and share with a number of other significant scholars and intellectuals, could be termed holistic, situational, contextual, relativistic or relational, cybernetic or a systems view, or ecological. Whatever the name that we give to it, the fundamental concern is with understanding what it means to be human; understanding ourselves as human beings, not in isolation, but in relation to our environments; understanding how we relate to our environments and how we *ought* to relate to our environments. For example, in the Introduction to the Second Edition of *Understanding Media*, McLuhan wrote:

> the section on "the medium is the message" can, perhaps, be clarified by pointing out that any technology gradually creates a totally new human environment. Environments are not passive wrappings but active processes. (McLuhan, 2003, p.12)

And in the Preface to the Third Edition of *Science and Sanity*, Korzybski wrote:

> The origin of this work was a new functional definition of 'man' . . . based on an analysis of uniquely human *potentialities*; namely, that each generation may begin where the former left off. This characteristic I called the 'time-binding' capacity. Here the reactions of humans are not split verbally and elementalistically into separate 'body', 'mind', 'emotions', 'intellect', 'intuitions', etc., but are treated from an organism-as-a-whole-in-an-environment . . . point of view. (Korzybski, 1993, p. xxxxii)

Ideally, we are concerned with how the organism-as-a-whole relates to the *total environment*, as McLuhan liked to put it. But in practice we may focus on a particular aspect of the environment, such as the cosmological or the geological, the physical or the chemical, the biological or the sociocultural. As an individual, the organism-as-a-whole exists in relationship to other individual human beings, in dyads and groups, in families and tribes, in organizations and associations, in cities and nations, in networks and in the global village. Every other organism-as-a-whole that the individual comes into contact with becomes part of the individual's environment. Of course, "organism" is a multiordinal term, referring to the individual, and also to the species-as-a-whole, the species as a social system. The human species, which is one of many social species, is distinguished by our unique capacity for symbolic communication, which grants us our potential for time-binding. And the environment for our species-as-a-whole is nothing less than what Buckminster Fuller (1971) called *spaceship earth*.

Individually and collectively, the relationship between human beings as systems and their environments is one that is fundamentally indirect. Externally, stimuli excite and irritate our sense organs and nervous systems, which constitute our informational boundary with our environment. Internally, we construct a map of the environment out of the various excitations and irritations that we experience, a map that may be more or less structurally homologous with the outside world, but a map that is, simply stated, not the territory itself. We therefore live in an inner environment, a perceptual environment, and a conceptual environment. And our relationship to the outer environment, being indirect, is therefore mediated, hence the medium is the message.

This is not a solipsistic point of view, I hasten to add. Our concern is with the *relationship*, or if you like, the *interface* between the inner environment of the map, and the outer environment of the territory. It is along this interface that Korzybski (1993) made reference to *verbal environments* and *semantic environments*, and *neurolinguistic* and *neurosemantic environments*. It is along this interface that we can then speak of information environments, communication environments, symbolic environments, and technological environments. It is along this interface that McLuhan (2003) talked about media environments, and Postman (1970) in turn defined media ecology as the study of media as environments.

In discussing the ways that we relate to our environments, Korzybski (1993) employed the key term of "abstracting." He used the verb form of "abstracting" instead of the noun form of "abstraction" because he did not want us to think about abstractions as things, but rather as processes, and activities. As a verb, "abstract" can be defined variously as summarize, remove, separate, steal, and purloin. And what we as organisms do when we abstract is take into ourselves something from the outside environment. Unlike the processes of ingesting and inhaling, abstracting does not involve absorbing any material substance from the environment; what we abstract is information, which provides us with a necessarily incomplete and selective summary, or map of our environment.

All forms of life engage in some form of abstracting, in that all forms of life respond to stimuli. Organisms with nervous systems engage in the form of abstracting that we call sense perception. And the human organism, the time-binding species, also engages in the form of abstracting that we call symbolic communication, employing language and other symbol systems to generate and accumulate knowledge. Korzybski was not alone in this linking of perception and language. Susanne Langer (1957) argued that perception is a symbolic activity, a form of metonymy where the fraction of the environment that we take in stands for the environment as a whole. McLuhan (2003) argued that language is a form of perception, indeed, that languages are organs of perception.

The process of abstracting, as it encompasses the processes of perception and symbolic communication, allows us to do more with less, and therefore represents enormous efficiencies, especially for organisms with complex nervous systems such as ourselves. And efficiency, as Jacques Ellul (1964) has made clear, is the basis of the technological imperative. Therefore abstracting, I would argue, is fundamentally associated with technological activity. And technological activity, I would suggest, can be traced back to the fact that all forms of life alter their environment, altering their environment to their own benefit, in theory if not always in practice, and altering their environment simply by their presence in the environment, and by their metabolism.

McLuhan (2003) used the term "technology" interchangeably with the term "medium" because all of our inventions and innovations are means by which we relate to our environment, by which we mediate and interface with our environment. Our technologies and techniques help us to abstract information from our environment; help us to accumulate, share, and preserve knowledge; help us to communicate and commune with one another; and help us to act upon our environment and alter it for better or for worse. We can study an individual medium or technology, its unique characteristics, biases, and effects. And we can also study the media-environment-as-a-whole, recognizing that the individual medium does not exist in isolation, but in complex interaction with other media. But going beyond the media-as-environments point of view, I want to suggest that McLuhan's approach can best be understood when we employ the verb form of *mediating*. Along these lines, the French media ecologist Regis Debray (1996, 2000), drawing on the field of *semiology*, which is concerned with the process of *signification*, calls his field of study *mediology*, which is concerned with the process of *mediation*. Admittedly, there is some potential for confusion with the ways in which the terms mediation and mediating are used in the legal sector, but there is also some benefit from associating media with activities such as negotiation.

With this way of understanding media, we can say that we relate to our environments through a process of *mediating*, of *interfacing*, of *abstracting*. From a systems perspective, as sociologist Niklas Luhmann (1982, 1989, 1995, 2000) explains, we can only take in part of our environment through abstracting because its totality would overwhelm us. All systems must maintain boundaries with their environments in order to establish and maintain their integrity as systems. Indeed, as biologists Humberto Maturana and Francisco Varela have argued (1980, 1992), it is only by closing itself to its environment to a significant degree that a system can organize itself, that is, that an independent system can come together as a system in the first place in the process termed autopoiesis. We create barriers for our own protection, biologically, psychologically, and sociologically. And we do so technologically as well, or as Max Frisch observed in his cybernetics-inspired novel *Homo Faber* (1959), "technology is the art of never having to experience the world" (p. 178).

McLuhan (2003) regarded media and technology as extensions of the human organism, following a tradition that can be traced back to Edward T. Hall (1959), C. K. Ogden and I. A. Richards (1923), and Ralph Waldo Emerson. (1883). But McLuhan insisted that every extension is also an amputation. The medium that extends our reach into the world does so by situating itself between ourselves and the world, so that it also becomes a barrier between ourselves and the world. And as a barrier, the medium becomes part of our world, part of our environment, the boundary that separates system from environment. In sum, as we relate to our environment, we reject as well as select. We filter. We mediate. Or as I like to say, the medium is the membrane (and the membrane is us). We dance along the edge of chaos and order, opening and closing, extension and amputation, the external and the internal.

Both Korzybski (1993) and McLuhan (2003) were concerned with *differences that make a difference*, as Gregory Bateson (1972) liked to put it. But their point of view on these differences were somewhat... *different*. Korzybski, being an engineer, and of a scientific and mathematical bent, looked at the process of abstracting along a vertical axis of higher and lower levels or orders. Sense perception constitutes the lowest level of abstraction, symbols a higher level. Images are less abstract than words. Names that are attached to an individual are less abstract than labels that refer to an entire category. Following Korzybski's lead, we can say that television is less abstract than a book. And we can say that the written word is more abstract than the spoken word because, as Walter Ong (1982) explains, writing is a secondary symbol system that represents speech, our primary symbol system, in a visual form.

McLuhan, being a scholar of English literature, focused on qualitative rather than quantitative differences. With this in mind, we can add to the vertical axis of *level of abstracting* a horizontal axis that I would call the *mode of abstracting*. For example, television and movies are different media, and therefore represent different methods of abstracting. One is not particularly more or less abstract than the other, they are just qualitatively different modes. The same could be said of sound recordings and radio, or a magazine and a newspaper, or a parchment manuscript and papyrus scroll, or hieroglyphics and cuneiform, or a dialogue and a public address. Following the insights of Sapir (1921), Whorf (1956), and Lee (1959), we can also understand that different languages (e.g., English, Spanish, French, Hindi, Mandarin, Hopi), represent different modes of abstracting, and mediating. And the same can be said of different forms of sense perception. As McLuhan (2003) made clear, vision represents a different mode of abstracting than hearing, or touching, or smelling or tasting; moreover, senses trained in different ways represent different modes of abstracting, so that literates, for example, use their eyes differently from nonliterates, and this in turn alters the way all of the other senses are used in concert.

Taking into account the mode of abstracting as well as the level of abstracting gives us a better handle on the process of abstracting, and the process of mediating. We mediate with our bodies, our sense organs and nervous systems. We mediate through our languages, art forms, and symbol systems. And we mediate through our technologies, techniques, and technical systems. We relate to our environment, not as separate entities, but as interdependent parts of an ecosystem. What that means is that the organism-as-a-whole is influenced and shaped by its environment, which is, as McLuhan (2003) noted, not a passive wrapping but an active process. And the environment-as-a-whole is influenced and shaped by the organisms that are a part of it. We have changed our environments radically through our inventions, through our ideas, and through our activities. But to change the world for the better, we must understand the world, understand how we relate to the world, how we can change the world and what the consequences of change might be.

What we need then is an ecology of mediating, an ecology of abstracting, an ecology of knowing. We need an ecology of knowledge, by which I mean both knowledge in the academic sense, and know-how in the everyday sense, knowledge that is both theoretical and practical, pure and applied, both theory and praxis. We need an ecology that incorporates both form and technology, the inner landscape and the outer environment, the map and the territory, the medium and the message. In other words, we need an ecology of Korzybski and McLuhan.

REFERENCES

Bateson, G. (1972). *Steps to an ecology of mind: Collected essays in anthropology, psychiatry, evolution, and epistemology.* Chicago, IL: University of Chicago Press. Philadelphia: University of Pennsylvania Press.

Debray, R. (1996). *Media manifestos: On the technological transmission of cultural forms* (E. Rauth, Trans.). New York: Verso.

Debray, R. (2000). *Transmitting culture* (E. Rauth, Trans.). New York: Columbia University Press.

Ellul, J. (1964). *The technological society* (J. Wilkinson, Trans.). New York: Knopf.

Emerson, R. W. (1883). *The conduct of life and society and solitude.* London: Macmillan and Company.

Frisch, M. (1959). *Homor faber: A report* (M. Bulloock, Trans.). San Diego: Harcourt Brace Jovanovich.

Fuller, R. B. (1971). *Operating manual for spaceship earth.* New York: E.P. Dutton.

Gorman, M. (1962). *General semantics and contemporary Thomism.* Lincoln: University of Nebraska Press.

Hall, E. T. (1959). *The silent language*. Garden City: Doubleday.

Korzybski, A. (1993). *Science and sanity: An introduction to non-Aristotelian systems and general semantics* (5th ed.). Englewood, NJ: The International Non-Aristotelian Library/Institute of General Semantics. Original work published in 1933, Third Edition in 1947.

Langer, S. K. (1957). *Philosophy in a new key: A study in the symbolism of reason, rite and art* (3rd ed.). Cambridge, MA: Harvard University Press.

Lee, D. (1959). *Freedom and culture*. Englewood Cliffs, NJ: Prentice-Hall.

Logan, R.K. (2004). *The alphabet effect: A media ecology understanding of the making of western civilization*. Cresskill, NJ: Hampton Press.

Logan, R. K. (2007). *The extended mind: The emergence of language, the human mind, and culture*. Toronto: University of Toronto Press.

Luhmann, N. (1982). *The differentiation of society* (S. Holmes & C. Larmore, Trans.). New York: Columbia University Press.

Luhmann, N. (1989). *Ecological communication* (J. Bednarz, Jr., Trans.). Chicago: University of Chicago Press.

Luhmann, N. (1995). *Social systems* (J. Bednarz , Jr. with D. Baecker, Trans.). Stanford: Stanford University Press.

Luhmann, N. (2000). *The reality of the mass media* (K. Cross, Trans.). Stanford: Stanford University Press.

Maturana, H. R. & Varela, F. J. (1980). *Autopoiesis and cognition: The realization of the living*. Boston: D. Reidel.

Maturana, H. R. & Varela, F. J. (1992). *The tree of knowledge: The biological roots of human understanding* (revised ed., R. Paolucci, Trans.). Boston: Shambhala.

McLuhan, M. (1962). *The Gutenberg galaxy: The making of typographic man*. Toronto: University of Toronto Press.

McLuhan, M. (2003). *Understanding media: The extensions of man* (Critical Ed., W. T. Gordon, Ed.). Original work published in

1964.

McLuhan, M. (2006). *The classical trivium: The place of Thomas Nashe in the learning of his time.* Madera, CA: Gingko Press.

McLuhan, M. & McLuhan, E. (1988). *Laws of Media: The new science.* Toronto: University of Toronto Press.

McLuhan, M. & McLuhan, E. (2011). *Media and formal cause.* Houston: NeoPoiesis Press.

Ogden, C. K. & Richards, I. A. (1923). *The meaning of meaning: A study of the influence of language upon thought and of the science of symbolism.* New York: Harcourt, Brace. Ithaca, NY: Cornell University Press.

Ong, W. J. (1982). *Orality and literacy: The technologizing of the word.* London: Routledge.

Postman, N. (1970). The reformed English curriculum. In A.C. Eurich (Ed.), *High school 1980: The shape of the future in American secondary education* (pp.160-168). New York: Pitman.

Postman, N. (1974). Media ecology: General semantics in the third millennium. *General Semantics Bulletin 41-43*, 74-78.

Postman, N. & Weingartner, C. (1969). *Teaching as a subversive activity.* New York: Delta.

Sapir, E. (1921). *Language: An introduction to the study of speech.* New York: Harcourt, Brace Jovanovich.

Strate, L. (2006). *Echoes and reflections: On media ecology as a field of study.* Cresskill, NJ: Hampton Press.

Strate, L. (2010). Alfred Korzybski and Marshall McLuhan. *General Semantics Bulletin 76*, pp. 56-59.

Strate, L. (2011). *On the binding biases of time and other essays on general semantics and media ecology.* Fort Worth, TX: Institute of General Semantics.

Whorf, B. L. (1956). *Language, thought, and reality.* Cambridge, MA: MIT Press.

CHAPTER 12: KORZYBSKI AND CULTURAL STUDIES

Geraldine E. Forsberg

THIS ESSAY CONSIDERS KORZYBSKI'S theory of abstraction as it relates to language, television, and culture.

Writing in the early 1900's, Alfred Korzybski, a Polish engineer, set out to discover what makes the human being unique, what distinguishes humans from other forms of life? In his book, *Manhood of Humanity: The Science and Art of Human Engineering* (1921), Korzybski set forth the idea that what makes humans unique is their ability to "bind-time." Human beings are able to preserve their language, their creative endeavors, their heritage, and pass their knowledge on to future generations. Humans can critique their language, their symbolic works, and can make revisions if needed. We can learn from our past and we can build off the labors of previous generations. Korzybski labeled animals as "space-binders" because animals are able to move about in space. However, animals are not able to symbolize. Animals cannot create libraries, museums, books, or art. They can abstract at lower sensory levels, but not at higher verbal levels. Korzybski labeled plants as "chemistry-binders" because they take energy from the sun and convert it into organic chemical energy. After establishing the functional uniqueness of human-beings, Korzybski went on in his book, *Science and Sanity: An Introduction to Non-Aristotelian Systems and General Semantics* (1933), to consider how people symbolize and how they create language.

Korzybski believed that there is a structural relationship between the natural environment and the symbolic environment. The structure of the natural environment forms the foundation of accurate language evaluation. In the natural environment there are many structural principles which can guide our evaluation of language, principles such as: uniqueness, complexity, change, order, interconnectedness, levels, and context.

For example, in the natural world everything is unique—every person, place, mountain, and stream. Language, however, enables us to label and categorize. When we use language we abstract out of the infinite world and ignore differences. We label in such a way that we forget the uniqueness of people, places, and events. For instance, we use the word "student" and forget that each student is unique with his or her own backgrounds, skills, and abilities.

In the natural environment the world is very complex. However, language enables us to simplify. In the medical profession, for example, doctors often specialize on one part of the body—the foot, the eye, skin, the heart, etc. This can lead to overlooking the complexity and interrelatedness of the human body.

In the natural environment everything is constantly changing, but language labels in such a way that we can forget or ignore change. We talk about the "United States", but the United States, today, is very different from the United States in the 1800s.

The natural environment is coherent. There is an order, and pattern, that exists within the natural environment. We move from summer to fall to winter to spring yearly in a repeated pattern. Language, however, can become disordered and even incoherent. We can talk about summer and winter, fall and spring, without following the natural order.

In the natural environment everything is interconnected, nothing exists in isolation. With language, however, we are able to separate what in nature is inseparable.

In the natural world everything exists on levels. There is a submicroscopic level, a microscopic level, a macroscopic level and object level. Language often keeps us focused on one level.

In the natural world everything exists within a context. Language enables us to isolate what in reality can only be understood in context.

Korzybski emphasized that the natural environment can never be fully known or perceived—it is an infinite world. In the same way, language can never communicate all there is to communicate about anything. These structural principles of the natural environment formed the foundation for Korzybski's theory of language evaluation.

In order to help people evaluate their use of language, Korzybski recommended using some practical devices such as indexes, dates, quotes, hyphens, and etc. These devices were to be used to remind people that language is not reality. Language, however, should relate closely to reality if it is to be reliable. In order to explain this, Korzybski provided the map/territory analogy. A map is not the territory. It is only a representation. A map cannot represent all of a territory. There will always be certain things left off of a map. A map is self-reflexive in that we can make maps of maps indefinitely.

Language is like a map. Language is not the object it labels. Language cannot communicate everything about an object. Language enables us to speak about language, critique our thinking, analyze our theories, and examine our philosophies. In other words, language is self-reflexive. We can create maps of maps indefinitely; we can abstract on and on indefinitely. (1933, pp. 58, 247, 498, 750)

Abstraction and Language

Abstraction as explained by Korzybski is a process of omitting or leaving out details of reality: "The standard meaning of 'abstract', 'abstracting' implies 'selecting', 'picking out', 'separating', 'summarizing', 'deducting', 'removing', 'omitting', 'disengaging', 'taking away', 'stripping', and, as an adjective, not 'concrete'" (1933, p. 379).

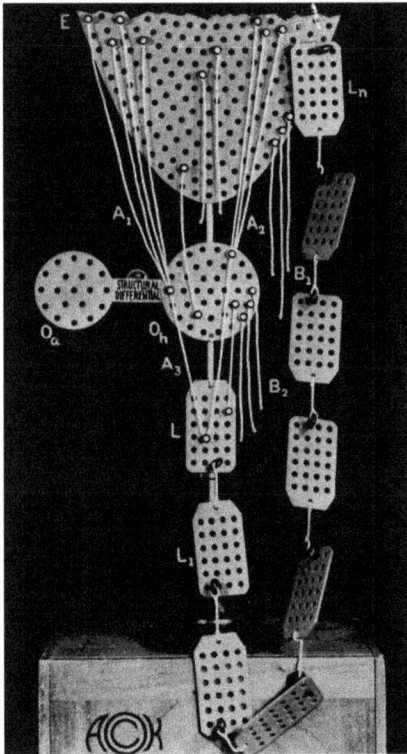

Figure 1: Alfred Korzybski's Structual Differential[1]

Korzybski developed a model of the process of abstracting called the "structural differential." The "differential" refers to the difference between animal abstracting and human abstracting. Humans alone can abstract at verbal levels. Abstracting occurs on a physiological-neurological-and non-verbal event level as well as on a symbolic and verbal level. It is a process that the entire body-brain-nervous system is continuously doing.

The structural differential, as shown in Figure 1, depicts the limitless natural environment by a parabola, the submicroscopic world, the process and event level (E). The circle (Oa) represents animals which are unable to abstract on verbal levels. The circle (Oh) represents the object, human, situation, etc. that we perceive with our senses— the macroscopic level. (L) Represents the labels we give to people, objects, experience. Korzybski believed that as we label, the correct order is to move from lower levels of abstraction to higher levels of abstraction and, then, back down to lower levels again—to move from facts, to descriptions, to inferences. Korzybski believed this to be an ongoing, continuous process of the entire organism. We abstract at non-verbal and verbal levels. The holes in the diagram (B) represent characteristics that are left out as we move from lower to higher levels of abstraction. The strings illustrate how more and more characteristics are left out the more abstraction takes place (Korzybski, 1933, pp. 386-411; Johnson, 2004, p. 20).

Figure 2: Hayakawa's Abstraction Ladder[2]

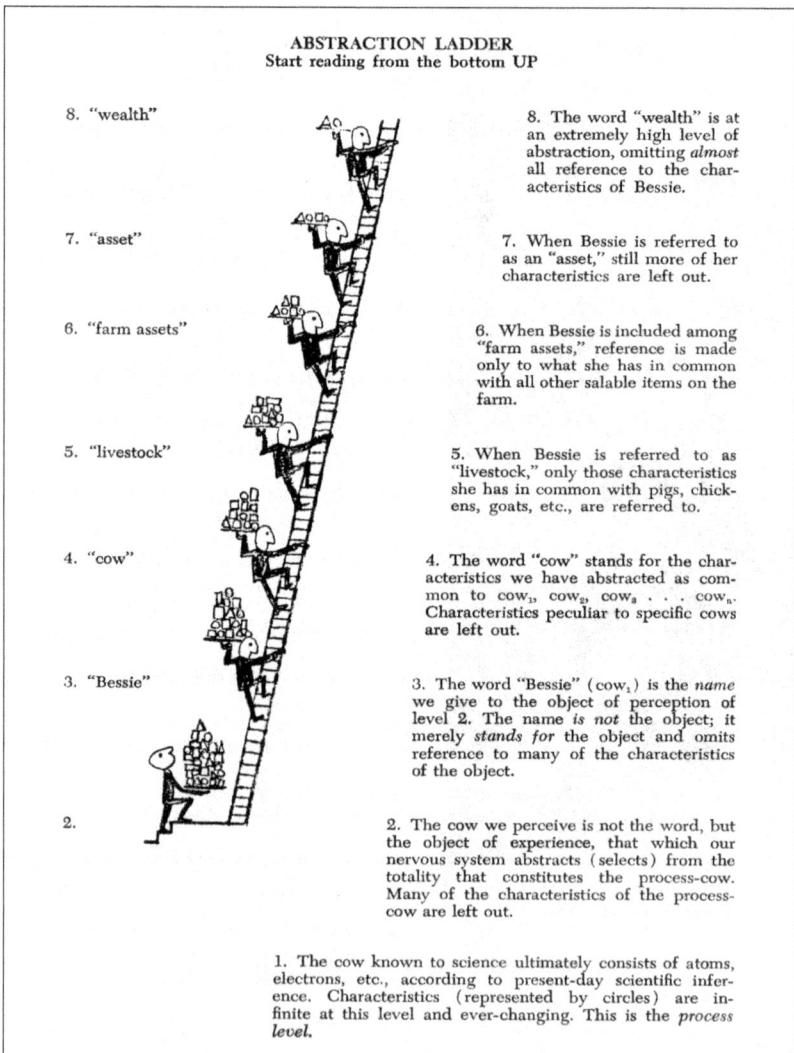

ABSTRACTION LADDER
Start reading from the bottom UP

8. "wealth"

8. The word "wealth" is at an extremely high level of abstraction, omitting *almost* all reference to the characteristics of Bessie.

7. "asset"

7. When Bessie is referred to as an "asset," still more of her characteristics are left out.

6. "farm assets"

6. When Bessie is included among "farm assets," reference is made only to what she has in common with all other salable items on the farm.

5. "livestock"

5. When Bessie is referred to as "livestock," only those characteristics she has in common with pigs, chickens, goats, etc., are referred to.

4. "cow"

4. The word "cow" stands for the characteristics we have abstracted as common to cow_1, cow_2, cow_3 . . . cow_n. Characteristics peculiar to specific cows are left out.

3. "Bessie"

3. The word "Bessie" (cow_1) is the *name* we give to the object of perception of level 2. The name *is not* the object; it merely *stands for* the object and omits reference to many of the characteristics of the object.

2.

2. The cow we perceive is not the word, but the object of experience, that which our nervous system abstracts (selects) from the totality that constitutes the process-cow. Many of the characteristics of the process-cow are left out.

1. The cow known to science ultimately consists of atoms, electrons, etc., according to present-day scientific inference. Characteristics (represented by circles) are infinite at this level and ever-changing. This is the *process* level.

S. I. Hayakawa's Abstraction Ladder

In 1939, S. I. Hayakawa wrote *Language in Action*, and in 1941 he published an expansion, *Language in Thought and Action*. In those books, Hayakawa popularized Korzybski's theory of abstracting by setting forth his own conception called the "abstraction ladder." The abstraction ladder was meant to more clearly explain how we abstract in relation to language.

As shown in Figure 2, Hayakawa explained how we move from lower to higher levels of abstraction as we create language. First, there is the process level. He used a cow as an example. The "cow known to science ultimately consists of atoms, electrons, etc." Second, there is the actual cow—"the object of experience." Third, there is the label, or the word for cow. In this case, the cow was named "Bessie." The name is *not* the object: It merely stands for the object and omits reference to many of the characteristics of the object. As we continue to label we move farther and farther away from reality. Our language becomes more and more abstract. As the diagram depicts, "the word 'wealth' is at an extremely high level of abstraction, omitting *almost* all reference to the characteristics of Bessie." The circles represent infinite characteristics that are ever changing.

Korzybski was not too pleased with Hayakawa's depiction of his theory since it did not illustrate the process nature of abstracting with the continuous feedback loop to the real life object or to the natural environment. Nevertheless, the abstraction ladder does help explain how we create language in progressively higher levels of abstraction by leaving out details.

One of the major dangers in the abstracting process is when people settle at one level of abstraction and do not move up or down. Wendell Johnson, in his book, *People in Quandaries* (1946), called this "dead-level abstracting." Dead-level abstracting can occur at any level: lower, middle, or higher levels of abstraction. Johnson gives the example of people who talk on and on without coming to some conclusion as those being stuck at lower levels of abstraction. "They go on indefinitely, reciting insignificant facts, never able to pull them together to frame a generalization that would give meaning to the facts" (Hayakawa, 1941, p. 164). People can also get stuck at high levels of abstraction. For example, philosophers who go to very high level generalizations, but do not come back down and give specific concrete examples and facts to support their generalizations. In either case, dead-level abstracting can be a symptom of mental illness.

In *Science and Sanity*, Korzybski discussed mental illness as it relates to semantic reactions. He actually studied schizophrenia and discovered that people with this disease speak of things which do not exist in reality and are disconnected from reality. In contrast to schizophrenics, scientists use a method based on verifying theories in reality. Scientists evaluate what is taking place in the real world and, then, create theories about what is taking place. Or, scientists create theories and, then, examine what is taking place in reality to see if it corresponds. According to Korzybski, if we could only follow the scientific method of verification, our thinking would be more accurate, we would become less confused, less disoriented, and we would be less likely to lose our way as individuals and as a society.

Abstraction and Television

Korzybski's theory of abstraction is considered in relation to television in *Critical Thinking in an Image World: Alfred Korzybski's Theoretical Principles Extended to Critical Television Evaluation* (Forsberg, 1993). In that book, it is suggested that abstraction relates to both the way television is created, or encoded, and the way people relate to, or decode, television. The focus model of TV image abstraction, as shown in Figure 3, illustrates how television goes through layers and layers of abstraction before the final image is transmitted on television.

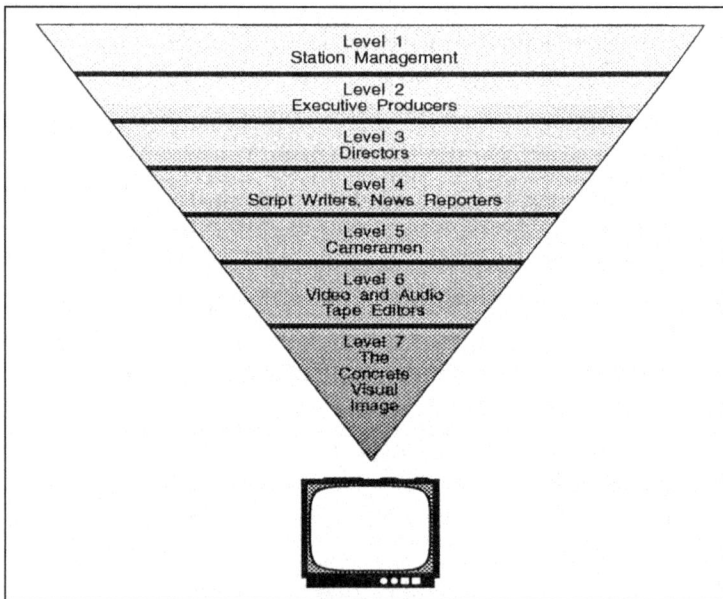

Figure 3: The Focus Model of TV Image Abstraction[3]

The station management and owners make decisions about what programs will and will not be broadcast. The executive producers and directors make decisions about what stories to cover and what stories not to cover. The scriptwriters and news reporters decide what facts to include and what facts to exclude. The cameramen abstract out of the environment the images to photograph. The video and audiotape editors splice and edit until often only a very few seconds of material actually makes it on. Finally, the viewer sees the visual image, an image which has been abstracted through layers and layers of decision-making. Unfortunately, television images often replace real life as the foundation for language abstraction.

Figure 4: Television and Abstraction: Images replace real life as the foundation for abstraction[4]

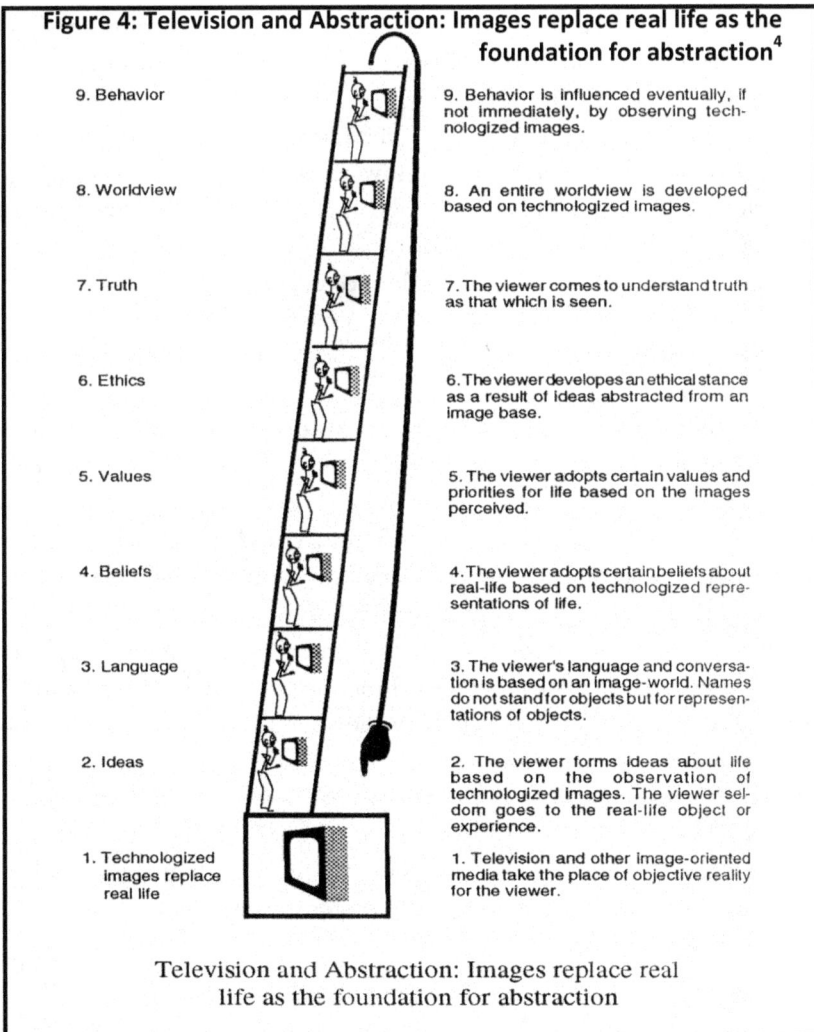

9. Behavior — 9. Behavior is influenced eventually, if not immediately, by observing technologized images.

8. Worldview — 8. An entire worldview is developed based on technologized images.

7. Truth — 7. The viewer comes to understand truth as that which is seen.

6. Ethics — 6. The viewer developes an ethical stance as a result of ideas abstracted from an image base.

5. Values — 5. The viewer adopts certain values and priorities for life based on the images perceived.

4. Beliefs — 4. The viewer adopts certain beliefs about real-life based on technologized representations of life.

3. Language — 3. The viewer's language and conversation is based on an image-world. Names do not stand for objects but for representations of objects.

2. Ideas — 2. The viewer forms ideas about life based on the observation of technologized images. The viewer seldom goes to the real-life object or experience.

1. Technologized images replace real life — 1. Television and other image-oriented media take the place of objective reality for the viewer.

Television and Abstraction: Images replace real life as the foundation for abstraction

In Figure 4, the author illustrates how instead of going to reality, viewers often mistake television for reality. Television forms the basis of our ideas, language, beliefs, values, ethics, and understanding of truth, our worldview, and behavior. Images end up replacing reality as the foundation for abstraction.

For Korzybski, this would be a very dangerous phenomenon because it violates the correct order of abstracting and creating language. One should go first to the real-life object and, then, create a label for it. "If we reverse the correct order of symbolizing, Korzybski warned, we risk becoming confused, disillusioned, and mentally insane" (Forsberg, 1993, p. 130).

Television also keeps us thinking at a concrete level of abstraction and does not foster higher levels of thinking. Neil Postman noted this in *The Disappearance of Childhood*. According to him, "…the business of television is to show—to forgo abstraction, to make everything concrete" (Postman, 1982, p. 117).

We know Korzybski's model of abstraction has provided a means of evaluating language and television. But how does it relate to understanding our technological culture? Can Korzybski's theory of abstraction provide a framework for cultural analysis? Before discussing that question, let me first briefly explain how technologies can influence culture.

Technology and Culture

Media ecologists know that when a new technology enters a culture it changes everything. A study done in the late 1960s provides a real concrete example of how technologies can change a culture. In 1969, Canadian anthropologist Edmund Carpenter carried out a study in New Guinea. He and fellow researchers went to a tiny, secluded, primitive tribe … many in the tribe practiced cannibalism. The natives had never seen movies or television. They had never seen themselves in a mirror, never seen a photograph, never heard a tape-recording of their voices. In an article titled, "Television Meets the Stone Age," Carpenter recounts how they introduced various technologies to the tribe and the effects.

First, the researchers gave the natives a mirror. Up until that time the natives had never seen their reflections in a mirror. They were paralyzed. Carpenter writes, "They stood transfixed, staring at their images. Only their stomach muscles betrayed their great tension. They became acutely self-conscious" (1971, p. 14).

Second, they gave the natives a Polaroid picture of themselves. The natives could not "read" the pictures. As Carpenter reflects:

> A photograph is black and white, flat, static, odorless. It is far removed from any reality they know. We had to teach them how to see the pictures. I pointed to a man's nose in the photograph; then I touched his real nose. Gradually they began to catch on. Recognition grew and so did fear. Pressing his photograph against his chest, each man would stand frozen. Then he would slip away to study his portrait alone. (ibid., p. 14)

Third, the researchers took motion pictures of the natives. Then, they showed the natives pictures of a neighboring tribe. Finally, they recorded the natives' voices. After their study they left the tribe. When they returned six months later, Carpenter and his research team did not even recognize the village. It had completely changed. As Carpenter writes:

> Houses had been rebuilt in a new style. The men wore European clothes, carried themselves differently, acted differently. They had left the village after our visit and, for the first time, traveled outside the world they had previously known. (ibid., p. 16)

With exposure to the new technologies there came a new self-awareness as well as a different view of others. Eventually there was a breakdown of the tribal community. Carpenter concludes by saying, "Our actions had produced instant alienation. They had destroyed the natives' old, strictly tribal self-concept." Carpenter was horrified about the results. But, he said, the same type of transformation is occurring in American culture with the adoption of television.

When technologies are introduced into a culture they change the way people think, the way people view themselves, the way people view others, and the way people behave (McLuhan and Fiore, 1967). When a technology enters a culture everything changes—the level of thought, innovation, creativity, logic, and rationality are all influenced (Eisenstein, 1979). New technologies affect the way we abstract information from our environment and the level in which we abstract. And, our underlying, often unconscious, assumptions about both time and space change.

Korzybski's theory of abstraction can help us better understand this change. I believe Korzybski's theory can give us a framework for cultural analysis and a framework for analyzing our use of technologies. His theory, which has been used to help people understand and evaluate our use of language and television, can also help us evaluate our evolving technological culture.

Korzybski's Theory of Abstraction and Culture

In his book, *Time Wars: The Primary Conflict in Human History* (1987), Jeremy Rifkin discussed the gradual evolution of culture as it relates to time. In his introduction he refers to Korzybski's concept of human beings as the "time-binding" form of life. Human beings can look forward in time, they can look back in time, and they can evaluate the present situation as it relates to time. They can also invent time-space technologies which order and re-order social life. They can preserve and pass on their best works from generation to generation. In Rifkin's insightful analysis of time and culture, he implicitly refers to time as it relates to the theory of abstraction. However, he does not explain Korzybski's model of abstraction nor does he explain how Korzybski's theory of abstraction forms the theoretical foundation for his analysis. This is an attempt to make Korzybski's theory of abstraction explicit as it relates to Rifkin's study of time; and, more specifically as it relates to cultural analysis in general.

Korzybski's theory of abstraction is based on the natural world—the natural universe. The natural environment also forms the foundation for Rifkin's cultural analysis. Rifkin begins his book by explaining how early societies thought of time in relationship to the natural environment. There was a strong tie between the temporal patterns of social life and the temporal patterns of the earth's ecosystem. Societies organized their lives by the seasons, the rooster's crowing, the rising and setting of the sun, the movement of the constellations, the migration of birds, etc. (1987, p. 27). However, with the invention and adoption of each new time technology, we have become more and more abstract as a culture. We have moved from societies closely connected to the rhythms of the natural universe to highly abstract nano-second cultures. Rifkin's main thesis as he states it is:

> While our biological life remains set to the unchanging rhythms of
> the natural world, our social life has become more and more

acclimated to the nanosecond time frame of the computer. The ever-widening schism between the natural time and social time is setting the stage for a dramatic confrontation over temporal choices and priorities in the years ahead. (ibid., p. 27)

The cultural movement from lower levels of abstraction where a society is closely connected to nature to highly abstract computer run societies follows the abstraction theory set forth by Korzybski. As shown in Figure 5, cultures move through levels of abstraction in relation to both time and space. It is important for cultural awareness to be conscious of our cultural level of abstraction. It is also important for mental health that we come back down to lower levels of abstraction—that we constantly reconnect with the natural environment. Just as with language, this movement needs to be a continuous process.

Figure 5: Abstraction and Culture[5]

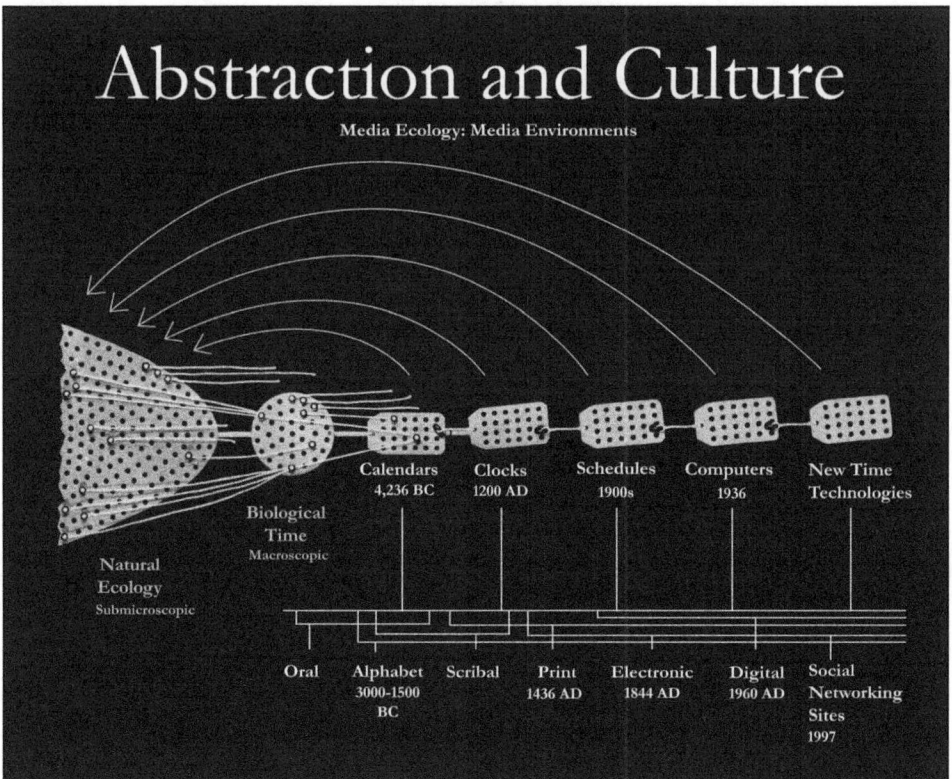

The model of abstraction and culture, illustrates how culture has moved from technologies which closely relate to the natural environment to technologies which are far removed from the natural environment. With the invention and adoption of various technologies our culture has moved to higher levels of abstraction. The lines illustrate the need to continuously move back down to the natural ecology.

Korzybski's model of abstraction emphasized levels of abstraction. In Rifkin's discussion of time, he uses these levels as a framework for cultural analysis. The following seeks to explain how Rifkin has used Korzybski's theory of abstraction.

First, Korzybski's theory of abstraction emphasizes the submicroscopic level. In the natural environment, the submicroscopic world forms the foundation of abstracting. Rifkin begins his discussion of time and culture by discussing the submicroscopic level. He describes the submicroscopic level as a world of "vibrating forces, a world of energy pulsations interacting rhythmically in an elaborately choreographed dance that seems to spread out and give order and meaning to the whole of the universe" (ibid., p. 29). Rifkin quotes John E. Orme who states:

> The physical universe is basically rhythmic in nature. The moon revolves around the earth, the earth around the sun, and the solar system itself changes spatial position with time. All these phenomena result in regular rhythmic changes, and the survival of biological species depends on the capacity to follow these rhythms. (1987, p. 36)

Throughout *Science and Sanity*, Korzybski discussed the submicroscopic world as it relates to human beings and time. In his words, "'Time' seemingly represents a general characteristic of *all* nervous tissue...We are made up of very long chains of atomic pulsating clocks on the submicroscopic level" (1933, p. 230).

Second, Korzybski's theory of abstraction emphasizes the macroscopic level. Speaking about the macroscopic level as it relates to time, Korzybski states, "on the macroscopic level, we have also to deal with periodic occurrences of hunger, sleep, breathing, heart beats...on objective levels we deal with times, and we feel 'time', when the times are rapid enough." (1933, p. 230) Rifkin also refers to the macroscopic level as he discusses time.

According to him, the human body is a perfect example of all that needs to be coordinated and timed out to function properly—heartbeat, blood pressure, sleep patterns, metabolic rates, all need to be in sync for optimum health. (Rifkin, 1987, p. 36-37) We function in both the biological world and biological time and the cultural world with cultural time. Rifkin explains this relationship. According to him,

> The human species is unique, then, in that it creates its own time…As our children grow up, they are entrained to live in two time worlds simultaneously: the biological time world they inherit and the social time world they learn. Until recently these two time worlds were closely attuned. The accelerated time frame of the modern age, however, is beginning to drive a permanent wedge between the rhythms of culture and the rhythms of nature, threatening a complete break in temporal bonds between the two worlds. (ibid., p. 47)

Third, Korzybski's theory of abstraction emphasizes the object level—that which can be seen with the naked eye. At the object level we find our various time technologies. Rifkin discusses the invention of astronomical calendars, clocks, schedules, and computers. Each technology changes the way people organize their lives, relate with others, view themselves, view others, and organize work. Each time technology changes the level in which people abstract. According, to Rifkin, with the invention of each new time device people move to higher and higher levels of abstraction. With the invention of computers, people are living at an extremely high nano-second level of abstraction.

Fourth, Korzybski's theory of abstraction emphasizes levels of language whereby we omit more and more details from reality as we move through higher levels. Our media and technologies are like language—they not only influence how we think and what we think about, but they also influence the level of abstraction at which we think. As various time-technologies have been introduced into society—calendars, clocks, schedules, and computers we have moved progressively from lower to higher and higher levels of abstraction. In fact, as each new type of calendar was invented there was a movement from lower to higher levels of abstraction. Over thousands of years, human beings developed different types of clocks. As clocks were invented there was also a movement from clocks that more closely connected to the natural universe to clocks that are very far removed from the natural universe. For example, there were early water clocks, sundials, astrological clocks, analogue clocks, and digital clocks. With each new invention we move further and further away from reality. With the invention of the computer, time is totally removed from the natural environment. As Rifkin explained,

> The clock dial is an analogue of the solar day, an acknowledgement that we perceive time revolving in a circle, corresponding to the rotation of the earth. In contrast, computer time is independent of nature; it creates its own context. A digital timepiece displays numbers in a vacuum—time unbound to a circadian reference. Computer time, then, is a mathematical abstraction that attempts to separate us from the pulls and periodicities of the natural world. (1987, p. 102)

Postman (1979) referring to Mumford and Ellul also noted the abstraction levels of the clock:

> Both Lewis Mumford and Jacques Ellul have shown how the invention of the mechanical clock, by totally reconstructing our image of time and space, laid the foundation of all modern forms of social organization. A sundial does not give you the same information as does a mechanical clock. The difference in their level of abstraction, their precision, and the context in which the information becomes accessible gave us a new metaphor for the universe. (p. 46)

As schedules were invented they also became increasingly abstract. The first schedules more closely related to the natural environment. More recent schedules are farther removed from the natural environment. As Rifkin noted, "With the introduction of each new device, the human species has detached itself further from the biological and physical rhythms of the planet. We have journeyed from close participation with the tempo of nature to near isolation from the earth's rhythms" (1987, p. 69). With an understanding of levels of abstraction, we can analyze at what level of abstraction a technology or medium operates. According to Postman (1974), this is a question of media ecology. Korzybski's theory of abstraction can help us address this question.

Finally, Korzybski's theory emphasizes the importance of coming back down to lower levels of abstraction and connecting with the biological world. In his analysis of time, Rifkin emphasized the importance of culturally coming back down and reconnecting with the rhythms of the natural environment. He believes the choice is ours. We can stay at this high-level of abstraction as a culture, where we are immersed in a fast-paced, simulated environment; and, an artificially controlled environment. Or we can choose a slower-paced, natural, and sacred environment—an environment connected to the natural world.

Rifkin believes many people are currently choosing what he calls the "empathetic time dynamic" in contrast to the "power time dynamic." He refers to the ecological stewardship movement, the movement toward holistic medicine, the movement in architecture to create buildings in tune with the natural environment, the movement in engineering to create wind, solar, and water technologies that are in harmony with the natural environment, the movement in the workforce to be more in line with human values; and, the growing movement in agriculture toward organic foods (1987, pp. 204-205).

Rifkin also mentions the movement in education to embrace empathetic knowledge rather than power-based knowledge—knowledge which helps everyone understand that we are all connected to one another—no one lives in isolation; each person's actions affect others. In politics there is also a movement to get back to community-based values and relationships—the politics of empathy and participation instead of power and domination (ibid., p. 205). In our twenty-first century, there is a growing awareness of the importance of reconnecting with our natural ecology, the importance of face-to-face communication, the importance of community, the importance of interdependence and accountability. The theory of abstraction and culture provides a powerful tool for cultural analysis. The theory can be used to help us evaluate our cultural, political, economic, spiritual, educational, and social life.

The theory of abstraction can not only help us evaluate a culture's understanding of time, but it can also help us evaluate a culture's relationship to space. In fact, Korzybski would say that in reality time and space are connected. Only through language can we separate them. As we consider space, we know that we have culturally moved from small tribal communities that were very connected to the natural environment, to city-states, to nation states, and to a global society. Historically, we have created more and more abstract conceptions of social space. Walter Ong, in *Orality and Literacy: The Technologizing of the Word*, explained how oral cultures are closely related to the natural environment whereas scribal and print cultures move progressively away from the natural environment. Electronic cultures are even further removed from the natural world.

According to Jacques Ellul, images have replaced the natural environment. In *The Humiliation of the Word* (1985), Ellul writes:

> ... We live increasingly separated from the natural environment (we frantically try to rediscover it when we go on vacation). When we lose contact with this reality, which used to be the essential reality of our lives, we develop an extremely deep need for another reality. Modern people are the only living beings in a nonliving environment. Because they live in a new abstract, theoretical milieu, unrelated to their tradition, they cannot yet conceive of this technical milieu as reality. (p. 207)

Lewis Mumford in *Technics and Civilization* (1934) also analyzed culture based on its connection and disconnection with the natural environment. He considered the effects of the use of print and paper on thinking and noted the change in our levels of abstraction in the print era. According to Mumford, "Through the habit of using print and paper thought lost some of its flowing, four-dimensional, organic character, and became abstract, categorical, stereotyped, content with purely verbal formulations and verbal solutions to problems that had never been presented or faced in their concrete inter-relationship (p.137).

Neil Postman (1982) also discussed the abstract nature of print. As he stated, "...reading people develop the capacity to conceptualize at a higher level of abstraction than do the illiterate" (p. 39). Postman's *Disappearance of Childhood* was an examination of what happens when a culture moves back to a concrete television image-dominated level of abstraction. According to his analysis, children become more like adults, adults become more like children, and the entire nature of social relationships change. In *Amusing ourselves to Death* (1985), Postman continued to examine what the concrete medium of television is doing to the way we think.

The theory of abstraction has already been used to evaluate culture. With a more explicit understanding Korzybski's theory, we can more consciously evaluate the relationship between our biological world and symbolic world; our natural environment and our media environment.

What Does Korzybski's Theory of Abstraction Provide for Cultural Analysis?

Korzybski's theory of abstraction provides a complete framework for analyzing culture. It is a framework that can be used to evaluate every aspect of social and cultural development. His theory can be used to address many important questions, such as: At what level of abstraction are we currently living? Is society functioning at a low-level, mid-level, or high-level of abstraction? Is society developing movements to come back down to lower levels of abstraction? Are we reconnecting with the biological world? How do our technologies help or hinder us from connecting with the natural world? What is the impetus in culture that creates the need to move back down to lower levels of abstraction? What are the consequences of moving to progressively higher levels of abstraction without coming back down to connect with our natural ecology? What eventually happens to a culture which lives disconnected from reality? Is it possible for a society to lose all sense of reality?

Korzybski emphasized the importance of developing a consciousness of abstracting. This theory can be used to educate ourselves on our cultural and societal levels of abstraction. It can lead us to ask such questions as: How is our nano-second, global society, changing our values? How are definitions of what it means to be human influenced by a highly abstract culture?

The theory of abstraction emphasizes the dangers of dead level abstraction. Is our contemporary American culture settling at a high-level of abstraction? Or, is American culture settling at a low concrete level of abstraction with the use of visual media?

The theory of abstraction emphasizes the structural principles inherent in the natural universe as a basis for the evaluation of language. How can these principles help us evaluate the technologies we use? How can these principles further inform our evaluation of culture?

Korzybski's theory of abstraction can help us more thoroughly address all of these questions. It is an older theory that has renewed significance and relevance for us today. It can continue to help us evaluate our use of language and television. It can also help us evaluate our technological culture.

NOTES

[1] From *Science and Sanity: An Introduction to Non-Aristotelian Systems and General Semantics* by A. Korzybski, 1933. P. 393. Copyright 1933 by The International Non-Aristotelian Library Publishing Company. Reprinted by permission.

[2] From *Language in Thought and Action* 4th Ed. By S. I. Hayakawa, p. 155. 1941 by Harcourt Brace Jovanovich. Reprinted by permission.

[3] From *Critical Thinking in an Image World: Alfred Korzybski's Theoretical Principles Extended to Critical Television Evaluation* by G. E. Forsberg, 1993. P. 128.

[4] From *Critical Thinking in an Image World: Alfred Korzybski's Theoretical Principles Extended to Critical Television Evaluation* by G. E. Forsberg, 1993. P. 140.

[5] Geraldine E. Forsberg: Adapted from Alfred Korzybski's Structural Differential by Permission.

REFERENCES

Carpenter, E. (1971, January). Television meets the stone age. *TV Guide,* 14-16.

Eisenstein, E. L. (1979). *The printing press as an agent of change.* New York: Cambridge University Press.

Ellul, J. (1985). *The humiliation of the word.* Grand Rapids: Eerdmans.

Forsberg, G. E. (1993). *Critical thinking in an image world: Alfred Korzybski's theoretical principles extended to critical television evaluation.* Lanham: University Press of America. Ph.D. diss., New York University, 1991.

Hayakawa, S. I. (1941). *Language in thought and action.* (4th ed.) New York: Harcourt.

Johnson, K. G. (2004). *General semantics: An outline survey.* (3rd ed.) Fort Worth: The Institute of General Semantics.

Johnson, W. (1946). *People in quandaries: The semantics of personal adjustment.* New York: Harper and Row.

Korzybski, A. (1921). *Manhood of humanity*. Lakeville: Institute of General Semantics.

Korzybski, A. (1933). *Science and sanity: An introduction to non-aristotelian systems and general semantics*. Lakeville: Institute of General Semantics.

McLuhan, M. and Fiore, Q. (1967). *The Medium is the massage: An inventory of effects*. New York: Bantam.

Mumford, L. (1934). *Technics and civilization*. New York: Harcourt.

Ong, W. J. (1982). *Orality and literacy: The technologizing of the word*. New York: Methuen.

Postman, N. (1974). Media ecology: General semantics in the third millennium. *General Semantics Bulletin*.

Postman, N. (1979). *Teaching as a conserving activity*. New York: Dell.

Postman, N. (1982). *The disappearance of childhood*. New York: Vintage.

Postman, N. (1985). *Amusing ourselves to death: Public discourse in the age of show business*. New York: Viking.

Rifkin, J. (1987). *Time wars: The primary conflict in human history*. New York: Henry Holt.

CHAPTER 13

KORZYBSKI AND A NEW VISUAL LANGUAGE

John S. Caputo, Robin Wynyard and Heather M. Crandall

> *"Unconscionable maps no longer satisfied,*
> *and the Cartographers Guilds struck a Map of the Empire,*
> *and which coincided point for point with it.*
> *The following Generations...saw that vast map was Useless."*

—J. L. Borges, *On Exactitude in Science*

THIS CHAPTER IS ABOUT the work of Alfred Korzybski and the impact of his work in General Semantics on contemporary social science and specifically the field of communication. Although *Time* magazine listed Korzybski as one of the most influential thinkers of the twentieth century, it can be difficult to actually see where others have built upon his work. However, from the time of his early writings and the 1933 publication *Science and Sanity*, Korzybski has influenced many others, including: Kenneth Burke, William S. Burroughs, Albert Ellis, Gregory Bateson, Buckminster Fuller, Stuart Chase, S.I. Hayakawa, Alvin Toffler, and Alan Watts. He also influenced the Belgian surrealist writer of comics Jan Bucquoy in the seventh part of the comics series *Jaunes: Labyrinthe*, with explicit reference in the plot to Korzybski's famous description, "the map is not the territory". By the 1970s, Korzybski's work fell out of fashion, as contemporary social science began to follow the very rational world paradigm that Korzybski was critiquing. Philosophy fell by the wayside as numbers and data became central. Now a resurgence of interest in his work seems to be occurring and the evidence of such a resurgence is the publication of this new volume. This essay will explore the work of Korzybski and particularly his connections to contemporary writers or painters such as Merleau-Ponty, Robert A. Heinlein, Jorge Borges, and Mark Rothko. Specifically, this essay is a critical comparison of the literature of Heinlein with that of Borges. Heinlein, a minor writer of science fiction, tried to incorporate Korzybski directly into his novel and failed because of any real insights into Korzybski's work, and Borges a great writer (who doesn't) but in whom we can understand much more at a higher level of meaning when reading his work after Korzybski's.

231

To understand the value of the work of Korzybski it has to be seen in the light of social context. His service in the Russian army during the First World War showed him first hand, the devastation and inhumanity that could be wrought by man on man. This devastation had a lasting impact on him and through his later theoretical work he wanted to provide the basis for societal intervention so that such social tragedy on a grand scale might not happen again.

Korzybski is interesting in what he has to say about the relation between language and thought and in this he is particularly damming of the systems of Aristotle, seeing these as producing stasis and an illusory nature which locks us into our own little linguistic cages.

In Korzbyski's view the "isness of language" implies a static quality of illusory permanence, and leads man into erroneous inferences and judgements. It was Korzybski's boast that he changed the structure of language without changing the language. He did this by introducing a series of extensional devices. An extensional device functions to make the structure of language resemble the structure of reality and to help men stop and think before acting (Winetrout & Pratte, 1973).

He acknowledges a debt to Wittgenstein, inasmuch as we must think before we open our mouths, and that what cannot be shown cannot be said. It has been known for some years that we cannot speak sense about man in the old language. Although Wittgenstein has proved this point, he did not show us the way out (Korzybski, 1950, p. 65). It is the very "isness" of language that traps us in the cage of the ordinary and the mundane, barely above the level of the animalistic. We must invent language anew with one not simply based on the relation between the signified and the signifier, but one, which is based on total perception of the world and the harmonies within it. The old Aristotelian categories that have been embedded in thought and language for centuries must be overturned if society is to progress. Positivistic thought based on cause and effect barely rises above that of the knee jerk of stimulus/response. The point in question is that to understand "space," "time," "infinity," etc. we need asymmetrical relations, which are totally excluded by the Aristotelian subject-predicate form of presentation (Korzybski, 1950, p. 123).

Korzybski was rarely concerned with the specific content of people's beliefs-whether people were religious or unreligious, liberal or conservative. He was concerned, rather with how people held their beliefs and convictions: whether with a two-values orientation ("I am right and everybody else is wrong") or a multi-valued orientation ("I don't know—let's see"). Korzybski saw the two-valued orientation as an *internalization* of the laws of Aristotelian logic … He therefore called his own system *non-Aristotelian*. This has led some people to say Korzybski was fighting Aristotle. He was not. He was simply fighting insanity…. As for Aristotle, he must have been one of the sanest men of his time; but anyone whose knowledge and thinking are limited to Aristotle's can hardly behave sanely in *our* time (Hayakawa, 1964, pp. 241-2).

Korzybski advocated training. He conceptualized that training the person will make us aware of what we do and of the potential traps and pitfalls along the way. These we have to avoid, as humanity does not come cheaply. He believed that consciousness of the whole world of abstraction could give insights into the world of information distortion: "Humans achieve full sanity only when the consciousness of abstracting becomes constant and a matter of reflex. It is a self defense kit against manipulative semantic disorders e.g. advertising, religion, etc." (Anton, 2009).

Korzybski thought that training could significantly improve the quality of life of the individual to free him from the confusions engendered by language. He stressed training in awareness of abstracting, using techniques that he had derived from his study of math and science. In terms of interventions he wants to see societal changes in behaviour, in this he is advocating a total epistemological break between signifier and signified.

> But there are no limits to the human capacity to abstract and organize and make use of abstraction. Hence, if human beings find problems insoluble because of fixed reactions—if they are frustrated because they can respond in only one way, regardless of context or circumstances, to certain symbolically defined situations—they are functioning at a less than full human capacity. They can be said, in Korzybski's suggestive phrase, to be 'copying animals in their reactions.' Wendell Johnson summarized this idea aptly when he said, 'To a mouse, cheese is cheese; that's why mousetraps work.' How do these fixations occur in human beings? (Hayakawa, 1964, p. 299)

Korzybski provided a simple technique for preventing such directives from having their harmful effect on our thinking by suggesting that we add "index numbers" to our terms, thus: Englishmen 1, Englishmen 2, Englishmen

3...cow 1, cow 2.... The terms of classification tells us what individuals in that class have in common; the index number reminds us of the characteristics left out....This rule, if remembered, prevents us from confusing levels of abstraction... (Hayakawa, 1964, p. 220).

No matter how great a thinker Korzybski undoubtedly is, many saw the major flaw in his work was the total lack of any methodology grounded in the "new" social sciences of the 1970s and '80s with its emphasis on statistical data. He placed great emphasis on social science yet seemed very reluctant to pursue any fundamental principles of social scientific research. One example is concerning the point he is making on intervention in society needed to bring about change. The majority of societal interventions fail because they are aimed at changing human behaviour, but they are fundamentally flawed due to targeting incorrect aspects of it. With any societal intervention we must identify the underlying cause and beliefs of the population you want to change. Korzybski's empathy with those he observed is just not enough. What one needs for an intervention to work is the strength of belief of the population under study, not just the beliefs of one man, no matter how well meaning.

Although Korzybski stresses we must always refer to facts, his writings sometimes display an inexcusable non-reliance on fact. To be fair, this may be in someway due to the mindset he had to work within during the years of his life. But going through the corpus of his work the following list are some of the highly dubious statements made by Korzybski.

i. *... it should be remembered that the child has an advantage over the imbeciles, idiots, and mentally ill who have stopped development or who have regressed to the age of the infant or the child (2000, p. 509).*

ii. *Many women at present are still infantile, very little developed as human beings (2000, p. 521).*

iii. *Criminals who are condemned to death should be given to science for experimenting...they would probably die, but the benefits to the rest of mankind through scientific discoveries would be very important (2000, p. 525).*

iv. *From an engineer's point of view humanity is apparently divided into three classes (1) the intellectuals; (2) the rich; and (3) the poor (1921, p. 108).*

v.   *The latest, most important non-aristotelian institution is found in the League of Nations, which embraces practically the whole civilized world with the exception of a very few nations who display infantile and Aristotelian aloofness (2000, p. 558)*

Just to take this last point alone, history shows that the League of Nations was totally ineffectual, it was unable to stop the Italian invasion of Abyssinia, or the rise of Fascism in Italy and Germany. In the end it was just a club for rich nations who had license to do whatever they wanted.

The Strength of the Work

So if Korzybski's thought has flaws where do the strengths of his work lie? How can his anti-Aristotelian stance be put to good use? The area where it seems applicable lies in one that has been totally ignored by all. "The very world around us is of pictures not words; visualization lets us fill our minds with these pictures" (Falconer, 2007, p. x). Persistent thinking in words causes the exact opposite: it more or less alienates us from reality" (Falconer, 2007, p. xi).

The salient rule of non-Aristotelian thinking and the basis behind Korzybski's training, is to look at the object or problem with the utmost attention as if it had never been seen before. In this there is perhaps a nod in the direction of the East, the emphasis being on perception and a oneness with the Cosmos. Pursuing this line of reasoning the theorist who comes closest to Korzybski would be Merleau-Ponty.

There is a tacit language Merleau-Ponty insists where, "we must consider speech before it is spoken, the background of silence without which it would say nothing" (Ashton, 1983, p. 121).

Merleau-Ponty like Korzybski is arguing that being in the world is not a matter of strictly measurable relationships. The body's spatiality is not geometrical, but spatiality of situation, an orientation towards a possible world. This was a view, which was to influence the writers of science fiction like Robert Anson Heinlein and L. Ron Hubbard. The perceptual object is never finally constituted, but always, spatially and temporally, a compound of perspectives open to further exploration. We are always in a continual process of self-constitution. We bring to the perceptual and behavioral field that is our own history, and in so doing bring an element of choice to our world. "When I glance rapidly about at the objects surrounding me in order to find my bearings and locate myself among them. I scarcely can be said to grasp the world in some instantaneous aspect" (Merleau-Ponty, 1962, p. 43).

Korzybski has influenced some popular writers of fiction, the science fiction writer R. A. Heinlein (1977) being one. His novel *Assignment in Eternity* mentions Korzybski directly and the whole novel is a restating of Korzybski's basic ideas and a direct homage to his thought. For example, regarding the Aristotelian versus the non-Aristotelian world Heinlein (1977) writes, "If the average man thinks at all, he does silly things like generalizing from a single datum. He uses one-valued logics. If he is exceptionally bright, he may use two-valued 'either-or' logic to arrive at his wrong answers. Still rarer is the man who thinks habitually, who applies reason rather than habit patterns, to all his activity" (pp. 59-60).

In the creation of a new language to inspire higher thought patterns Heinlein (1977) in true Korzybski fashion embodies a critique of the verb "to be."

> A symbolic structure, invented instead of accepting without question, can be made similar in structure to the real world to which it refers...The world--the continuum known to science and including all human activity--does not contain 'noun things' and 'verb things': it contains space-time events and relationships between them...Even before World War II Alfred Korzybski had shown that human thought was performed, when done efficiently, only in symbols: the action of 'pure' thought, free of abstracted speech symbols, was merely fantasy. The brain was so constructed as to work, without symbols only on the animal level: to speak of reasoning without symbols was to speak nonsense. (Heinlein, pp. 69; 74)

Heinlein tries to match the narrative structure of the novel directly with the words of Korzybski. So the best we can say is, that it might capture in some way the thought of Korzybski, but in terms of literature it just doesn't work. What Heinlein failed to realize was that good literature embodies a different language that escapes the logocentric fallacy of believing itself capable of capturing events, things and ideas perfectly. Heinlein makes the mistake of believing that he can capture the reality of Korzybski's thought, without realizing how a fictive text plays with the reader in setting up oppositions and binary concepts. Popular writers like Heinlein who want to change the way people think don't succeed too well. In this case any serious content involving Korzybski's thought is merely read as entertainment, not as reaching a higher level of abstraction. Thus making it susceptible to multiple readings not just uni-dimensional reading.

A much more serious and important writer is the Argentinean Jorge Luis Borges. At the lowest level of reading if you try to read Borges like Heinlein you would probably get little entertainment and a lot of confusion. Reading Borges and Korzybski together, Korzybski's thought becomes crystal clear. With Borges's emphasis on the *labyrinth, knots* and a playful language of words, Korzybski's work has an important resonance. So we have a case of direct influence of Korzybski on the writer Heinlein. With Borges, who never influenced Korzybski, but who read in the context of Korzybski's work can be seen to be saying something profound. The symmetry between the two writers is exciting and revelatory for both.

Borges, in his fiction, takes the expansion of a purely poetic consciousness to its furthest limits. Most of his popular stories concern the nature of time, infinity, labyrinths, reality, philosophy and identity. Borges saw man's search for meaning in a seemingly infinite universe as a fruitless one, and as a maze we have to think our way through.

In *On Exactitude in Science* (Borges, 1999) one immediately identifies with Korzybski's well-known statement, *the map is not the territory.* In this, Borges wrote of an empire whose ambition to map the entire world in all its detail and variations led it to gradually increase the scope and complexity of its maps, until maps became maps of maps. And in their attempt to correspond the nature of the mapped territory to reality, the maps became totally useless. An excerpt follows:

> Unconscionable maps no longer satisfied, and the Cartographers Guilds struck a Map of the Empire, and which coincided point for point with it. The following Generations...saw that vast map was Useless. (p. 181)

Hayakawa (1964) also speaks to this when he writes:

If our ideas and beliefs are held with consciousness of abstracting, they can be changed if found to be inadequate or erroneous. But if they are held without consciousness of abstracting—if our mental maps are believed *to be* the territory—they are prejudices. …But if we teach them to be habitually conscious of the process of abstraction, we give them the means with which to free themselves from whatever erroneous notions we may have taught them.…The picture of reality created inside our heads by the lack of consciousness of abstracting is not a 'map' of any existing 'territory.' It is a delusional world.…How do we reduce such areas of infantilism in our thought? One way is to know deeply there is no 'necessary connection' between words and what they stand for. (p. 208)

In stating three fundamental new non-Aristotelian semantic premises, Korzybski is saying exactly the same as Borges. 1. A map is not the territory. 2. A map covers not all the characteristics of a territory. 3. A map is self-reflexive because an ideal map would include the map of the map, etc. (Korzybski, 1950, p. 222).

Korzybski (1950) goes on to say, "I use the map territory relationship because the characteristics are general for all existing forms of representation which include the structure of language" (p. 275).

Although written by Borges (1970), the following could easily have been written by Korzybski: Locke in the seventeenth century postulated (and rejected) an impossible language in which each individual thing, each stone, each bird and each branch would have its own name (p. 93).

The third scenario by using Korzybski's theory as an explanatory template in understanding art and its abstractions comes from the visual arts, i.e. the work of the American abstract artist Mark Rothko. Abstract painting is difficult to comprehend and is easily dismissed by many people, who at best see it as colorful and at worse rubbish, either phoney or childlike daubing. It is never made easier by the fact that artists are not the most articulate when it comes to explanations of their own work. If you read Korzybski and then go to what Rothko and those around him say concerning his pictures, Korzybski's thought on the nature and importance of abstraction makes perfect sense and enables a much-heightened level of understanding of Rothko's painting.

To this point we mean to show that we cannot look for a direct connection between fiction and Korzybski's work as the writer Heinlein thought. But we can look to an explanation of the work of writers like Borges when we compare what he writes to the writings of Korzybski. We now argue that greater understandings of the abstract paintings of Rothko are possible when we look at what Korzybski had to say about the nature of abstract thought. Korzybski (1950) said, "as a matter of fact all human life is a permanent dance between different levels of abstraction" (p. 113).

> The finding of structural means of representation facilitates visualization …The higher centres produce the 'very abstract theories,' which cannot be visualized for a while. The lower centres, which are involved in visualization can deal only with structures which can be 'concretely pictured.' (Korzybski, 1950, p. 454)

You only have to stand in front of them to suspect that Rothko's abstracts have a depth of meaning that in some way relates to the core of human values. This however is difficult to express and act upon. The contention here is that Korzybski's work helps us both to understand the work more and to operationalize the feelings into our psyche, which adds to the nature of humanity, which Korzybski saw as so important on a larger societal scale.

This view seems to be shared by commentators on Rothko's work, "What Rothko needed was not the literary allusions so much as a new way…of controlling and ordering his experience in a time out of join" (Ashton, 1983, p. 41). Korzybski's mission as an intervention through training practices was to achieve precisely this, i.e. to restore a new and higher stability and sanity to society. In discussing Rothko, Schama (2006) writes, "Only a completely new visual language of strong feeling, Rothko thought, could wake us from moral stupor"(p. 398).

Korzybski wanted to strip away the total grip that the old way of thinking had over us thus to inaugurate a new non-Aristotelian way of thought, based not on what was earlier myth, nor what was 'common-sense', nor cause-effect relations. A new language was needed, based on the old, but with a new structure of meaning built on what might be silences in the text. Adding this to the facts of a situation that are usually hidden by generalizations of taken-for-granted notions. For Korzybski speech is not spontaneity, it is based on thinking about what we need to say before we say it. This is precisely what Rothko had in mind when he painted; he had to strip away extraneous detail so that the viewer might be permitted the space to construct new kinds of associations through a new visual language. Uniting both the artist and the viewer in a new language were the pauses and the silences of the text, the silences built into the paintings. Rothko's approach was contemplative rather than physical ... Rothko, according to Waldman (2000), proceeded from long periods of meditation to the physical act of painting.

Rothko posits that the familiar identity of things must be pulverized in order to destroy the finite associations with which our society increasingly enshrouds every aspect of our environment (as cited in Causey, 1972).

Korzybski (1950) puts it in a different way but with the same meaning: "If we 'think' verbally, we act as biased observers and project onto the silent levels the structure of the language we use, and so remain in our rut of old orientations, making keen, unbiased, observations and creative work well-nigh impossible" (p. 653).

The argument we have been pursuing is that art is an intervention in society aiming to bring about changes in the way we think. Perhaps very little literature and painting has the power to do this, but great art whether the writing of Borges or the painting of Rothko, if given the chance to do so, can. Borges and Rothko were bold in what they wanted to achieve, as was Korzybski. Korzybski like these two great artists had the boldness and foresight to see aspects of change that society needed. He thought training in his methods of General Semantics could bring about change, but his thought has reached relatively few people and has been superseded by new developments in philosophy, social science, and psychology. Strangely in a field where he still has resonance today he has been totally neglected, that is, in the world of painting and literary theory.

Some scholars of visual rhetoric, without using Korsybski directly, have helped expose the ways in which the visual (photographs, X-rays, television, memorials, museum exhibits) are also abstractions rather than the reality people take them to be. Korsybski desired a move away from the perceptual traps of language through consciousness of the workings of abstraction. The scholarship in visual culture and visual rhetoric has made strides in directing attention to the perceptual traps in image. As Bruce E. Gronbeck (2008) states, "[t]he potential for radically new visual rhetoric is today being operationalized, incident by incident, election by election. Time can be stretched or compressed; space can be recontoured or evaporated. The eye cannot trust, the mind cannot verify, what it sees" (p. xxiv). It is possible that Korzybski's ideas could dovetail nicely with such scholarship. And that could be the work of another day.

REFERENCES

Anton, C. (2009, Dec. 18). Korzybski, E-prime, Map & Territory [Video file]. Retrieved from www.youtube.com

Ashton, D. (1983). *About Rothko*. New York, NY: Oxford University Press.

Borges, J. L. (1970). *Labyrinths*. Harmonsworth, London: Penguin Books.

Borges, J. L. (1990). *Collected fictions*. London: Penguin Books.

Borges, J. L. (1999). *The Aleph*. London: Penguin Classics.

Causey, A. (1972). Rothko through his paintings. *Studio International*. 183(943), Retreived from http://www.studiointernational.co.uk/archive/causey_1972_183_943.asp

Falconar, T. (2007). *Creative intelligence and self–liberation: Korzybski, non-Aristotelian thinking and enlightenment*. Carmarthen, Wales: Crown House Publishing.

Gronbeck, B. E. (2008). Visual rhetorical studies: Traces through time and space. In Olson, L.

Hayakawa, S. I. (1964). *Language in thought and action* (2nd ed.). New York, NY: Harcourt, Brace & World

Heinlein, R. A. (1977). *Assignment in eternity*. New English Library. London. Originally printed in 1971.

Korzybski, A. (1921). *Manhood of humanity: The science and art of human engineering*. New York, NY: E. P. Dutton & Company.

Korzybski, A. (2000). *Science and Sanity: An introduction to the non-Aristotelian systems and general semantics*. Brooklyn, NY: Institute of General Semantics.

Korzybski, A. (1950). *Collected writings, 1920-1950*. Collected and arranged by M. Kendig (1990). Institute of General Semantics. Pittsboro, NC: Town House Press.

Merleau-Ponty, M. (1962). *Phenomenology of perception: An introduction*. London: Routledge and Keegan Paul Ltd. London.

Morain, M. S. (Ed.) (1969). *Teaching General Semantics: A collection of lesson plans for college and adult classes*. San Francisco, CA: International Society for General Semantics.

Olson, L. C., Finnegan, C. A., & Hope, D. (Eds.), *Visual rhetoric: A reader in communication and American culture* (pp. xxi-xxvi). Los Angelos, CA: Sage Publications.

Schama, S. (2006). *Power of art*. London: BBC Publications.

Waldman, D. (2000). *Mark Rothko*. London: Thames and Hudson.

Winetrout, K., & Pratte, R. (1973). General semantics: a neglected method in philosophy of education. *ETC. A Review of General Semantics*, XXX(1), pp. 9-20.

CHAPTER 14: KORZYBSKI AND CARTOGRAPHY

Bini B.S.

INTRODUCTION

I EXAMINE THE IDEAS OF time-binding and consciousness of abstracting suggested by the aphorism "Map is not the Territory" with reference to contemporary linguistic and cultural phenomena. It is also a reflection on the relevance of General Semantics in a world submerged in proliferating communication and information and confusing consumerism. General semantics is an interdisciplinary/ multi-disciplinary methodology that derives insights from linguistics, behavioral sciences, physiology, philosophy, neuroscience, etc. By adding the epithet, 'general,' Alfred Korzybski diversifies the scope of meaning of semantics to implicate a general theory of communication, perception and nuances of human evaluation. Korzybski recommends a clear awareness of limitations, uncertainty and the grey zones that one passes through while using a language or any system of symbols as a medium of communication and a tool for knowledge acquisition and dissemination.

The analogy "Map is not the Territory; Word is not the Thing Defined" has to be interpreted in relation to the idea of time-binding. My analysis in the light of this analogy brings into its theoretical framework the factors that impact the circulation and transmission of knowledge and information and ventures into the disciplinary, cultural and political implications of time-binding. Map/territory analogy also implies that knowledge and information get obliterated and distorted in the linguistic and other representations we use. Korzybski warns us about misevaluation, misunderstanding and misjudgment through this analogy. The concept of time-binding may appear to be biologically deterministic since in formulating it Korzybski relies on a neuro-linguistic and psycho-logical exposition. But a careful perusal of Korzybski's works, especially *Science and Sanity*, permits a glimpse of the pathways opened if one sets out to explore the nuances of time-binding. Even in such an epistemological journey, one has to keep in mind the map/territory analogy. Robert Pula's observation : "By 'maps' we should understand everything and anything that humans formulate- including this book and my present contributions, but also including (to take in alphabetical order) biology, Buddhism, Catholicism, chemistry, Evangelism, Freudianism, Hinduism,

243

Islam, Judaism, Lutherianism, physics, Taoism, etc ; etc ;... !" (*Science and Sanity,* Preface to the Fifth Edition xvii) indicates how the map territory analogy traces the complex relation between the world(s) humans inhabit, knowledge and time-binding.

It has to be noted that Korzybski, though he emphasizes the importance of language as a time-binding tool, does not want to attribute any metaphysical dimension to it and wanted to maintain the non-theological orientation of General Semantics. General Semanticists take a more 'practical' stance and emphasize that language, as a time-binding tool, intervenes between human beings and the world. General Semantics as a methodology recommends a reform of our verbal behavior to negate the linguistic distortion of 'reality.' The 'consciousness of abstracting' becomes a useful tool for avoiding the confusion between *higher logical types* and *lower logical types*. Analyzed in this light, one may say that a map that represents a territory or a word that represents a thing is of a higher and more general logical type than the territory or the thing.

Korzybski's attempt was also to develop a theory of human nature which implies the aphorism, "Know yourself." This theory of human nature is neuro-linguistic in orientation and is also imbued with psychological insights. The intention of Korzybski was to provide the vision and methodology essential for evaluating the appropriateness and inadequacies of different linguistic means in accomplishing communicative ends in different contexts and their impact on time-binding.

Map/Territory Analogy: Attempting a Nuanced Understanding

Korzybski's analogy, "Map is not the Territory," deceptively simple, makes one plunge into the poetics and politics of map making in a metaphorical sense and contemplate on the purposes of 'mapping' a territory and functionality of the map that claims to represent the territory. The process of making a verbal or visual map through language or any other means of representation and communication involves perception, interpretation and representation. The unstable nature of both map and the territory and their 'constructedness' implied in the aphorism inspire one to engage with nuances of reception, perception, interpretation and utilization of the map and the problems that arise while trying to comprehend or reconstitute the changing territory with the help of it. A map fails to capture the territory 'fully.' "Map is not the Territory" alludes to the 'non-identity' and 'non- allness' of the map that cannot depict the territory as it 'really' is in terms of size, shape, other physical and cultural features, climatic or socio-political conditions, etc. As a map freezes into a completed image, it cannot reflect the changes happening to the territory. "Word is not the thing defined" follows the map/territory analogy and the principles of non-allness and non-identity are relevant in this context also. When this analogy is transposed to the domains of art, media, politics, cyberspace, etc, the profoundness of its implications can be glimpsed.

Mapping: The Play of Subjectivities and Perspectives

Mapping in this sense is not an objective, disinterested activity. The relation between the map and the cartographer makes one consider issues like limits of perception, strategies, possible manipulations and lapses (deliberate or inadvertent) and limitations in the process of representation or depiction. The point-of-view of the cartographer impacts her/his perception and comprehension of the territory and the process of map making. In this era of mass media culture, when instead of reality, humans have to tackle virtuality and are thus plagued by fantasies, (as Zizek puts it), map/territory analogy acquires new dimensions.

The map/territory analogy has cultural and political implications while it is examined with reference to propaganda, freedom of speech, democracy, the process of indoctrination and even entertainment and commercials. The deliberate distortions of the map owing to 'vested interests' and oversight on the part of the map maker cannot also be disregarded and this further complicates the process of 'mapping'. When one gazes at a territory which has segments that are inaccessible and hence incomprehensible and tries to map it with available 'tools' despite the lacunae in seeing and knowing, the map is bound to have discontinuities, gaps, fissures and thus a fragmentary nature. This insight on the inadequacies of the map makes one aware of the limitations of media in understanding and interpreting an event.

On the other hand, when one looks at the map thinking that it is a complete and true depiction, understanding of the territory can but be naïve and uninformed. In the above mentioned contexts, the one who thinks that the map is territory is deceived by his/her inability to distinguish between the two and comprehend the limitations of the former in capturing the latter. Korzybski gives an interesting analogy of a traveler with a map in which all towns are marked in the wrong order. This map does not help one travel or progress in the journey so that a desired destination can be reached. What such a map lacks, according to Korzybski, is predictability and the traveler using that map will wander aimlessly thinking that he/she is on the right path. At a symbolic and metaphoric level, this is a problem with human language and perceptions also.

The nuances of perception of the one who looks at the map and the mechanisms of reception, interpretation and utilization are also implicated in the Korzybskian analogy. One who traces the map as a cartographer and the other who looks at the map as an explorer project their own views or mental structures into it. The territory is unpredictable, in a state of flux, fluid and unstable. The map tries to stabilize it as an ossified, fixed image that exudes the impression of finality.

Time-binding: Problematizing Maps and Mapping Tools

Language appears to map an event, person, place, activity, etc and the one who uses the map uncritically and without caution is lost and confused in the wilderness of words and ideas. This confusion is contagious. Consciousness of abstracting is that awareness and alertness about map/territory distinction and the instability of territory and the deceptive nature of maps. It makes one cautious of how information gets erased and distorted in the linguistic and other representations we use. General Semantics, while it discusses the thought-feeling-speaking-listening-reading-writing-action dynamics of communication, warns that a person should critically evaluate (one's own and others') thoughts, emotions, verbal or non-verbal expressions and actions while taking single or multiple roles such as speaker, listener, writer or reader in any process of communication. Korzybski warns about the dangers of intensional thinking and recommends an extensional approach to comprehension. His critique of Aristotelian and Euclidean systems does emphasize the pitfalls of identifying the map as territory and believing that the map represents all of the territory. The extensional devices suggested by Korzybski are meant to bring in changes in one's perception, outlook, interpretation and reception, besides making one cautious about the limitations of communication.

Coming back to the map/territory analogy, since the territory is seen and understood through the eyes of the map maker(s) and represented as the map hence, one can only say that it is true according to the map makers(s)' belief, provided he/she has not deliberately or flippantly erred. It also implies that the one who views the map and uses it should be conscious about the abstractness of it and cautious about its unreliability because the territory as such could have deceived the eyes of the map maker(s).

Maps and Territories: Insights from Saussure, Derrida and Foucault

Saussure's analyses linger around the connections between words and ideas, also metaphorically maps and territories. He theorizes on the duality between a word and the concept it represents, and how this duality as a relationship transmutes with time. Saussure affirms that language is form, a system of sound-images linked to concepts. The non-identity of sign and signified is found in the writings of Saussure also.

Saussure discusses the concepts of synchronic and diachronic relationships to account for the changes and variations in/of a language. Saussurian concept of diachrony analyzes changes in the meaning of words over time. It is also a study of language in terms of how it visibly changes in usage. The concept of diachrony introduces the phenomenon of 'change' into the realms of *langue* and *parole*. Korzybski's major concern is that language does not reflect the rapid changes in the world and society and thus does not change at an accelerating rate. We live in a world of flux and language is relatively static.

Why the relatively stagnant nature of language in comparison to rapidly changing world and expanding knowledge became a matter of concern for Korzybski can be explained with reference to the idea of time-binding. Human beings are time-binders because they have the power to use language and other signs to record, communicate and disseminate information and knowledge. As language fails to capture the nuances of change due to its static nature, it becomes an inadequate time-binding tool.

In the conceptual framework of Saussure, the components of language namely *langue* (the abstract system of language that is internalized by a given speech community) and *parole* (the individual acts of speech or the actual use of language) give it both homogeneous and heterogeneous characteristics. One can say, ideally *Parole* is heterogeneous and *langue* is homogeneous and systematic. Saussure's idea is useful in understanding how language is strongly affected by the social context. Modification of *langue* at the point of *parole* may be used to create new meaning in instances wherein the speaker has little grasp of language or deliberate distortion is used by him/her.

Each signifier and signified implies difference from every other signifier and signified in the system. *Langue* has several elements that constitute meaning(s) and in the construction of any shade of meaning, the deployment of these elements and the relationships between them play a role. Meaning is thus a process with a strategy. By drawing a demarcating line between *Langue* and *Parole*, Saussure makes a distinction between language as a system and how it is used, and calls for the need to study these as two very different and separate entities. Being a structuralist, Saussure's concern was more with langue than parole. He was more interested in the system by which meaning could be created. Individual instances of language use were not explored much by Saussure and his followers. Korzybski's conceptualizations were more in relation to *parole* than *langue*. He did see the imperfections of *langue* and suggested how while using it, one should exercise caution and care. Consciousness of abstractions is one kind of caution that a language user should exercise.

While trying to understand the idea of 'consciousness of abstractions,' an analysis of the shortcomings of Saussure's conceptualizations may prove useful. Saussure did not make distinctions between concrete words such as book, pencil, etc. and abstract ones like mind, beauty, sublime and the like. In the consciousness of the language user, both concrete and abstract words represent a tangible 'signified.' Sign, as represented in the *Course in General Linguistics* is not an abstraction, but a real, concrete entity that stands for an object. According to Saussure, "The signs of which a language is composed are not abstractions, but real objects." (1977, p. 144). Paradoxically, he says that signifier and the signified are pure abstractions. "The linguistic entity exists only through the association of the signifier and the signified... ; take only one of these elements and the linguistic entity vanishes ; instead of a concrete object, you no longer have before you anything but a pure abstraction" (ibid., 144). The idea of the signifier actually indicates the acoustic pattern of a word in mental projection or in actual, physical realization as part of a speech act. Saussure's emphasis was more on phonic signs.

The abstractness of signifier and signified and the concreteness of the sign discussed by Saussure will help us engage with the notion of the 'consciousness of abstraction' from a different perspective. Saussure's analysis in the work *Course in General Linguistics* of the relationship between language and 'reality' using the terms signifier and signified and the consequent theorization about language in terms of signs rather than words make one confront the paradox of the concreteness of signs and the abstractness of both signifier and signified.

Saussure's theory of *language* as a system of signs (basic unit of language) that expresses meanings/ideas also argues that it is a socially shared and psychologically imbibed system. The sign is not conceptual or phonic; it is neither thought nor sound whereas the signifier can be understood as sound and the signified as the thought. According to Saussure: "A sign is not a link between a thing and a name, but between a concept and a sound pattern" (ibid., p. 66). Referentiality may be a function of language but it is only one of its functions. These signs comprise the arbitrary conjunction of abstract concept and sound-image (acoustic image). The meanings of signs may be arbitrary, but the process of *assigning* meaning is not so. It is an unending activity in which the entire language community consciously or unconsciously partakes. There is no intrinsic link between the concept and the acoustic image (ibid., p. 101). Saussure did not see language as a static entity; he opined that though the linguistic sign is arbitrary, it is practically impossible for anyone to change it (ibid., p. 104). Time can change a sign, by bringing about a shift in the relationship between the signified and the signifier (ibid., pp. 108-9). Individuals may contribute some new meanings or coin new words. As James Harkness opines, "In Saussurian Linguistics, words do not "refer" to things themselves. Rather they have meanings as points within the entire system that is a language- a system, further conceived as a network of graded differences" (Foucault, 2008, p. 5). It is evident from Saussurian formulations that the relationship between the signifier and the signified is circumstantial and is a convention that can be traced using etymological evidences. This argument leads to the assumption that language as a system of signs can be studied as an entity at any given point in time *only*. Saussure saw the signifier and the signified as *inseparable* by formulating the idea of 'sign' though their relationship is *arbitrary*.

According to Saussurian linguistics, ideas are connected to sound-images and written words are connected to spoken words. Derrida disapproves of the theory of Saussure on language for its validation of logocentrism and phonocentrism. Writing may also have a multi-dimensional structure which may not be subordinated to the temporality of sound (Derrida, 1998, p. 85). Derrida disagrees with the Saussurian view that writing exists with a purpose to represent speech. Derrida argues that a single phonetic signifier may have multiple phonetic values and Saussure does not consider the range of differences which may occur between phonetic signifiers. According to Derrida, any linguistic sign, irrespective of the fact whether it is spoken or written, acquires meaning or significance, from conventions. While meaning itself is a matter of convention rather than nature, the sign can only be conceived as 'arbitrary.' One can say through the time-binding mechanism, the convention is passed on from one generation to the next in a linguistic community. Derrida refers to this convention as the "instituted trace" and according to him, "the trace is nothing, it is not an entity, it exceeds the question What is? And contingently makes it possible;" (1998, p. 75) and also "the instituted trace is 'unmotivated' but not capricious" (ibid., p. 46).

Derrida's theory asserts that meaning is never fixed and hence indeterminate. He critiques intentionality because it does not operate in the way as it has been traditionally conceived in the philosophy of language since Plato ; our intention has little decisiveness as far as the meaning of what we are saying is concerned. Derrida questions the very nature of communication itself and suggests a pluralistic way of looking at communication which implies the possibility of reinterpretation and multiple meanings of words. He observes that language users use words in different contexts or frames of references and that is how they arrive at meaning(s) which are unstable and in a state of flux. The contexts that we relate to meaning(s) are so vague, unstable and indeterminate and cannot be used as a foundational principle for meaning. The polysemy of communication implicates its uncertainty and indeterminate nature. In other words, the territory, unstable as it is cannot have the certainty of only one map representing it. A map does not correspond to a single territory, but what it should remind us is the polyvalent nature, and multiplicity of the territory and the map's own ineptitude in capturing the plurality of territory. A map cannot claim to reconstruct the territory ; but the very process of mapping is a deconstruction which destabilizes the territory which as such is boundless, indeterminable and unfathomable. Derrida is not concluding here that intentionality plays no role in meaning ; he is opposing the primacy attached to it in any communicative process.

Derrida discusses the free play of signifiers in the sense that they are not fixed to their signifieds, but point beyond themselves to other signifiers in an "indefinite referral of signifier to signified" (1978, p. 25). He blatantly denies that there are any determinable meanings, thus deconstructing the western semiotic system. Derrida gives emphasis to the need for a new "rationality" which would "deconstruct" the Platonic view of language that affirms that conventions are and should be based on "real" meaning.

> … Language itself is menaced in its very life, helpless, adrift in the threat of limit-lessness, brought back to its own finitude at the very moment when its limits seem to disappear, when it ceases to be self-assured, contained, and guaranteed by the infinite signified which seemed to exceed it. (1998, p. 6)

Foucault's engagement with signifier and signified with reference to the enunciative dimension of language opens a different avenue of exploration when we use a map to understand the territory. According to Foucault, "the signifying structure of language always refers back to something else; objects are designed by it; meaning is intended by it; the subject is referred back to it by a number of signs even if he is not himself present in them" (1972, p. 111). He adds:

> If one wishes to describe the enunciative level, one must consider…the question of language, not in the direction to which it refers, but in the dimension that gives it; ignore its power to designate, to name, to show, to reveal, to be the place of meaning or truth, and, instead turn one's attention to the moment – which is at once solidified, caught up in the play of the 'signifier' and the 'signified'- that determines its unique and limited existence. (ibid., p. 111)

Foucault observes in his work, *The Order of Things*, that while using any language in depicting the 'visible,' one strays into zones of inexplicability. The title in French of this work was *Les Mots et les choses* and in order to avoid confusion with two other books that had already appeared under the same title: *Words and Things*, the title of the French original was not translated literally. He sheds light on the inadequacies of the 'nomenclature' function of language thus which will help us look more insightfully on "word is not the thing defined":

> The proper name…is merely an artifice: it gives us a finger to point with, in other words, to pass surreptitiously from the space

where one speaks to the space where one looks; in other words, to fold one over the other as though they were equivalents. (1994, p. 9)

The Order of Things shows how constrained by the inadequacies and limitations of words in depicting things and also due to the plurality of meaning generated in word-thing associations, communication through signs, visual or verbal, becomes highly unstable and problematic. According to Foucault:

> It is not that words are imperfect, or that, when confronted by the visible, they prove insuperably inadequate. Neither can be reduced to the other's terms: it is in vain that we say what we see; what we see never resides in what we say. And it is in vain that we attempt to show, by the use of images, metaphors, or similes, what we are saying; the space where they achieve their splendor is not that deployed by our eyes but that defined by the sequential elements of syntax. (ibid., p. 9)

By venturing into these realms of analysis about language, meaning and interpretations, one is able to see the nuances and implications of the map/territory analogy. The concerns about the inadequacy of language as a means of time-binding are justified in the light of these views. Besides, one cannot turn a blind eye to the possibility that language can be strategically used to impact the process of time-binding. Here I bring in the mechanisms of power that affects the selection, dispersion and sustaining, obliteration and marginalization of knowledge. The analysis of language operates on words. Foucault's analysis of discourse is indebted to Saussure's insights about the construction of meaning. Foucault shows how discourses regulate what can be said, what can be thought, and what is considered true or correct. I begin with the Foucauldian formulation on statements generated within discursive formation and the networks of power that play a decisive role in determining the epistemic conditions of the formation and ratification of truth. According to this view, language may be regarded as a system for constructing possible statements. Foucault examines "statement" as the basic unit of discourse that he believes has been ignored due to the emphasis on words. He affirms that:

A statement is not the direct projection of signs onto the plane of language of a particular situation or a group of representations. It is not simply the manipulation by a speaking subject of a number of elements and linguistic rules. At the very outset, from the very root, the statement is divided up into an enunciative field in which it has a place and a status, which arranges for its possible relations with the past, and which opens up for it a possible future. (Foucault, 1972, p. 99)

Foucault argues that a statement may not necessarily have the 'grammatical structure' of a sentence or the 'logical configuration' of a proposition, but that it must have a referent, a subject, an associated enunciative field (because there is no statement that does not presuppose others ; all statements are surrounded by a field of coexistence) and materiality or means linguistic or other through which it can be expressed. It is against this background of enunciative coexistence that "the grammatical relations between sentences, the logical relations between prepositions, the metalinguistic relations between an object language and the one that defines the rules, the rhetorical relations between groups or elements of sentences" and the like stand out. (ibid., p. 99).

According to Foucault, statements engender a network of rules establishing what is meaningful; in other words, these rules are preconditions for propositions, utterances, or speech acts to have meaning. His formulation in *Archaeology of Knowledge* about how statements are dependent on the conditions/contexts in which they emerge and exist in relation to a field of discourse helps one glimpse into a hitherto unexplored aspect of time-binding and its relation to power. One should keep in mind that these conditions or contexts of discourse formations are plural and often indeterminate. Foucault analyzes the process and consequences of discursive formations which results from a conglomeration of statements and explores the inevitable connections between knowledge and discourse. Knowledge may be seen as a kind of discursive practice. Foucault ushers the notion of 'truth' into this theoretical framework and shows how it is a construct along with meaning. In his *Archaeology of Knowledge*, Foucault is not digging discourses to unearth a deeper meaning; nor is he looking for the origin of meaning in some transcendental subject. His attempt is to reveal the futility of such endeavors. By analyzing the conditions of existence for meaning, he hints at the play of power and thus politicizes and problematizes the process of discursive formations and emergence of something as the 'truth.' To substantiate the principles of meaning production in various discursive formations, he illustrates how truth claims emerge during various epochs on the basis of 'dominant discourses' at any point in time.

The conditions of the existence, circulation and sustenance of statements are indicative of how claims of truth are constructed and valued. How, why when and where do certain statements gain prominence and certain other statements are rejected. Foucault looks at breaks, fissures, mutations, and discontinuities instead of homogeneity and continuity in discursive formations. The production of meaning and knowledge are determined by various factors and in order to comprehend the political implications of time-binding, these factors must be taken into account. An Epistemic violence is involved in the formation and circulation of knowledge. Foucault uses an interesting imagery from battle to highlight this idea:

> Here I believe one's point of reference should not be to the great model of language (*langue*) and signs, but to that of war and battle. The history which bears and determines us has the form of a war rather than that of a language: relations of power, not relations of meaning. (1980, pp. 114-115)

Discursive rules that attain dominance determine the identity and status of the statement at any given point of time. New statements are continuously generated; so are discursive formations. Foucault's major concern was obliterated and forgotten discourses. Their difference to the dominant discourse may account for this process of systematic and strategic obliteration. In understanding time-binding, these insights are helpful. Foucault makes a sarcastic statement about those who do not admit the role of power in discursive formations and validation of something as truth:

> They have probably found it difficult enough to recognize that their history, their economics, their social practices, the language that they speak, the mythology of their ancestors, even the stories that they were told in their childhood, are governed by rules that are not all given to their consciousness;... So many things have

already eluded them in their language: they have no wish to see
what they say go the same way. (1972, p. 211)

This remark makes us aware of the territories that were obliterated while
mapping. In other words a realm of knowledge can be excluded from the
time-binding process by deliberately not mapping it. Instances of
obliterated knowledge and texts are not rare in the history of human
civilization.

The Poetics and Politics of Mapping: The Poststructuralist Impasse

In this section I discuss *This is not a Pipe* and *Fearless Speech* by Foucault and
Simulations and Simulacra by Baudrillard to understand the implications the
map/territory analogy in the context of literary and artistic representations
and other aesthetic expressions. I also look at the implications of this analogy
with reference to the 'construction' of 'truth' or 'reality' and strategies of
ratifying a statement with reference to political situations and representations
by media. I would also like to discuss the function of the 'author' of the map
or the map-maker. Foucault, whom John Harkness describes in the
introduction to his translation of *This is not a Pipe* as a 'cartographer of
Heterotopia,' engaged in a historic-epistemological critique of language,
emphasizes the arbitrariness of sign in a similar fashion as Saussure did.

Foucault's long article on the Belgian artist, Rene Magritte exemplifies
how the map territory analogy can be used to subvert the presumptions on
artistic representations often accepted as truth in an uncritical manner.
Magritte challenges the assumptions of realism by using a technique of paradox
employing both language and visual representation through many of his
paintings. Foucault sees a visual critique of language and of several suppositions
underlying representational art in the compositions of Magritte, especially
"This is not a Pipe." Magritte, in a letter to Foucault agrees on the preference
for the notion of similitude over resemblance in the discourse of
representation in art. Magritte's paintings can be interpreted as attempts to
destabilize the traditional links of language and the image. In his painting, "This
is not a Pipe" the calligraphy below the image asserts autonomy with respect to
the image. The paradox of the statement, "This is not a Pipe" below an image
of a pipe leads to challenging our assumptions about the relationship between
image and language; object and representation; life and art, etc. In Magritte

paintings, the fragmented and jumbled 'paraphernalia of everyday life' is given an abstract expression drawing our attention to the deceptive familiarity that conceals the alienness. The heterotopias constructed in a visual way by Magritte in "This is not a Pipe" destabilize several myths which are taken for granted.

Magritte denies the viewer the certainty of calling the map the territory or even something that resembles the territory. The destruction of the contextual, conventional, historically validated association between the word and the object represented in linguistic or artistic terms also conveys the fundamental idea of map/territory analogy. When surrealists like Dali and Tanguy, who used the technique of blatant fantasy and defamiliarization, Magritte tried to highlight the alienness that is concealed beneath the familiar surface of daily life. Through the banishment of the "referential" from visual production, Magritte questions our simplistic interpretations. Foucault, while trying to see into the subversive and paradoxical art of Magritte, affirms that interpretation cannot survive the blind faith in signs which are taken to be static, coherent, and systematic symbols. There is no ossified model that an interpretation must conform to; there are only a variety and multiplicity of possible interpretations. A map is just one way of interpreting the territory and through numerous possible maps, the territory ceases to be a fixed model; in other words, a territory is open to several and endless interpretations. Ultimately we are left with abstract interpretations of a seemingly concrete territory or maps of the territory. The territory is lost somewhere in the process of interpretations. This awareness is "consciousness of abstracting."

Representation, verbal, written or visual, is not an apolitical activity. Foucauldian conceptualizations on the process and politics of 'truth telling' discussed in the Seminar, *Fearless Speech* in which he explores the implications of the term 'truth' and the process of verbalizing or giving it a tangible expression through the act of 'telling' makes one think of another dimension of the map/territory analogy wherein the territory itself could be a 'construct.' Telling is analogous to mapping if we consider truth as a territory, unstable and indeterminate in many contexts. The power/knowledge dynamics that goes into the projection of something as 'true' or 'reality' reminds that one should be conscious about not only abstractions, but also of the very nature of truth, reality or event which one may try to map through visual and verbal expressions. Foucault builds his argument around the Greek word *parrhesia*. He interprets its meaning in the Greco-Roman tradition thus: "The one who uses *parrhesia*, the *parrhesiastes*, is someone who says everything he has in mind: he does not hide anything, but opens his heart and mind completely to other people through his discourse.

In *parrhesia*, the speaker is supposed to give a *complete* and *exact* account of what he has in mind so that the audience is able to comprehend *exactly* what the speaker thinks" (Foucault, 2011, p. 12 emphasis added). In such a situation, it goes without saying that the speaker is revealing what is true in his opinion and his perspective manifests. While a *parrhesiastes* thus uses transparent and clear expressions without any rhetorical flourishes, he unrolls the map of a territory as he has seen it and interpreted it. Foucault's analysis of whether the *parrhesiastes* is telling the truth or what he believes as true leads to the imagining of a situation wherein there is exact coincidence between belief and truth for which dependence on and evaluation of reliable evidence are required. In the light of Map/Territory analogy, this would mean that the process of mapping should 'ideally' be systematic and conscious which include seeing and measuring the territory ensuring accuracy and at each stage the process has to be monitored. Truth teller and the listener of truth may form a hierarchy which would also determine the 'constructed' quality of truth and bring in values like 'courage,' 'sincerity,' 'integrity,' 'dutifulness,' and the like to the discursive realm of telling and reception of truth. In the Greco-Roman sense, a *parrhesiastes* takes a risk by uttering a truth and it demands some courage in the face of danger. Foucault's question, 'how is it that the alleged *parrhesiastes* can be certain that what he believes is, in fact, the truth' (ibid., p. 15) is pertinent with reference to speech activity in a political situation. Coming back to the map/territory analogy, since the territory is seen and understood through the eyes of the map maker(s) and represented as the map hence, one can only say that it is true according to the map makers(s)' belief, provided he/she has not deliberately or flippantly erred. It also implies that the one who views the map and uses it should be conscious of the abstractness of it and cautious about its unreliability because the territory as such could have deceived the eyes of the map maker(s). As Foucault rightly says:

'Truth' is to be understood as a system of ordered procedures for the production, regulation, distribution, circulation and operation of statements. 'Truth' is linked in a circular relation with systems of power which produce and sustain it, and to effects of power which it induces and which extend it. A 'regime' of truth. (1980, p. 133)

Simulations, Heterotopias and Mapping the Virtual

Postmodernism poses the question, what is real and true in a language of paradox and sarcasm. Postmodernist imagination captures the nuances of the dystopic and it is expressed blatantly and subtly in art, media and films. The imagined world of high and impossible fantasy turns out to be a telling metaphor for our ordinary, everyday lives. This situation is opposed to utopia. Our contemporary films and writings capture dystopic experiences. For example, we can read the film, *Inception* as a metaphor. Implanting an idea in another person's mind through several mechanisms involving different dreamscapes, or in other words giving a person some kind of "prosthetic" thought, metaphorically suggests the effects of propaganda and demagoguery. So an improbable situation here actually is a metaphor for a very strong possibility and an observable phenomenon. The strategies of propaganda and indoctrination alter our perception of the territory drastically.

Imagine situations wherein a cartographer maps a heterotopia (in a metaphorical sense) with the help of available linguistic or artistic tools. Foucault uses the concept of Heterotopia to describe places and spaces of otherness, which are neither here nor there or both here and there. Heterotopia is not confined to the 'spatiality' of existence and perception. The Hererotopic spaces are simultaneously physical and psychological, such as the space of a chat-window, a game in the virtual space, a phone call and even a social networking site where islands of isolation appear to be a virtual continent of togetherness. Our contemporary media and modes of communication and human interaction have exposed us to many heterotopias. Heterotopia is a spatial-temporal experience of flotation and non-fixity. When one considers the possible attempts to map, make sense of and interpret for oneself the flood of information, images and entertainment through various types of media, the nightmare of heterotopia begins. Media traps us in a nowhere-land. Foucault observes in his 1967 article, "Of Other Spaces, Heterotopias," "The heterotopia is capable of juxtaposing in a single real place several spaces, several sites that are in themselves incompatible" and "The heterotopia begins to function at full capacity when men arrive at a sort of absolute break with their traditional time.[1]

How would general semantics interpret the territory and map of a heterotopic experience? A situation which poses some difficulty in placing oneself or making sense of the experience one undergoes is gaming. The graphics-based computer games entertain the player in part by presenting him or her with a simulated space, an imaginary two or three dimensional region. Its visual appearance is mapped onto the two dimensional surface of the video screen. The player enters this space and time, moves in that virtual space and spends time there. This is a space of fantasy and imagination constructed by human beings. It takes one through a vicarious experience. In the spaces one is ushered to through gaming and such realms of experience, human beings taste, virtually and vicariously, adventure, cruelty, fantasy, etc.

Let's imagine an impasse in the map/territory relationship by analyzing a possibility suggested by Baudrillard: signs were invented to signify 'reality.' The connectedness between signifier and signified eventually wear out. According to him, advertising, propaganda and commodification hide reality. He interprets the multiplicity and mimesis of representations or 'simulacra' as a means for concealing the absence of reality. Thus, in the age of hyper-reality, signs conceal the absence of reality and only pretend to mean something. Our knowledge of the world is not firsthand, unmediated and direct. Our perceptions are mediated by media and communication systems and hence we have access to only simulations of 'reality.' Representations are not neutral, objective or apolitical. They construct their versions of 'reality.' General Semantics makes us aware that such representations should not be mistaken for 'reality' and train us to analyze whose realities they represent and why.

I think this analysis, which is done as a collage to juxtapose various implications of map/territory analogy in a fragmentary way form will take a new direction if we bring in the maverick philosopher of our times. Baudrillard's argument that postmodern societies are organized around simulation and the play of images and signs offers a new dimension to map/territory analogy. He portrays an alarming situation in which signs are the organizing forms of a new social order where simulation dominates everything else giving way to a condition in which territories are obliterated by maps. Mode of simulation or stratagems of mapping and maps themselves determine how and why goods are consumed, the happenings in politics and public response, and worse, even how everyday life is lived. Baudrillard discusses the disappearance of the difference between map and territory that takes away the charm of abstraction. The concept and the real become suddenly indistinguishable from their representation. Or in other words, the map becomes the territory. If a superimposing of the map on territory is possible in a mad project coextensivity, their distinctions disappear. The virtual and the real cannot be identified and classified as different in the realm of simulation. In this context, I would like to allude to a story by Louis Borges. "On Exactitude in Science" or "On Rigor in Science" is a one-paragraph short story by Jorge Luis Borges, about the map/territory relation with a reference to which Jean Baudrillard's *Simulations and Simulacra* begins. The Borges story imagines an empire where the science of cartography insists on exactitude in such a way that only a map of the same size as the empire would suffice. Baudrillard contemplates on this map when the territory ceases to be. Here the map engenders the territory, map remains even when and where the territory ceases to be. The real is substituted by the signs of the real and it is a state wherein all referentials are liquidated.

Thinkers like Baudrillard lament that our society has become so dependent on maps that we have lost all contact with the territory that ideally precedes the map. He warns that we have lost the ability to see the distinction between nature and artifice. We depend on the media not only for information, but we let the media interpret our most private selves for us. We see ourselves, others and the world through the kaleidoscope of these media images. Our needs and desires are determined by commercials. Media culture deprives us of historicity. Movies, documentaries and television transform history to viable, 'retro' recreations of the past the function of which is recreational (everything becomes entertainment, even holocaust and wars). Media make us forget history; Television, film, and the internet, due to their very form and function, separate from the real as they attempt to reproduce it more fully or faithfully: The map is more real and interesting than the territory. Real is turned into hyperreal. More real than real, that is how the real is abolished" ("*The Implosion of Meaning in the Media*" p. 81). In a society of simulation and hyperreality, economics, politics, culture, religion, language, sexuality, etc. implode into each other. Media plays a major role in 'hardening of categories' and generating and sustaining stereotypes. People are labeled and classified according to their political stands, and terms like "terrorist" are used uncritically.

The realm of hyperreality is one in which entertainment, information, and communication technologies abundantly supply such experiences which are more intensely engaging and engrossing than the scenes of banal everyday life. It controls our thought and behavior. Individuals run away from the "desert of the real" or boring quotidian realities in search of hyperreality into the realms of computer, media, and technological experience. Symbolically, locations of entertainment, commodification and ecstasy are prominent on the map of the world provided by the media. Violence, death, war and famine turn into visuals that one enjoys and seeks for; media commodifies catastrophes. The resulting fragmentation of subjectivities, short attention span and insensitivity to gross and unjust events usher us to a new terrain of experience that leaves previous and familiar territories of experience obsolete. We are in a state of "ecstasy of communication" due to the proximity to instantaneous images and prolific information. Humans, in the ecstatic realm of communication, have become schizophrenic because of over-exposure to information and spectacle; moreover, we are slaves to gadgets which are schizo-functional.

In the age of media and consumerism, spectacle which has little relationship to 'reality' prevails. According to Baudrillard, media saturated consciousness is narcoticized and mesmerized and is in a state of perpetual hunger and fascination for image and spectacle. At this state, meaning dissipates, both in reality and as metaphor. As boundaries, structures and consensus cease to be in the media-dominated world, meaning(s) also die. In this alarming situation, the referents disappear; territories are obliterated and maps prevail in abundance. Alluding to the statements of McLuhan, "Medium is the message (mess-age)" and "Medium is the Massage," Baudrillard discusses how shut in the universe of simulations, the "masses" are "bathed in a media massage" that has neither messages nor meaning; it is a mass age where classes go unnoticed, and politics is dead. Hence there is no space for the grand dreams of liberation, and revolution.Baudrillard observes that the content of communication is emptied of meaning and consequent action.

Information and News spread like metastases. Maps proliferate, many distorted or fantasized ones. The relevance of territory is lost. Today media has increased indiscriminately the quantity of signs and spectacles, and produced a proliferation of sign-value. Commodities are not to be understood by their use-value and exchange value. Sign-value, an increasingly important aspect of the commodity and consumption, obliterates them. Commodities are signs through which individuals achieve and hoard prestige, identity, and social recognition.

CONCLUSION

In this attempt to map the territories of language, knowledge, information and media, in the light of map/territory analogy and 'consciousness of abstracting' several disjointed aspects are juxtaposed in the paper without trying to link them. What remains to be explored is how General Semantics can be useful in surviving in a world plagued by fantasies wherein human beings inhabit realms of virtuality, a world in which consumerism has commodified our everyday lives. General semantics if properly understood teaches one to become aware of the abstraction process, to identify assumptions, test our assumptions and hold all beliefs conditionally. But as Korzybski rightly understood, it does not offer instant solutions and should not be interpreted as a panacea. Developing the consciousness of abstracting, using extensional devices, being aware of the neurolinguistic dimension of communication, etc. prescribed by Korzybski and other General Semanticists have the potential to act as defense mechanisms in several environments of knowledge, information and communication.

The world has seen numerous rises and falls of ideas and ideologies after Korzybski. In a true time-binding spirit, one has to expand the scope of General Semantics to incorporate insights from new ideas and think of its implications in other epistemological realms.

NOTES

[1] http://foucault.info/documents/heteroTopia/foucault.heteroTopia.en.html

REFERENCES

Baudrillard, J. (1981). *For a critique of the political economy of the sign.* St. Louis: Telos Press.

Baudrillard, J. (1983). *Simulations.* New York: Semiotext(e).

Baudrillard, J. (1983). *In the shadow of the silent majorities.* New York: Semiotext(e).

Baudrillard, J. (1983). "The ecstasy of communication." *The Anti-Aesthetic.* Hal Foster (Ed.), Washington: Bay Press, 1983.

Baudrillard, J. (1996). *The perfect crime.* London and New York: Verso Books.

Debord, G. (1970). *The society of the spectacle.* Detroit: Black and Red.

Derrida, J. (1978). *Writing and difference* (Bass, A., Trans.). Chicago: University of Chicago Press.

Derrida, J. (1998). *Of grammatology* (Spivak, G. C., Trans.). Baltimore & London: Johns Hopkins University Press.

Foucault, M. (1972). *The archaeology of knowledge : The discourse on language.* (Sheridan, A. M., Trans.). New York : Pantheon Books.

Foucault, M. (1980). *Power/Knowledge: Selected interviews and other writings, 1972-1977.* New York: Pantheon.

Foucault, M. (1994). *The order of things : An archaeology of the human sciences* (Sheridan, A. M., Trans.). London : Vintage.

Foucault, M. (2001). *Fearless speech.* New York: Semiotext (e).

Foucault, M. (2008). *This is not a pipe* (Harkness, J., Trans.). Berkeley: University of California Press.

Korzybski, A. (2000). *Science and sanity: An introduction to non-Aristotelian systems and general semantics* (5th ed.). USA: Institute of General Semantics.

Saussure, F. de. (1977). *Course in general linguistics,* Bally, C. & Schehaye, A., (Eds.), (Baskin, W., Trans.). Glasgow: Fontana/Collins.

Saussure, F. de. (2006). *Writings in general linguistics.* Oxford: Oxford University Press.

CHAPTER 15: KORZYBSKI AND CYBERCULTURE

Thierry Bardini

THIS CHAPTER IS ABOUT maps and territories, but about special kinds of maps and territories: digital (and not virtual) maps and territories. So I start with a serious question: say at the satellite resolution of Google maps, for instance, doesn't the map look like the territory? And if the territory itself is digital (as in cyberspace), isn't the map the territory? In order to give some elements of answer to these questions I examine here the direct and indirect influences Alfred Korzybski had on contemporary cyberculture. In this process, I draw a genealogical map. But first, the obvious question: "What is cyberculture?" or more accurately if I follow the e-prime directive: What do I mean by "cyberculture" here?

I would like to avoid any essentialist bias, and, in a way true to Korzysbski's teachings, also avoid at any cost an improper use of the verb "to be." This is why I feel that I must answer that cyberculture is no-thing, i.e. not a thing, but rather a complex *assemblage* of discourses and ideas, *dispositifs* and artifacts, practices and materialities, human and not...but most crucially for my talk today: cyberculture is a process, what they made and we make of it. So it begs the next question: Who, "they?"

They are a whole bunch of people, singular individuals who contributed to this collective production of discourses and ideas, *dispositifs*, etc. Note here that if I consider (cyber-)cultural production a collective process, I no less insist that its expression stems from the workings of *singular individuals*, actual people who lived and wrote, filmed or designed the discourses and ideas, *dispositifs* etc. that actually constitute cyberculture. In other words, in spite of the death of the author and his replacement by a function, I still personalize the issue here. So I will talk about some of these singular individuals, and, most importantly, about the links between them, with the following hypothesis: They are somehow all related to Alfred Korzybski.

I.

Starting with a bold proposition: cyber-culture is, above all, a reflection on the world Philip K. Dick (PKD hereafter) made. This speed intoxicated

265

pulp writer *actually created* this cyber-world, or in his own words, *remembered* it first. PKD first saw through the iron cage of reality, got the first glimpse of the final *anamnesis*. From the power invested in him by the Logos, he actually created this world. He felt it in his bones and in his mind, and he recognized it like some long gone impression, like somebody who would wake up from a long cultural coma (and this coma was named *modernity*). He is the mastermind behind it all, the paranoid writing android, the schizophrenic demiurge who first remembered it into being. Cyberculture is a figure of his anamnesis.

But you might ask: what is the link with the strange count? The short answer: through Alfred Elton van Vogt, one pioneer of the kind of pulp science fiction PKD enjoyed so much:

> There's no doubt who got me off originally and that was A. E. van Vogt. There was in van Vogt's writing a mysterious quality, and this was especially true in *The World of Null A*. All the parts of that book did not add up; all the ingredients did not make a coherency the thing that fascinated me so much was that this resembled reality more than anybody else's writing inside or outside science fiction.[1]

Van Vogt (1912-2000) was a Canadian-born science fiction author, and one of its early pioneers. Born in Winnipeg, the son of a lawyer, he grew up in a rural Saskatchewan community. Without money for education (like many children of the great depression, his father lost a good job), he did not attend college. He worked at a series of jobs and then started writing true confessions, love stories, trade-magazine articles, and radio plays. In the late 1930s, he switched to writing science fiction, influenced by his teenage passion for fairy tales. In 1939, he published his first two SF story, entitled "Black Destroyer" and "Discord in Scarlet," in John W. Campbell's *Astounding Science Fiction*, the ultimate science-fiction serial of all time. In the same issue appeared Isaac Asimov's first *Astounding* story, "Trends"; Robert Heinlein's first story "Lifeline" appeared a month later and Theodore Sturgeon's "Ether Breather" a month after that. In his numerous production, van Vogt showed PKD the way to create this unstable reality, this consensual hallucination (William Gibson's very definition of cyberspace) that redefined reality, albeit in a digital way (and again not virtual), and, as we shall see, this way was a null-A way.

Van Vogt was a General Semantics alumnus; moreover, he is this alumnus who actually popularized G.S. into S-F pulp and thus into pop culture (that and being the missing link between G.S. and Dianetics, for instance). Not only through his famous null-A trilogy, but also through his first short story, which eventually became his first novel (*The Voyage of the Space Beagle*). In this novel, G.S. appears as "Nexialism" and his protagonist, Elliot Grosvenor (a clear allusion to the relationship between G.S. and cybernetics[2]) is the first graduate of the Nexial Institute. Van Vogt defined Nexialism as "the science of joining in an orderly fashion the knowledge of one field of learning with that of other fields. It provides techniques for speeding up the processes of absorbing knowledge and of using effectively what has been learned." In fact, "nexialism" is van Vogt's fictitious rendering of two of his main influences: Korzybski's general semantics and Alfred North Whitehead's process philosophy. It is a little known fact that this first story eventually turned into…*Alien*, the 1979 Ridley Scott movie. Believe it or not, Sigourney Weaver actually enacted a G.S. graduate!

Ridley Scott, of course, went on making *Blade Runner*, three years later, thus adapting for the screen Philip K. Dick's novel, *Do Androids Dream of Electric Sheep?*, and thus giving our cyberculture its look and feel. Androids, and thus replicants, are the ultimate representation of artificial life, the merging of cybernetic circuits and organic life (the infamous cyborg). As such, they carry the representations ascribed to machines since the dawn of the mechanical age, and, especially as "perfect" replacement of human labor, i.e. slaves. In fact, the name chosen by PKD to call the ultimate generation of replicants, the "more human than human" *Nexus-6*, happens to be highly evocative of their function, since from the time of early Roman Law, *nexi* are quasi-slaves, free persons unable to pay their debts and given (annexed) to their creditors. In PKD's Gnostic worldview, these are names that can be given by extension to the human person still captive of the iron jail of reality, somebody who needs awakening to find redemption. But there is yet another connection to the strange count at play here…

Blade Runner, the title of Scott's movie, came from another screenplay that was never shot: a screenplay by William Burroughs. In Burroughs' adaptation of Alan E. Nourse's eponymous book, a "blade runner" is an underground trafficker in medical equipment. The screenplay is set in New York in 2014, a city that "has less a look of having been rebuilt than resettled," and the general ambiance is also built around decay and debris, "derelict skyscrapers and public transport."[3] The movie's title, but also its overall ambiance, the Mayan architecture of the Tyrell Corporation, the ruins and junk, all this belong to Burroughs's vision. So if PKD created this world, Burroughs named it, and refined its look and feel.

William Burroughs was yet another General Semantics graduate: he took Korzybski's seminar in 1939. In his Cut-Ups trilogy of the first half of the 1960s (*The Soft Machine*, *The Ticket that Exploded* and *Nova Express*), he experimented with the stuff of words. In the early 1970s, he eventually synthesized the experiment in one fundamental thesis: language (and especially written language) as virus. The use of the verb "to be," the first of the forms of the virus, was, of course, highly problematic for him, to the point that it is quite accurate to consider him the detective-doctor of the antiviral fight. In the true tradition of G.S. the principals of this fight began with a reform of language itself.

Burroughs's emphasis on the virus strengthened the series of equivalences that eventually got to be buried deep into the heart of cyberculture and has served since then as its ontological axiom:

LANGUAGE = VIRUS = JUNK CODE[4]

Through Burroughs's mediation, GS indirectly influenced many a philosopher, including most of the representative authors of the so-called "French Theory".[5] This is the case for instance of Jacques Derrida, who realized only later that his whole philosophy was nothing but a virology. Between *Of Grammatology* (1967) and *The Dissemination* (1972), Jacques Derrida started a philosophical enterprise attempting to introduce the Other in the I, a redefinition of the subject. Eventually, this "introduction" became translated into "infection", and the Other was radically recast as the virus.[6] Like Burroughs, Derrida first found traces of the process in writing itself. This is also the case of Gilles Deleuze, and his famous understanding of our present condition as subjects of societies of control, a term he borrowed directly from Burroughs.[7] This is finally (or maybe even terminally) the case of Jean Baudrillard for whom PKD and Burroughs' influences are so strong in his work that a citation would beg here for a *passim*.

Or maybe not... Here the genealogy of ideas becomes quite complex. In my knowledge, Baudrillard never actually quotes Korzybski directly. In the famous opening lines of his groundbreaking *Simulacra & Simulation*, instead, he refers to Jorge Luis Borges' short story entitled "On Rigor in Science."[8] This four-sentence short story, itself an apocryphal quote, evokes a long-past historical episode where the "Art of Cartography" reached such a level of perfection that geographers created "a map of the Empire which had the size of the Empire itself and coincided with it point by point." Baudrillard considered that this fable "has nothing but the discreet charm of second-order simulacra," an industrial era obsession with production, and especially with serial reproduction. And it seems indeed that the origins of this fable are to be found at the acme of the industrial revolution: Borges seems to have gotten it from the works of Josiah Royce, a pupil of William James and long-time friend and intellectual opponent of Charles Sanders Peirce.[9]

In his 1899 book entitled *The World and the Individual*, Royce muses on the logical conundrum created by a thought experiment where he imagines that "a portion of the surface of England is very perfectly leveled and smoothed, and is then devoted to the production of our precise map of England." Every student of logics since the Greeks knows this logical inconsequence as a set of paradoxes connected with the notion of the infinite regression. Royce was fast to remark, of course, that if it were to be done, "This representation would agree in contour with the real England, but at a place within this map of England, there would appear, upon a smaller scale, a new representation of the contour of England. This representation, which would repeat in the outer portions the details of the former, but upon a smaller space, would be seen to contain yet another England and this another, and so on without limit." Actually, Royce's invention seems to be an instance of Zeno's paradox of place, where "place" is equated with "map". Aristotle gave the following formulation of the paradox of place: "… if everything that exists has a place, place too will have a place, and so on *ad infinitum*."[10]

Korzybski too, it seems, followed on Royce's steps. He actually dedicated *Science and Sanity* to the works of various individuals, and among them Royce, "which have greatly influenced [his] inquiry." In the first section where he develops fully the analogy of the map and the territory, he wrote:

> A map is *not* the territory it represents, but if correct, it has a *similar structure* to the territory, which accounts for its usefulness. If the map could be ideally correct, it would include, in a reduced scale, the map of the map; the map of the map, of the map; on so on, endlessly, a fact first noticed by Royce.[11]

Korzybski was right to insist that these propositions amount to "*two* important characteristics of maps" (my emphasis): (1) the structural similarity, and (2) the metonymic recursion.[12] I will come back to structural analogy later but first let me say a word of metonymic recursion. It usually is of no concern to the mapmaker (or for that matter to the map-user). At a "normal" scale, the map itself cannot be represented on the map—it is too small a detail on the territory—and the infinite regress is but an impracticable after-thought. Like in all instances of Zeno's paradoxes—and maybe even in all instances of calling on the figure of the "infinite" on which depends the recursion[13]—reality has a way to ignore the subtleties of the mind.

There are in fact two different criteria for the usefulness of a map: (1) accuracy, of course, since you probably want to find on the map something that you look for on the territory, and (2) scale.[14] A pocket-map is also useful because you can put it in your pocket (and a printed book was a revolution *because* you could carry it on the pockets of your saddle, thanks to the 12-point font, not so much to the Gutenberg Press). Precision and scale can go hand in hand, but not necessarily so. In Borges's version, this lack of practicality actually means the end of the cartographic enterprise:

> The following Generations, who were not so fond of the Study of Cartography as their Forebears had been, saw that that vast Map was Useless, and not without some Pitilessness was it, that they delivered it up to the Inclemencies of Sun and Winters. In the Deserts of the West, still today, there are Tattered Ruins of that Map, inhabited by Animals and Beggars; in all the Land there is no other Relic of the Disciplines of Geography.

This lack of practicality in the "real world", however, depends in turn on a certain conception of "the real". Charles Sanders Peirce, reflecting on Royce's conundrum, merged it with Carroll's insight and reached the following conclusion:

> If a map of the entire globe was made on a sufficiently large scale, and out of doors, the map itself would be shown upon the map; and upon that image would be seen the map of the map; and so on, indefinitely. If the map were to cover the entire globe, it

would be an image of nothing but itself, where each point would be imaged by some other point, itself imaged by a third, etc. [15]

Ivan Almeida, to whom I owe this quote, argues convincingly that if it is so, the map "becomes not only a self-representative (solipsist) representation, but also an infinite representation of itself"; but quite crucially, he adds: "*consequently, it is possible and justifiable to conceive a map without territory, in which each enclosed map represents the next enclosing map in a universe in which there is nothing but maps.*"[16] This, he keeps on arguing with success, is the presumption (not to say the axiom) that makes possible the Borgesian universe: "what is supposed to be 'the real' is only 'a dream' (fiction, representation) that encloses another dream."[17] Moreover, I will argue here that to understand this point, theoretically and practically, is particularly helpful when one wants to understand cyberspace and cyberculture. I will sum up it in three propositions:

i. Cybernetics is (and is not, but is, after all) a science of codes, i.e. mappings
ii. Recursivity is (and is not, but is, after all) its operating concept.
iii. Cyberspace is (and is not, but is, after all) this map without territory (and hence, no space at all)

Cybernetics, the word, was not coined in the twentieth century. Plato first, in the old age, and André-Marie Ampère[18] (1775-1836) second, at the interface of classical and the modern ages, had already used it. To them, it meant the governance of men, the steering of people. This world, of which the Subject was once the measure, became a loopy machine inasmuch that he, in return, needed to be steered, cared for, disciplined and punished.[19] The loop, it is said, came with the steam engine and its regulator, Watt's governor.[20] Under a new name, the loop became one of the key concepts of a formidable synthesis, uniting animal and machine under the hospices of this great mechanism: *feedback*.

Feedback is indeed another name of the loop, the technical name under which went this other key concept of cybernetics. Cybernetics, the science of communication and control, rests on these two pillars: a theory of communication (information and code) coupled to a theory of control (feedback). Control is of major importance; it is the insurance of performance, the process of maintaining equilibrium or aiming towards something. Thus control and regulation go hand in hand in the virtuous circle of *negative feedback*: "when we desire a motion to follow a given pattern the difference between this pattern and the actually performed motion is used as a new input to cause the part regulated to move in such a way as to bring its motion closer to that given pattern."[21]

Cybernetics finally reached its metaphysical accomplishment when both of its main theories, through their conceptual foundations on communication ("code") and control ("feedback"), successfully redefined the living, when it thus managed to fulfill its boldest pronouncement: to be an adequate theory for both the machine and the animal. That happened not so much through computer science and technology at first,[22] but rather through the formidable fable of the molecular biology of the gene. This is why DNA, and not the computer, is the true "prophet" of the metaphysics of code (says Baudrillard).

What is especially ironic about this fable, is the fact that biologists and historians of science still debate whether the so-called "genetic code" is actually a code in the sense of the cybernetic theory of information![23] Here two basic definitions of "code" are worth recalling: (1) code as algorithm, i.e. "a method for solving a mathematical problem (...) in a finite number of steps that frequently involves repetition of an operation" (Webster's), and (2) code as a table of equivalences.[24] In Shannon's information theory, "code" is the algorithm solving the "problem" of the relationship between the message alphabet and the signal alphabet: this method works on a set of rules that establish the relationship as a set of equivalences. Some, including Lily Kay, have argued such is not the case of the so-called "genetic code": "this critique applies also to the use of 'code' in information theory (but not a Morse code) where, according to Weaver, it is used to change a 'message' into a 'signal.' But a code is a relationship between two distinct linguistic systems; it does not 'change' anything into anything else, neither do encoding and decoding. They simply amount to more metaphors."[25] Umberto Eco concurs and writes that "the so-called 'genetic code' seems to be a system like I," i.e. "a set of possible behavioral responses on the part of the destination" and thus an "s-code" rather than a "code" proper.[26]

In the terms of interest here, "code" can thus be defined alternatively as map or mapping. The second option supersedes the first since "mapping" both means the process and result of map-making (and such is also the case of Eco's /code/ and /s-code/[27]). So when Baudrillard says that it is no more a question of map and territories, he might still mean that it is a question of "mapping," with a specific proviso that actually dates the so-called "simulation" era: the criteria here for mapping is not reference (i.e. "accuracy") but rather *generation,* as is intended in the virtuous understanding of recursion, the always possible nesting of a further map inside the map. This, however, requires a different metaphysics, or to put it in slightly different terms, *a different logic.* That this logic requires a different relationship between identity and difference, between cause and consequence, in other words *a non-Aristotelian logic,* is the focal point of this paper; but before we establish this, we need to address yet another difference where Korzybski's influence partially made a difference: that of medium and message.

II.

It is maybe Bateson's take on cybernetics, and more crucially his Korzybskian re-articulation of the concept of information as a "difference which makes a difference," that epitomizes the best this intersection between the two contingencies, between cybernetics and relativism. Here is the key to the notion of "structural similarity" that I evoked previously: the structural similarity between map and territory is the result of the transcription on the map of actual differences present in the territory. Such is Gregory Bateson's take on this idea, in his Korzybski memorial lecture:

> Let us go back to the map and the territory and ask: 'What is it in the territory that gets onto the map?' We know the territory does not get onto the map. That is the central point about which we here are all agreed. Now, if the territory were uniform, nothing would get onto the map except its boundaries, which are the points at which it ceases to be uniform against some larger matrix. What gets onto the map, in fact, is difference, be it a difference in altitude, a difference in vegetation, a difference in population structure, difference in surface, or whatever. Differences are the things that get onto a map. [28]

Bateson was also very interested in the recursive conundrum that we addressed previously. He devoted much of his thinking to paradoxes and loops, and most famously recurred to Russell's theory of "logical types" to try to "solve" them. The theory of logical types, in Bateson's translation, is "the theory that asserts that no class can, in formal logical or mathematical discourse, be a member of itself; that a class of classes cannot be one of the classes which are its members."[29] Bateson used this theory to formulate his ideas about content and meta-content: in other words, paradoxes could be avoided, claimed Russell, if no error of logical typing was made, i.e. if no proposition held simultaneously statements of different logical types, no content and meta-content, statements and statements about statements. But Bateson also understood early on that "Russell's rule cannot be stated without breaking the rule."[30] So the aporia persisted.

It is also such a sense of aporia that Bateson found in General Semantics. Korzybski, he wrote, "was, on the whole, speaking as a philosopher, attempting to persuade people to discipline their manner of thinking. But he could not win."[31] But he also provided the most general translation of Korzybski's aphorism, and the point of view, the all-encompassing metaphor, which will allow me to tie-up all the remaining knots:

> Korzybski's statement asserts that in all thought or perception or communication about perception, there is a transformation, a coding, between the report and the thing reported, the *Ding an sich*. Above all, the relation between the report and that mysterious thing reported tends to have the nature of a *classification*, an assignment of a thing to a class. Naming is always classifying, and mapping is essentially the same as naming.[32]

Thus are the relationships between mapping, naming and coding. The metaphor I alluded to here, however, is not that of the map and the territory, nor that of the map and the name. There is yet another, more encompassing metaphor that characterizes Bateson's contribution to this whole debate: the ecological perspective. In the nested hierarchy of metaphors, this set of maps inside maps, the ecological perspective appears as the most encompassing level: whatever the map or the territory, the name or the symbol, *they always belong to an ecology*; an ecology of bodies and minds, an ecology of ideas and behaviors:

> At the root it is the notion that ideas are interdependent, interacting, that ideas live and die (...) You've got the sort of complicated, living, struggling, cooperating tangle like what

you'll find on any mountainside with the trees, various plants and animals that live there—in fact, an ecology.[33]

In his Korzybski Memorial Lecture, the notion of "an ecology of ideas" was already present, and Bateson credited Sir Geoffrey Vickers for it.[34] It was itself an idea whose time had come, and that would be rich of further developments. So, let us consider now a final line of development in our genealogy: if Dick made this universe, and Burroughs named it, then Postman et al. further refined the study of its means of expression. "Media Ecology," "the study of media as environments" in Postman's own terms, is "General Semantics writ large." In his contribution to the twenty-third Korzybski memorial lecture, Postman wrote that he merely tried to improve on a map, the map made by Korzybski, who, according to him, had "a most curious and paradoxical blockage in his vision: he did not see that media must be considered as languages and therefore did not seriously reflect on how their structures influence the perceptions and values of an historical epoch."[35] In his "Notes Toward an Intellectual History of Media Ecology," Casey Man Kong Lum summarizes the ensuing research tradition around three main theoretical propositions:

(1) "A medium's symbolic form entails the characteristics of the code in which in the medium presents information (...) and the structures in which symbols are put together. Similarly, a medium's physical structure refers to the characteristics of the technology that carries the code and the physical requirements for encoding, transmitting, storing, receiving, decoding, and distributing information";

(2) "Each medium's unique set of physical, as well as symbolic characteristics carry with them a set of biases";

(3) "Communication media facilitate various psychic or perceptual, social, economic, political, and cultural consequences that are relative to the media intrinsic biases."[36]

Casey Man Kong Lum further insists that three theoretical propositions must be located into a larger perspective describing a continuum going from soft to hard (technological) determinism, and centered on "culture/technology symbiosis,"[37] "a perspective on looking at human culture as the result of the ongoing, interdependent and therefore mutually influential interaction between people and their technologies or media."[38] So when considering media as languages, Postman's original intuition pushes a nod further Korzybski's thesis by adding technology to the equation. In other words, the media ecology tradition focuses on the form and the consequences of the form of linguistic mediation, and thus on the technological configuration (both as process and result) of the forms of expression. In fact, Postman did to General Semantics what Douglas Engelbart, an early pioneer of personal computing and the inventor of the mouse, did to the Whorfian hypothesis: extend it to media and tools, and thus to cyberculture.

> The Whorfian hypothesis states that "the world view of a culture is limited by the structure of the language which this culture uses." But there seems to be another factor to consider in the evolution of language and human reasoning ability. We offer the following hypothesis, which is related to the Whorfian hypothesis: Both the language used by a culture, and the capability for effective intellectual activity, are directly affected during the evolution by the means by which individuals control the external manipulation of symbols.[39]

This connection would prove especially crucial for cyberculture: it shows that the notion of cultural (or linguistic) relativity was there as much in the mind of this theoreticians as it was in the hands of its engineers. The Whorfian connection did not escape Postman's theorizing either, and he wrote on his second book about "the Sapir-Whorf-Korzybski-Ames-Einstein-Heisenberg-Wittgenstein-McLuhan-Et.Al. Hypothesis...that language is not merely a vehicle of expression, it is also the driver; and that what we perceive, and therefore can learn, is a function of our languaging processes."[40] The inclusion in this list of the names of Einstein and Heisenberg—two physicists who did not write much about media and/or language—firmly locates Postman's theoretical proposition inside a more global perspective which begs for the name "relativism." This identification was by no means new to the late '60s; in fact it was there from the start for what concerns us here: cyberneticians, and especially social scientists among them, had already noticed that the conflation of Einstein and Heisenberg's (physical) relativism and Whorf-Sapir's (cultural) relativism was both a very potent and potentially dangerous idea.[41]

Whatever be the dangers and confusion of physical/cultural relativism, it is however this broad perspective that allows to understand how Postman and his fellow media ecologists could enroll Marshall McLuhan in the list of "hypothesers" founding their research tradition. According to Lance Strate, it was Louis Fordale's[42] comprehension of McLuhan that "his understanding of media is essentially an extension of the Sapir-Whorf hypothesis.[43] Postman himself credited McLuhan for coining the very expression "Media Ecology" around 1962-1964.[44] Since then, McLuhan seems to have been regularly included in the list of "founding fathers" of the Media Ecology field of study. If there is not much doubt about this understanding of media and environment and his sharing of the three theoretical propositions introduced previously, his position on the topic discussed here is however less obvious. McLuhan was obviously aware of the existence of the Sapir-Whorf "hypothesis"[45]; his proximity to the ideas and theses of Alfred Korzybski is, however, more doubtful.

I am not aware of a direct reference to Korzybski in Marshall McLuhan's writings. The only reference I found was in his son Eric and Franck Zingrone's introduction to an anthology of his key ideas entitled *The Essential McLuhan*: they wrote "in the information age we should remember Korzybski's notion of 'a world of words and a world of not words.' Paradox and ambiguity must exist if the interplay between these two worlds is to be balanced humanely."[46] It might be exactly because of this kind of interpretation of Korzybski's ideas that McLuhan never actually quoted him. McLuhan would have never agreed on a "two-worlds" theory, nor would he have ever been comfortable with a non-Aristotelian logic. Marshall McLuhan could have never agreed with some version of a Gnostic heresy. Or maybe, he would have, and would have not.

I would not dare claiming here that Korzybski was himself a Gnostic.[47] I feel pretty confident that Benjamin Lee Whorf would not have condoned such a misreading of his specific—and not so deterministic—notion of cultural relativism.[48] But most of their followers, and especially many of the writers discussed in the present paper, definitely fall into his category. It is the case of Philip K. Dick, without a shadow of a doubt.[49] William Burroughs was also suspected of such an affinity, and Borges wrote about his admiration for the "desperate and admirable men the Gnostics were" and confessed having studies their "passionate speculations."[50] The case of Gregory Bateson is not too doubtful either. In his Korzybski Memorial Lecture, he actually characterized his reading of Korzybski's ideas following this tradition:

> Let us go back to the original statement for which Korzybski is most famous—the statement that the map is not the territory, This statement came out of a very wide range of philosophic thinking, going back to Greece, and wriggling through the history of European thought over the last 2,000 years. In this history, there has been a sort of rough dichotomy and often deep controversy. There has been a violent enmity and bloodshed. It all starts, I suppose, with the Pythagoreans versus their predecessors, and the argument took the shape of, "Do you ask what it's made of—earth, fire, water, etc.?" Or do you ask, "What is its pattern?" Pythagoras stood for inquiry into pattern rather than inquiry into substance. That controversy has gone through the ages, and the Pythagorean half of it has, until recently, been on the whole the submerged half. The Gnostics followed the Pythagoreans, and the alchemists follow the Gnostics, and so on. [51]

Anyways, it is not much news anymore to repeat that cyberculture as a whole is Gnostic through and through.[52] Have you ever asked a cyberaddict if he enjoyed coming back to this world? Ever heard of the Matrix?

Since his conversion to Roman Catholicism in the end of March 1937 (he was then 26 years old), Marshall McLuhan remained a devout believer, whose main theological inclination was towards Thomism. He was also, however, a "trickster," probably as paranoid and schizoid as William Burroughs or Philip K. Dick ever were. He did not make much mention of Korzybski, but here is what he wrote about Dr. Junk: "Burroughs is not asking merit marks as a writer; he is trying to point to the shut-out button of an active and lethal environmental process."[53] On the same occasion, he provided yet another meaning to his most famous aphorism that seems a far cry away from the beatific optimism many ascribe to the father figure of the "global village": "it is the medium that is the message because the medium creates an environment that is as indelible as it is lethal", he wrote.

McLuhan was either a Thomist, i.e. an Aristotelian onto-theologian, or an artistic gadfly prone to Luciferian probes and other Menippean satires. He was "bipolar," which might explain why he could simultaneously "influence" the

French Theorists[54] and the Media Ecologists, the Borgesians and the Korzybskites (without mentioning too much the staff and readers of *Wired*); thus achieving the goals he had picked for himself, in the mapping metaphors of the period: "I'm making explorations. I don't know where they're going to take me," he once said, "I want to map new terrain rather than chart old landmarks."[55] Many still vacation by his maps, be it on the secure shores of the Omega Point[56]… or the bleak shoal waters of the Neuromancers:

> It's our nature to represent. We're the animal that represents, the sole and only maker of maps. And if our weakness has been to confuse the bright and bloody colors of our calendars with the true weather of days, and the parchment's territory of our maps with the land spread out before us…never mind. We've always been on our way to this new place, that is no place, really, but is real.[57]

III.

Now that it is time to conclude, I want to attract your attention on Bruno Bosteels's recent reading of "the entire field of critical theory and cultural studies" as being "split among the melancholy admirers of McLuhan, for whom *the medium is the message*, and the hopeful followers of Korzybski, for whom *the map is not the territory*." Bosteels follows up on this polemical characterization with an attenuating gesture that seems crucial to me: "the irreconciliation of both positions is perhaps only a lure, as such inseparable from the kind of semiology for which radical alternatives are also available. Perhaps Baudrillard's descriptions of simulation should then be reread in light of a different semiotic framework altogether.[58] Jean Baudrillard was indeed an admirer of Marshall McLuhan. He credited him with having coined the definitive aphorism of the Hyperreal, "the key formula of the era of simulation,"[59] *The medium is the message*. Gregory Bateson was an admirer of Alfred Korzybski. The instances of his reflection on the famous aphorism of the Count are countless in his work: *The map is not the territory*.

But rather than talking about Bosteels's "different semiotic framework," we might want to ponder about a different logic. For that was, after all, the most important proposal Korzybski ever made: move from an Aristotelian to a non-Aristotelian logics (that and the synchronous moves to a non-Euclidian mathematics and a non-Newtonian physics). That means concretely to replace, displace or plainly do way with Aristotle's classic "three laws of thought": the law of identity,[59] the law of non-contradiction,[61] and the law of excluded middle.[62] Applied to language, Korzybski's main interest since he diagnosed at this level the root of all modern pathologies, the proposal goes as follows:

> (1) If the traditional Aristotelian metaphysics says that something (a word) is something else (a thing), then I say that something (a word) is "nothing" (that is, not a thing); (2) if Aristotelian grammar says that a word has a definite meaning (that is means what it means as a defined term), then I say that a word has an indefinite range of meanings (that is, means what it means as an undefined term in a particular context or structure); and (3) if Aristotelian logic asserts that something cannot both *be* and *not be* at the same time (that is, must be *either* one thing *or* not be that one thing), then I say that according to modern quantum physics and relativity theory, something (light) can both *be* one thing (matter) and *not be* that one thing (that is, it can a be quantum of energy) at the same time.[63]

Korzybski was thus aware that his proposal included three inter-nested epistemological levels: metaphysics, grammar, and eventually logics: a new image of the *Trivium* so dear to Marshall McLuhan (and the rest of the General Semantics program took care of the *Quadrivium*). Among these levels, that of metaphysics is indeed first, and now begs for a renewed conception of identity, a relative conception of identity: "relative to the history of the things considered, relative to the environment the thing is in, relative to our own practical purposes, relative to the frame of reference from which it is viewed, etc."[64] That this proposal has somehow become the basic mode of functioning of our present culture, under the rule of its most common prefix, *cyber* (or its alternative qualification, *post-*), is no news anymore. Consider for instance Frederic Jameson's conclusion to his "cartographic digression" at the end of his introduction to *Postmodernism. Or, The Cultural Logic of Late Capitalism*: "The political form of postmodernism, if there ever is any, will have as its vocation the invention and projection of a global cognitive mapping, on a social as a spatial scale."[65]

Jean Baudrillard, too, has noticed this elision of the Symbolic, and, moreover, made of the "origins of the semiotic in the abolition of the symbolic, [and] the characterization of our society as defined by this transformation," "the central organizing principles of his work."[66] His fate in the "representational dialectic," however, was long gone...instead, he, like McLuhan, recurred to satire and aphorisms, probes and provocations (and a photographic practice). It was no satire or provocation, however, when he found the metaphysical foundation of the Hyperreal in a move away from Aristotle:

> ... This is an Aristotelian logic which is no longer our own. Our virtual has definitively overtaken the actual and we must be content with this extreme virtuality which, unlike the Aristotelian, deters any passage to action. We are no longer in a logic of the passage from virtual to actual but in a hyperrealist logic of deterrence of the real by the virtual.[67]

But instead of "the deterrence of the real by the virtual", that leaves not much room for grace, let alone for hope, could one still, like William Gibson asserted, keep on going to "this new place, that is no place, really, but is real"? Could one find again "a sense of place"[68] in a place that is really no place? An element of a possible answer, I hope, is provided by the exploration I just offered on the null-A genealogical map of cyberculture. It is thus to Borges, this dreamer of dreams nested inside other dreams, that I will leave the last word, with his reaction to Coleridge's dream:

> If a man could pass through Paradise in a dream, and have a flower presented to him as a pledge that his soul has really been there, and if he found that flower in his hand when he awoke— Ay!—and what then?

I wonder what my reader thinks of such a fancy; to me it is perfect.[69]

NOTES

[1] "Arthur Byron Interviews Philip K. Dick," *Vertex*, 1(6), February, 1974.

[2] The governor is the name of flyball regulator on James Watt steam engine, usually considered as the first cybernetic device (i.e. working on the feedback principle).

[3] William S. Burroughs, *Blade Runner: A Movie*, Berkeley, Blue Wind Press, 1989, volume is not paginated.

[4] For the final term of this equation, see my book entitled *Junkware: The Coming of Homo Nexus*, University of Minnesota Press, 2011.

[5] François Cusset, *French Theory: How Foucault, Derrida, Deleuze, & Co, Transformed the Intellectual Life of the United States*, University of Minnesota Press, 2008.

[6] For a more detailed account of the importance of the trope of the virus in contemporary cyberculture, see my paper entitled "Hypervirus: A Clinical Report" in *Critical Digital Studies: A Reader*, edited by Arthur and Marilouise Kroker at the University of Toronto Press, 2008, pp. 143-157.

[7] See Gilles Deleuze, "Postscript on the Societies of Control," *October* 59: 3-7, 1992.

[8] Also translated by "On Exactitude in Science". The story was first published in the March 1946 edition of *Los Anales de Buenos Aires, año 1, no. 3* as part of a piece called "Museo" under the name B. Lynch Davis, a joint pseudonym of Borges and Adolfo Bioy; that piece credited it as the work of "Suarez Miranda," *Viajes de varones prudentes, Libro IV, Cap. XLV*, Lerida, 1658 (*Wikipedia*).

[9] Borges acknowledges this intellectual debt in a few instances in his work, including in "When Fiction Lives in Fiction" (*El Hogar*, June 2, 1939) and "Partial Magic in the *Quixote*" (*Otras Inquisiciones*, 1952).

[10] *Physics* IV:1, 209a25.

[11] Chapter IV, "On Structure", pp. 55-65 of the Fourth Edition, 1958, p. 58.

[12] I Borrow this term to Louis Armand, in a footnote entitled "a topographics of the virtual" in his introduction to *Rhizomes.06*, "Codeworks and Surveillance", Spring 2003 [web page] last accessed December 26, 2008 at http://www.rhizomes.net/issue6/armand5.htm.

[13] See Brian Rotman, *Ad Infinitum: the Ghost in Turing Machine. Taking God out of Mathematics and Putting the Body Back In*. Stanford: Stanford University Press, 1993.

[14] Actually one should add a third criterion, i.e. size, for size and scale do not amount to the same. For clarity and brievity's sakes, I will however conflate them here.

[15] Charles Sanders Peirce, *Collected Papers*. Vols. 1–8, edited by C. Hartshorne, P. Weiss and A. W. Burks. Cambridge, MA, Harvard University Press, 1935-1966, 3.609.

[16] "Borges and Peirce, on abduction and maps," *Semiotica* 140: 13-31, 2002, p. 24, my emphasis.

[17] Ibid., p. 25.

[18] *Essai sur la philosophie des sciences*. Paris, Bachelier, 1834.

[19] "Practically and historically, this signified the substitution of social control by the *end* (and by a more or less dialectical *providence* which surveys the accomplishment of this *end*) for social control by anticipation, simulation and programming, and indeterminate mutation directed by the code." "The order of simulacra", op. cit. p. 111. Or, more succinctly, "Sweep away teleology in favor of a teleonomic principle?" "DNA or the Metaphysics of Code," op. cit. p. 94.

[20] But it can also be argued that it was there since the dawn of the technological ages, with knitting: "The most distinctive feature of knitting is its loops," Sadie Plant, "Mobile Knitting" in *Information Is Alive*, pp. 26-37, Rotterdam, V2_/Nai publishers, 2003, p. 30.

[21] Norbert Wiener, *Cybernetics, or Control and Communication in the Animal and the Machine*, 2nd ed., Cambridge, MIT Press, 1994 [1948], pp. 6-7.

[22] Not at first, but eventually, when molecular biology turned to bioinformatics, and the gene reentered the hyperreal it should have never left, in the 1990s.

[23] See Lily Kay, *Who Wrote the Book of Life? A History of the Genetic Code*, Stanford University Press, 2000, and its review by Richard C. Lewontin, "Molecular Biology: In the Beginning Was the Word," *Science*, 291(5507): 1263-64, 2000. As Lily Kay so eloquently puts it: "the genetic code is 'a period piece,' a manifestation of the emergence of the information age." (p. 2). The genetic code is *the* period piece.

[24] This distinction is analog to the one Umberto Eco makes between /code/ and /s-code/. See *A Theory of Semiotics*, Indiana University Press, 1979, pp. 36-40.

[25] *Who Wrote the Book of Life?*, op. cit. p. 23.

[26] *A Theory of Semiotics*, op. cit. p. 37.

[27] "Since an s-code deserves theoretical attention only when it is inserted within a significant communication framework (the code), the theoretical attention is focused on its intended purpose: therefore a non-significant system is called a 'code' by a sort of *metonymical* transference, being understood as part of a semiotic whole with which it shares some properties." In other words, the recursion is pragmatically metonymical from the start, but these pragmatics are deeply paradoxical. Eco adds, "thus an s-code is usually called a 'code' but this habit relies on a rhetorical convention that it would be wise to eliminate." Ibid., p. 38.

[28] Gregory Bateson, "Form, Substance, and Difference," *XIXth Alfred Korzybski Memorial Lecture*, 1970, available on-line at the General Semantics website [last accessed December 28, 2008] : http://www.generalsemantics.org/misc/akml/akmls/37-bateson.pdf

[29] "The Logical Categories of Learning and Communication" in *Steps to an Ecology of Mind*, University of Chicago Press, 2000 [1964], p. 280.

[30] "A Theory of Play and Fantasy," in *Steps to an Ecology of Mind*, University of Chicago Press, 2000 [1954], p. 189.

[31] Gregory Bateson, *Mind and Nature: A Necessary Unity*, New York, Bantam Books, 1980, p. 33.

[32] Ibid., pp. 32-33.

[33] Gregory Bateson, "Ecology of Mind: The Sacred," in *A Sacred Unity: Further Steps to an Ecology of Mind*, edited by Rodney E. Donaldson, New York, HarperCollins, 1991 [1974], p. 265.

[34] In *Value Systems and Social Process*, New York, Basic Books, 1968.

[35] "Media Ecology: General Semantics in the Third Millenium," *XXIIIth Alfred Korzybski Memorial Lecture*, 1974, available on-line at the General Semantics website [last accessed December 28, 2008]: http://www.generalsemantics.org/misc/akml/akmls/41-43-postman-johnson.pdf

[36] In *Perspectives on Culture, Technology, and Communication: The Media Ecology Tradition*, edited by Casey Man Kong Lum, pp. 1-60, Cresskill, Hampton Press, 2006, p. 32-33.

[37] The use of the biological term "symbiosis" here is very representative of the "ecological' perspective and highly reminiscent of J.C.R. Licklider's 1960 paper, "Man-Computer Symbiosis" (*IRE Transactions on Human Factors in Electronics*, March: 4-11). This major contribution can be rightly considered as the founding paper for most of the 1960s research in computing in the U.S.

and thus of the then-nascent "cyberculture". Licklider would eventually contribute another major paper (with Robert Taylor) in 1968, "The Computer as a Communication Device" (*Science & Technology*, avril: 21-31), that would change forever the perception of the computer: from tool to medium.

[38] Lum, "Notes Towards an Intellectual History...", op. cit. p. 34.

[39] Douglas Engelbart, *Augmenting Human Intellect: A Conceptual Framework*, 1962. For more on Engelbart see my *Bootstrapping : Douglas Engelbart, Coevolution and the Origins of Personal Computing*, Stanford University Press, 2000, and especially its pages 36-56 for the relation between his framework for the Augmentation of Human Intellect and the Whorf-Sapir Hypothesis (which by the way is not an hypothesis at all, and even less a deterministic proposition).

[40] Neil Postman and Charles Wiengartner, *Teaching as a Subversive Activity*, New York, Delta, 1969, p. 101, cited in Lance Strate, *Echoes and Reflections: On Media Ecology as a Field of Study*. Cresskill, Hampton Press, 2006, p. 51.

[41] See for instance Margaret Mead, *Coming of Age in Samoa: A Psychological Study of Primitive Youth for Western Civilization* (second edition, New York, Morrow, 1928, p. 145), and Steve Joshua Heims' commentary in *The Cybernetics Group*. Cambridge, MIT Press, 1991, p. 269.

[42] Louis Forsdale was Postman and Weingarter's professor at Columbia University's Teachers College.

[43] Strate, *Echoes and Reflections...*, op. cit. p. 86.

[44] See Lum, "Notes Towards an Intellectual History...", op. cit. p. 9 for the contention that it could have been the case.

[45] Philip Marchand and Neil Postman dates this awareness from the early fifties, probably sometimes between 1953 and the 1956 posthumous publication of an anthology of Whorf's papers edited by John Carroll (*Language, Thought, and Reality*, New York, John Wiley &Sons). They characterized Whorf and Sapir work as having theorized that "human beings learn to perceive reality through language and that language shape the experience of the world" and add, "not a startling thesis for someone exposed to the work of I.A. Richards on language and communications or to the belief of the ancient grammarians that the order of language was analogous to the order of reality." *Marshall McLuhan: The Medium and the Messenger: A Biography*, MIT Press, 1998, p. 126.

[46] Eric McLuhan and Franck Zingrone, "Introduction" in *The Essential McLuhan*, Concord, Ontario, Anansi, 1995, pp. 7-8.

[47] Although some Gnostic interpretations of his thesis exist, and are even documented. See for instance the case of Ralph Moriarty deBit, aka Vitvan, the founder of the School of Natural Order in Baker, Nevada. See "Highlights of Vitvan's teachings, v. 1.3" in relation to General Semantics [webpage last accessed December 29, 2008] at http://m_euser.tripod.com/articles/vithl1.htm.

[48] Whorf was a Methodist, and as such, belonged to the Protestant Church the least amenable to such a characterization. For this theological insight, see for instance Michael J. Christensen, "John Wesley's Reformulation of a Patristic Doctrine" on the Wesley Center for Applied Theology Website [last accessed December 29, 2008] at http://wesley.nnu.edu/wesleyan_theology/theojrnl/31-35/31-2-4.htm

[49] PKD was indeed a self-proclaimed Gnostic, and even believed that he was the reincarnation of a Gnostic of the first Century.

[50] In "A Defense of Basilides the False," in Jorge Luis Borges. Selected Non-Fictions, edited by Eliot Weinberger, London, Penguin, 1999, p. 65.

[51] Bateson, "Form, Substance, and Difference", op. cit.

[52] See for instance Slavoj Zizek's "Against the Digital Heresy," chapter one of On Belief, London, Routledge, 2001, pp. 6-55, and Erik Davis, Techgnosis: Myth, Magic + Mysticism in the Age of Information, New York, Random House, 1999.

[53] "Notes on Burroughs", Nation, 28 December 1964, p. 519.

[54] See Donald F. Theall, The Virtual McLuhan (McGill/Queens University Press, 2001) and especially his chapters 6, "McLuhan and the Cults: Gnosticism, Hermetecism, and Modernism" pp. 108-124, and 7, "McLuhan as a Prepostmodernist and Forerunner of French Theory," pp. 125-137

[55] Marshall McLuhan, The Playboy Interview, March 1969.

[56] See Pierre Lévy (passim) and Douglas Rushkoff, announcing his 56th Annual Alfred Korzybski Memorial Lecture on Boingboing: A Directory of Wonderful Things, October 10, 2008 [website last accessed December 30] http://www.boingboing.net/2008/10/05/sets-and-settings.html

[57] William Gibson: No Maps for this Territory, a documentary by Mark Neale, this excerpt (with music from U2) available on YouTube at http://www.youtube.com/watch?v=dLmgrYS781A.

[58] Bruno, "A Misreading of Maps: The Politics of Cartography in Marxism and Poststructuralism" in Signs of Change: Premodern, Modern, Postmodern, edited by Stephan Barker, pp. 109-142, SUNY Press, 1996, p. 134

[59] Jean Baudrillard, "The implosion of meaning in the media," *In the Shadow of the Silent Majorities*, trans. Paul Foss, John Johnston and Paul Patton, New York, Semiotext(e), 1983 [1978], p. 101.

[60] "Whatever is, is."

[61] "Nothing can both be, and not be."

[62] "Everything must either be, or not be"

[63] Korzybski cited in R. E. Paulson, *Language, Science, and Action. Korzybski's General Semantics—A Study in Comparative Intellectual History*. Westport, Greenwood Press, 1983, p. 47, emphasis in the original.

[64] Oliver L. Reiser, "Résumé: Aristotle, Newton, and Einstein," in *Logic and General Semantics: Writings of Oliver L. Reiser and Others*, edited by Sanford I. Berman, pp. 80-88, San Francisco, International Society for General Semantics. 1989. [1940], pp. 85-86.

[65] Durham, Duke University Press, 1991, p. 54.

[66] William Merrin, *Baudrillard and the Media. A Critical Introduction*.London, Polity, 2005, p. 28.

[67] Jean Baudrillard, "The Gulf War Did not Take Place," in *Selected Writings*, edited by Mark Poster, Stanford University Press, pp. 231-253, 2001, p. 233.

[68] Joshau Meyrowitz, *No Sense of Place: The Impact of Electronic Media on Social Behavior*, Oxford University Press, 1985.

[69] Jorge Luis Borges, "Coleridge's Flower", in *Jorge Luis Borges. Selected Non-Fictions*, op. cit. p. 240.

CHAPTER 16

KORZYBSKI AND...

Deborah Eicher-Catt

INTRODUCTION

OF THE MANY APPARENT linguistic devices that Alfred Korzybski advocates, his appeal to the term *et cetera,* and its diagrammatical counterpart, the *ellipse,* have become standard, popularized representations for the General Semantics movement. It is no coincidence that the main journal published by the Institute is named, *ETC: A Review of General Semantics.* Nor is it surprising that this new book, intended to respond to the resurgence of scholarly interest in General Semantics, marks its efforts with an *ellipse* in the title. *Ellipse,* which appears most often in prose writing as "...", depicts its sister expression, i.e., the Latin expression *et cetera*, a word that simply translates "and the rest" of such things. While the term *et cetera* is a verbal designation, the *ellipse* often marks a non-verbal pause in discourse. Regardless of whether an addresser in a given interaction is using "....", or the term *et cetera*, both "signs of omission" (Eicher-Catt & Sutton, 2010) are typically theorized within General Semantics literature as mere referential devices meant to increase our "consciousness of abstraction" and the potential constraints imposed by our static, Aristotelian ways of thinking and reasoning. For example, Korzybski includes *et cetera* in his list of extensional devices in *Science and Sanity* (1994, p. lx) and many others advocate its use, especially when it comes to eliminating the sense of "allness" our language typically induces (see for example, Read, 1985; Johnson, 1946; and Lee, 1994). Therefore, seeing them as mere extensional devices has become our taken-for-granted sense of their linguistic and discursive importance.

In this chapter I argue that considering *et cetera* and its counterpart, *ellipse*, as mere referential devices is short sighted, especially given more current postmodern theorizing regarding discourse and action. Herein, I re-consider *ellipse* and *et cetera* by rendering a semiotic phenomenological interpretation of their discursive contours. Such an epistemological move provides a broader understanding I believe of Korzybski's overall philosophical yet pragmatic project. As I argue elsewhere (Eicher-Catt, 2010), bringing semiotics and phenomenology to a discussion of Korzybski's work is not new. In terms of semiotics, theoretical links are espoused by Sebeok (1982), Read (1983, 1987), Taylor (2002), Vassallo (2008) and Anton (2008), to name but a few.

Connections with phenomenological thought are found readily in the writings of E.W. Kellogg (1987, 1992) and in the foundational work of early proponent of General Semantics, Elwood Murray (1978). Most recently, Michael Cole, who holds the Dr. Sanford I. Berman Chair in General Semantics within the Department of Communication at the University of California, San Diego, clearly indicates the "interconnectedness" of General Semantics with not only semiotics and phenomenology but also pragmatism, social constructionism and structuralism (see http://communication.ucsd.edu/berman/).

As I aim to demonstrate herein, through a synthesis of semiotics and phenomenology (Lanigan, 1988, 1992) we discover a useful lens that helps contemporary thinkers of General Semantics to theorize more clearly various General Semantic concepts. In terms of *et cetera* and *ellipse,* a semiotic phenomenological investigation reveals their qualitative nature as *figures of speech* (Lanigan, 1992, p. 157) rather than mere stylistic devices. As *figures* (or *tropes*) *of speech*, we begin to appreciate their mediating capabilities as phenomenological semiotic enactments or *bodily gesture* (Merleau-Ponty, 1962). Such a theoretical shift thus highlights their operative qualities in shaping a discursive *logic of tropism* inherent in all discourse and action, as many postmodern theorists of language and culture suggest (see for example, Bakhtin, 1981; Burke, 1969; Cassirer, 1969, 1979, 1996; Eicher-Catt & Sutton, 2010; Foucault, 1972, 1973; Lanigan, 1988; 1992; Lefebvre, 1991; Sutton & Mifsud, 2002; White, 1978, 1999). I maintain that Korzybski names this interactive, *tropic* quality of speech our "*psycho-logic*" (Korzybski, 1994, p. 8). By reading *ellipse* (and *et cetera*) as semiotic and phenomenological enactments of *speech*, we expose the capability of humans to actively mediate (both physically and symbolically) the personal-natural-cultural interstices (Eicher-Catt, 2010) of our existence, a problematic that occupied Korzybski's "scientific" endeavors for his entire career.

So, while the writings of Korzybski address a number of topics for those interested in improving our understanding of "the science and art of human nature," (2008, p. 38), his use of *ellipse* (and promotion of the rhetorical expression, *et cetera*) proves heuristic for those who desire to delve deeper into the philosophical and epistemological tenets that I believe undergird General Semantics. For they expose his concern with our extensional abilities that results in a *tropic* thematic within his theorizing, and underscore his attempts to account for the embodied nature of discourse and action as mediating factors within any communicative or interactive exchange. Above all, Korzybski's work sought to problematize "the world within which language operates to *mediate* the relations of human beings with each other and the physical world" (Cole, http://communication.ucsd.edu/berman, italics mine). I advance my argument through a three-step reflection process (Lanigan, 1988) that, when synthesized as a whole, exposes our taken-for-granted assumptions concerning *ellipse* (and *et cetera*) that, as currently theorized, cast too narrow of an epistemological net.

I begin by discussing Korzybski's concern with errors in logic, errors that ignore what he identifies as the "dimensionality" within human existence (1994, p. 666-667). Taking up his arguments for a logic grounded within mathematical and geometrical models that conjoin space and time (provided by the "..." designation as discussed below), I argue that Korzybski understood that the dimensionality of human existence shares structural similarities to the physical-chemical-mathematical world in which we inescapably live. He identifies this pattern of affect *and* reasoning that frames our communicative approach to the world as a "living logic" (Bois, 1975) or *psycho-logic* (Korzybski, 1994, p. 9). Thereby, he accentuates the ways in which our semiotic and phenomenological interactions with the world (both physical, mental, and social) reflect *figural* or *tropic qualities*. We begin to see that *ellipse* (and its counterpart *et cetera*) represents a logical joining of space-time relations that affect or shape our interpretive yet embodied patterns. Rather than being mere linguistic devices, they are embodied practices of expression and perception (*speech*) and so are best understood, following Foucault, as *figures of language* and *tropes of speech* (Lanigan, 1992, pp. 155-177).

I continue and discuss more specifically how *ellipse* functions as an example of Korzybski's *psycho-logic*. Here I outline *ellipse* as a *trope of discourse* that operates semiotically and phenomenologically to induce particular explanatory effects in discursive practices (Eicher-Catt & Sutton, 2010). Regardless of the particular space-time configurations invoked by a situated user of *ellipse*, it operates to constitute a discursive economy (Eicher-Catt & Sutton, 2010). The positive or negative valence of a particular economy depends upon its space-time, i.e., semiotic and phenomenological, relations. At this stage in our reflection, we dismiss interpreting Korzybski's *psycho-logic* as merely a cognitive or psychological response to the world. Instead, we comprehend more fully Korzybski's *psycho-logic* as a living embodiment of *speech* as *bodily gesture* (Merleau-Ponty, 1962).

I end by addressing why a semiotic phenomenological reading of *ellipse* is important in furthering our postmodern conceptions of the essential intersections between person, socio-cultural world, and the physical-chemical world. I argue that, seen through the lens of semiotic phenomenology, we begin to grasp Korzybski's *psycho-logic* and the use of *ellipse* as signaling a potential, productive moment in discourse and action as embodied performance. This perceptual shift extends theorizing in General Semantics that typically frames *psycho-logic* and *ellipse* within cognitive or psychological meaning systems, i.e., as only "intellectual" maneuvers. As important, we find that in some discursive configurations, the use of *ellipse* invites an interlocutor to lend a semiotic and phenomenological "version" (Peeren, 2008) of the world, an epistemological move that is in sharp contrast to a mere "translation" process (Benjamin, 1992). Whereas translation signifies a modern, positivistic logic reminiscent of Aristotle's law of identity, "versioning" de-centers that logic. As a "sign of omission" (Eicher-Catt & Sutton, 2010) that is anything but "empty," as we shall see, *ellipse* forecasts a postmodern approach to understanding the role discursive practices play in constructing the "reality" or "semantic environment" we come to perceive and know. Rather than contextualizing Korzybski within a narrow social science perspective, we begin to appreciate his contributions to a "reflexive human science" (Eicher-Catt & Catt, 2010, p. 15). In other words, we come to a better comprehension of Korzybski's *psycho-logic* as a semiotic and phenomenological process of meaning making.

RECONCEPTUALIZING *ELLIPSE* AS A *FIGURE OF SPEECH*

Korzybski is concerned with errors in logic, errors that ignore what he identifies as the "dimensionality" within human existence (1994, p. 666-667). These errors are fundamentally grounded in our outdated Aristotelian and Euclidean thinking about time and space as one dimensional and distinct. Although he does not directly mention the non-dimensionality of Aristotelian logic per se, (for example, Aristotle's writings have no mention of space, see Sachs, 1995, p. 105), he does recognize the logical errors we commit with our false sense of time and space as distinct modes of existence which these outdated systems of thought promote. As he advocates, our terms such as matter, space, and time "should be completely eliminated from science because of their extremely wide-spread and vicious structural and so semantic implications, and that the terms 'events,' 'space-time,' …be used instead," (Korzybski, 1994, p. 235).

The inadequate Euclidean understanding of space as "emptiness," in particular, needs to be revised, according to Korzybski. Operating under the premise of space as emptiness, of course, leads us to conceive of it as merely a "container, *in* which both world and bodies are found" (Anton, 2002, p. 186). Space is better conceptualized as "fullness," an epistemological move characterized by the now socially-accepted collaborations in science between geometry and physics. Building upon the work of mathematician Minkowski who "fused geometry and physics structurally" (Korzybski, 1994, p. 666), Korzybski claims it makes no sense to talk about the "curvature of space-time" if we adopt the premise that space is emptiness. A "curve," in geometrical language, only makes logical sense when understood as marking the "fullness" of space-time relations of which it is a part. In other words, Korzybski appeals to a more sophisticated notion of space and time by advocating that we understand them only in relation to each other. As he claims, "in our experience, 'space' and 'time' can never be separated" (1994, p. 666). It should not go unnoticed, at this point, that *ellipse* has geometrical affinities with the oval; a shape that is, of course, curved (see http://oed.com).

Thus, space is conceptualized more accurately as "a network of intervals" (1994, p. 234) for Korzybski, a logical correction conveniently symbolized by the *ellipse*, ". . .". While our logical errors lead us to perceive this graphic typically as marking only a passage of "time," thinking with Korzybski, we begin to comprehend not an emptiness, omission, or erasure of space as our typical translations suggest. Rather, we see space acknowledged *between* the periods as a "fullness" of relations that evolve *through* time. Representing the full dimensionality inherent within space-time relations, we are led to a newer understanding of the typical meaning of *ellipse* (or its counterpart *et cetera*) as marking "something which cannot be exhausted" (http://oed.com). Space, like time, *forms* possibilities for the interacting agent, an idea elaborated thoroughly by Cassirer (1996). Although typically viewed as merely a "sign of omission," (Eicher-Catt & Sutton, 2010) or gap that represents an emptiness, this new perspective of space (and time) as fullness begins to *add* a whole new *dimension* to our thinking about what *ellipse* potentializes in its discursive use, as I detail below.

Moreover, we begin to comprehend that when space is theorized properly as fullness in relation to time, then it also carries a material weight or has a *body* (like "father time") that necessarily impacts or *figures* the "mental" or "verbal" world of humans. In other words, space and time conjointly *matter*, structurally, as we attempt to capture the seemingly "objective" or physical world around us and interpret its meaning. The *ellipse* (and its counterpart, *et cetera*), therefore, possess *figural* or embodied properties that shape discourse and action and are shaped by it. Paul Ricoeur's (1973, p. 143) remark that "originally the word *figure* was to be said only of bodies," now makes good sense. By advocating such a space-time perspective, therefore, Korzybski highlights the capacity of *ellipse* (and *et cetera*) to help us *turn* the brute "facts of life" (of the physical or mental world) as we experience them into the concepts of "reality" that we come to know, understand, and live. As J. Samuel Bois reminds us concerning the *figural* aspects of space-time, "all meaningful outputs or statements [we humans make] must be seen as the fruits of some human activity that took place somewhere, sometime, in a human being, whose *totality* was involved in the process" (1975, p. 165, italics mine). Korzybski's ideas are similar in scope, of course, to Bakhtin's theory of the *chronotopic* nature of discourse (Bakhtin, 1981). Accordingly, we recognize that any response we make is multi-dimensionally "situated."

In sum, rather than narrowly viewing *ellipse* as merely a stylistic device, we begin to appreciate that it carries epistemological weight and import and so is best understood as a *figure of language and trope of speech* (see Lanigan, 1992, pp. 155-177). By emphasizing that our experience of the world is a *configuration* of space-time relations and that reciprocally our *configurations* impact space-time relations, Korzybski is reminding us of the epistemological nature of our existence; the knower helps to shape the known. Above all, he is emphasizing that "objects are phenomena of reality connected to events, forces, mechanism, and networks ... [and that] their meaning or definition is never independent of this radical interconnectedness" (Cole, http://communication.ucsd.edu/berman). It is to a more thorough understanding of this interconnectedness that we now turn.

THE SEMIOTIC AND PHENOMENOLOGICAL

"Nature" of Korzybski's *Psycho-logic*

Marking *ellipse* as a *figure of speech* announces its full embodied nature, especially if we philosophically broaden typical definitions of speech to encompass the semiotic (including symbolic) and phenomenological (natural) qualities inherent in any act or response to the world (Lanigan, 1992, pp. 155-177). By viewing speech as *bodily gesture* (Merleau-Ponty, 1962), an inherently phenomenological move, we begin to recognize how Korzybski was attempting to extend his theorizing about the communicative dimensions of consciousness, experience, and action; in particular, by accounting for a *"body's* relationship to cultural signs and codes of discourse as *reflexive* performances of meaning making" (Eicher-Catt, 2010, p. 4). I contend that this communicative dimensionality induced by a combination of consciousness and experience of the world is identified by Korzybski as our *living logic* (Bois, 1975) or *psycho-logic* (Korzybski, 1994). By *psycho-logic* he refers to the wholistic pattern of interpretation and reasoning, in other words, that we employ—multi-dimensionally—as we make sense of or respond to the world. Bois (1975, p. 166) clarifies Korzybski's sense of our multi-dimensionality, we are "not strictly anatomical; [we are] not limited to a neural feedback firing in reverberatory circuits, cell assemblies, and phase sequences. [We] *integrate*, at a more comprehensive level of existence, the various aspects of our semantic reactions: thinking, feeling, self-moving, electro-chemical, environmental, past, and anticipated future" (italics mine). Another way to acknowledge this "integrative" capability is by way of semiotic phenomenology. *Ellipse* has given us an entry point into comprehending this *psycho-logic*.

Psycho-logic as a Semiotic Phenomenology

Support for a semiotic phenomenological reading of many of Korzybski's concepts is found most readily in Korzybski's discussion of his *living logic* (Bois, 1975). This *psycho-logic*, according to Korzybski, operates at the heart of our "natural" (physico-chemical) and "supernatural" (understood as symbolic) interconnections with the world around us. I contend that the *figural* or embodied nature of our *psycho-logic* is emphasized by Korzbyski when he claims that humans, unlike animals and plants, are both "natural," i.e., a part of the physico-chemical materiality of the world (an acknowledgement of our phenomenological entailments) *and* "supernatural" (an acknowledgement of our semiotic capabilities). According to Korzybski, the "natural" aspect is displayed within the physicality of all existence—including the supposed "objective" world of objects and physical forces of which our bodily "sensorium" is a part (the phenomenological). The "supernatural" aspect depicts the ability that only humans have, the ability to time-bind, i.e., "to digest and appropriate the labors and experiences of the past...the capacity to use the fruits of past labors and experiences as intellectual or spiritual capital for the developments in the present" (Korzybski, 2008, p. 35). This constitutes our semiotic enactments—the ability to "capture" the qualities of objects, events, or actions in the world and make them meaningful through "sign actions" (Peirce, 1955b). A Peircian semiotics identifies these "sign actions," which are correlatively understood as phenomenological enactments as well, as operating primarily through indexical, iconic, and symbolic signs (Peirce, 1955a).

Thus Korzybski recognizes, quite clearly, that humans "embody" the world around them—regardless of whether that embodiment is at the lowest discriminatory level of "sensing" or the highest—what he called the "verbal" or "mental." Moreover, he understood this embodied relationship as reciprocal and reflexive. As he goes on to say, "there is nothing mystical about the fact that ideas and words are energies which powerfully affect the physic-chemical base of our time-binding activities" (1921/2008, p. 42). This *is* the "supernatural" or "metaphysical" quality inherent in all human beings and is, consequently, represented in the very language and discourse we use. Later in our philosophical history, Gregory Bateson takes up this same theme concerning the interconnected "knowing" that transpires between the "natural" and "supernatural" aspects and calls it his "epistemology of the sacred" (Bateson & Bateson, 1987). Bateson interprets this interconnectedness as "the sacred unity," or the "pattern which connects" mind and nature (Bateson, 1991).

Viewing Korzybski's *psycho-logic* from this *figural* or embodied perspective also announces the spatial dimensions to his concept of "time-binding." While we easily understand his concept of "time-binding" as an attempt to emphasize how we create, through our process of abstraction, objectified "time*s*" out of seemingly continuous moments, as I read Korzybski, time-binding also implies its spatial dimensionality. To "bind" is to bring together both space and time—and for Korzybski, this togetherness entails a "fullness" of thought and action (possibilities), not an emptiness. A simple example illustrates this point. The way that I frame any experience of the world necessarily signifies my interpretations or thoughts (whether positive and/or negative) about it that *in turn* constitutes my "horizon" of understanding when it comes to both myself and the world around me. Any attempt to bind time or create a "crystallized" moment of conscious, reflective experience therefore, produces this "fullness" of thought and action that necessarily signifies a space-time, bodily relation toward the world.

In attempting to discover "the natural laws of the human class of life," (2008, p. 51) Korzybski correctly identifies the same *structural* regularities within our sensing, thinking or logic that he sees as naturally inherent within the mathematical, geometrical, physical-chemical relations with which he was so concerned as a physicist/engineer. While so often critiqued for seeming to posit a separate "objectified" world and a "mental" world, I believe, as noted above, Korzybski's goal, like phenomenological semiotician, C. S. Peirce, was to explore the *integrative* components of both that necessarily operate simultaneously in a dialectical movement that shapes our lived experience (on this point, see Eicher-Catt, 2010). This integrative component is what Korzybski meant when he discusses our *psycho-logic*. So, Korzybski's mission becomes not only increasing our awareness of this *psycho-logic* which we employ, but to grasp the ways in which our language and discursive practices (typically locked within outmoded Newtonian, Euclidean, and Aristotelian ways of thinking) are complicit in its unproductive manifestation. Speaking to the epistemological importance of properly recognizing this integrative potential for humans, Bois claims, "the *psycho-logics* of Korzybski is, in my judgment, more comprehensive than any other scheme of thinking I have encountered in my research for a substitute to the logic inaugurated by Aristotle" (1975, p. 168).

So as an example of his *psycho-logic*, (which is semiotically and phenomenologically constituted) *ellipse* is understood more clearly as a *figure of language* and *speech* that instantiates a *tropic* logic, an occasion that calls for a semantic reaction that is personally-culturally-socially situated. That is, a transformational process necessarily inheres within its arc and this transformational process is produced by the dialectical movement of "natural" (phenomenological) aspects and "supernatural" (semiotic) qualities of a speaking/listening subject responding to his/her world. As a *figure of speech*, *ellipse* thus imposes a structure and "impress[es] on us not only a metaphysical framework but also an affective one. [Such a figure] do[es] not only a good deal of our thinking for us, but also a good deal of our feeling" (Rapoport, 1955, p. 182).

Furthermore, Korzybski understood the contingent, open-ended nature of this autonomous, evolutionary *tropic logic* by appealing to what he called the "spiral theory" (2008, p. 152), a "working mechanism" at the heart of our time-binding abilities. Like communication theorist Gregory Bateson (1972), Korzybski understood that only living things (humans, for Korzybski) produced spirals (either physically or metaphorically) to mark their evolutionary arcs or trails of interaction or mediation with the world around them. Specifically focusing on time-binding as a *tropic logic*, he says, since "animals are *not* time-binding, they have *not* the capacity of the spiral; therefore, they have not autonomous progress" (2008, p. 152). Given its affinities geometrically with the oval, it is no wonder that Korzybski would appeal to the diagrammatical sign of *ellipse*, since it signifies the potential evolutionary arc of the spiral and thus marks the agential qualities of humans to create "reality" as we know it. As he says, "the spiral theory' explains how our reactions can be accelerated and elaborated by ourselves, and how truly we are the masters of our destinies" (2008, p. 160).

Moreover, Korzybski finds the "tropism theory of animal conduct, founded by Dr. J. Loeb [to be] of the greatest interest" (2008, p. 154). Attempting to characterize how an organism as a whole responds to the world, he outlines the "forced movements" or tropisms that animals display and that change their interactions with the world. Applying this theory to humans, Korzybski describes how this mechanism of change (*tropism*) "becomes in the time-binding class of life the instinct of creation, and is nothing else than the expression of the natural impulse of the time-binding energy" (2008, p. 162). As he summarizes these ideas, he says, "time-binding in its last analysis is creation" (2008, p. 163). So while the theory of tropism is more deterministic in animals, i.e., it more closely resembles the forces and impacts (reflexes) found in the supposed physical "objective" world, the theory of tropism announces the creative potential in humans. This creative potential manifests, of course, both positively and negatively in terms of our health and sanity.

Figuring *Ellipse* as a Discursive Economy

Given the above, we must ask: what are the qualities of discourse and action that the *ellipse* typically instantiates as a semiotic phenomenology? How does the *ellipse* function, in other words, to *figure* discursive practices as supernatural (semiotic) and natural (phenomenological) enactments? And what, if any, ideological components inhere within this *tropic* process?

With our broadened understanding of *ellipse* as a temporal and spatial *tropic form*, we can now briefly explore how it emplots human relations (as opposed to merely being a stylistic device). Foremost, *ellipse* represents, in other words, "a subtractive metataxeme" (Sloan, 2001, p. 237), by emplotting a discursive form "using a recognizable set of relations or syntax based on the mechanics of "omission" and "subtraction" of discursive elements, with hyperbole/amplification as potential opposite and counterpart," (Eicher-Catt & Sutton, 2010, p. 212). "As a generic form (replete with mode of argument and ideological implication), a discourse that is derived from *ellipse*, functions overall by syntactically deleting parts of the discourse for the sake of an economy characterized by separation and isolation" (Eicher-Catt & Sutton, 2010, p. 212). The result is a unique *discursive* economy that has ideological implications, a condition that did not go unnoticed by Korzybski.

Thus, as a *figure of speech* (or *trope of discourse*) *ellipse* induces (through its semiotic and phenomenological qualities) particular explanatory effects in discursive practices. As we shall observe, these explanatory effects are best understood as semiotic and phenomenological "events," a wholistic term meant to do "away with this old and vicious elementalism" (Korzybski, 1994, p. 243) displayed by Aristotelian thought. One of these main effects is explanation by omission. In prose writing designated as ". . .", we typically interpret this operation as simply an omission of words. In tropical terms, however, "omission is a general rhetorical strategy that is employed to create a sense of a whole, of a *full* form, or of a unity by avoiding or suppressing a part" (Dupriez, 1991, p. 149; Lanham, 1991, p. 62). One of the tropical operations or *logic of ellipse* thus entails speaking from part while conceptualizing the whole. When discussing part to whole dynamic relations, we typically think of metonymy. However, unlike metonymy, which enacts change by addition, *ellipse* enacts change by subtraction (Quintilian, 1921, 9.3.58). What this means is that either semiotic or phenomenological elements within discourse are reduced, as I describe below.

Regardless of its tropical operation or manifestation the omission that inheres within *ellipse* is, therefore, a strategy of "necessity:" the avoidance or the suppression of a part is needed for the sake of the whole. In this way, the whole achieves clarity or sense or understanding (Anderson, 2000, p. 41). It is also the representation of the "whole" (geometrically drawn as a circle or quasi-circle—*ellipse*) that renders this particular tropical operation as typically "brusque, authoritarian, or domineering" (Dupriez, 1991, p. 149). Thus, when employed by an interlocutor, the preceding cluster of terms (categories of things in a series) in an *elliptical* syntax tends to dominate the participating interlocutor's rhetorical choices for how to continue/complete the interpretive enactment. In this way, the *trope* of *ellipse* forces the hermeneutical moment toward a particular semiotic and phenomenological interpretation. For example, upon hearing someone say, "At the farm I saw pigs, geese, horses, cows.... (or *et cetera*)," we would not complete the interpretation with "curbs, gutters, and sewer drains." In this way, *ellipse* isolates and separates linguistic choice from an array of other possibilities. It exhibits a domineering absence/presence. Although this configuration operates on the basis of isolation, it does not always produce a "disturbed semantic reaction" as Korzybski defines it. It does, however, *force* a reaction/response resulting in a politicized discursive economy. The particular content nature of a given *elliptical* syntax, of course, determines the degree to which a discursive politic is recognized and experienced—positively or negatively.

While I argue that Korzybski definitely appreciated this tropical operation of *ellipse* to specify interpretive acts (something he would identify as lower-order abstracting), this domineering aspect of *ellipse* is not the only tropical function that interests him. Following Cassirer's understanding of a dialectical movement that inheres within all symbolic forms of existence (1996), we recognize that, although *ellipse* functions on the basis of omission, its corresponding counterpart—amplification—can also be possibilized within discursive relations (Anderson, 2000, p. 41; Lanham, 1991, p. 62; Lausberg, 1998, 838-39). So, while an omission typically signifies a gap that is full or pregnant with potential meaning, *ellipse* often accomplishes its rhetorical strategy through its opposite or counterpart—i.e., hyperbole/amplication as well. When amplification becomes the domineering tropical operation, the full potentiality of discourse and action is enhanced. In other words, the function of the omission is not so much to isolate and separate but to amplify the potentiality of creating a sense of completion or wholeness. In this way, *ellipse* announces an absence/absence. It is the use of *ellipse* in this manner (for example, as exemplified by the title of this book) that signals the most possibilizing aspects of perception and expression by a participating interlocutor. In other words, an omission affords a *turning* of context and meaning toward something new—the poetic function of language (Jakobson, 1971), and thus offers an interlocutor the opportunity to add a new "version" (Peeren, 2008) of perceptions and expressions to discourse and action. So regardless of the specific tropical operation that is activated (given the particular space-time relations at work), the use of *ellipse* thus constitutes an economy of discourse and action. That is, *ellipse* draws our attention to the underlying structural relations that are at play in a given linguistic, communicative exchange that may have ideological consequences.

On the negative side of this discursive economy, *ellipse* is domineering as it constrains discursive choices and closes off potentiality. Another way to understand this is to say that a person's semiotic and phenomenological freedom is denied. Ways of encoding and decoding by a body-subject are perceived as relatively fixed or static. On the positive side of this economy, *ellipse* can serve to highlight or amplify the inability to "exhaust" all possible meanings of an expression (its semiotic dimensions) and thereby emphasize the embodied (phenomenological) role the reader/listener has in the creative production of meaning. Thus, in its amplification mode, either the semiotic (consciousness) or phenomenological (experience) aspects of existence must be heightened. Foremost, we must keep in mind that these structural relations are enacted by the particular semiotic and phenomenological interpretations of a body-subject (Merleau-Ponty, 1962) who is situated within a particular space-time configuration.

As a synthetic theory and methodology, semiotic phenomenology thus provides us with a more comprehensive understanding of discourse and action as *bodily gesture* (Merleau-Ponty, 1962). As I discuss elsewhere (Eicher-Catt, 2010, p. 10), "*Gesturing*, after all, entails a body in language who speaks. Thus, semiotic [phenomenology] offers us an insightful way to extend our understanding regarding the complex dialectical nature of our symbolicity (our capacity to encode and decode our consciousness of experience) and our experience of consciousness (our existential nature as body-subjects who originate [discourse and action] as bodily gesture)". As a *chronotope* (or *trope of discourse*), we recognize that *ellipse* necessarily emplots not only what a "body" can and cannot do, but also a line of reasoning, affect, and values for understanding the world (Eicher-Catt & Sutton, 2010). This *is* the *psycho-logics* of which Korzybski speaks.

Ellipse and the Postmodern Turn to the *Tropological*

Korzybski's use of *ellipse*, "..." (and its counterpart *et cetera*) thus symbolically highlights the dimensionality of our existence as it theoretically joins space and time (both literally and figuratively) in a graphic representation that serves as a reminder of our existential situatedness (body, space, time, and relations). While it appears to be a one dimensional, linear graphic, the *ellipse* (or that which is *elliptical*) marks a geometric curve, with affinities with the oval that represents a fullness of thought and action that necessarily *figures* discursive practices. By advocating its use, Korzybski recognizes that the power of language and discourse (rhetoric) is not merely in its typical temporal conceptualization, as Aristotle theorized (Eicher-Catt & Sutton, 2010). Such a view of rhetoric as only temporality limits "the scope and function of rhetoric to mere instrumentality. Rhetoric becomes, in other words, merely a teleological device for accomplishing one's goals within a view of space as merely place," (Eicher-Catt & Sutton, 2010, p. 208), i.e., something empty that we occupy. A function of *ellipse* resides in its very *corporeality* or spatiality, i.e., its ability to constitute or *figure* reality as we know it as an *embodied* activity (Eicher-Catt & Sutton, 2010).

Thinking with Korzybski but also through the lens of semiotic phenomenology, we begin to appreciate how discursive practices are ultimately *corporeal* enactments; indeed, *full-figured* in their capacity to shape an always present/absence dialectical movement between lived-body and space-time relations. Bakhtin, of course, defines this important juxta-positioning of lived-body space-time relations as the *chronotope* (1981), in his efforts to advance our limited understanding of rhetoric in its temporal configuration. While Korzybski never uses the literary words the *figurative* or the *chronotope* to explain this lived-body mediation process between person-world (albeit physical or mental), there is little doubt that he spoke within their discursive parameters. As he says, "Man [sic], therefore, by the very intrinsic character of his [sic] being, MUST ACT FIRST, IN ORDER TO BE ABLE TO LIVE" (2008, p. 43). This originary act is the *figural* or the embodied component of our time-binding capabilities and is integral to our mediation process of the world. As he theorized, if the physical-chemical-mathematical-geometrical world is structurally characterized by space-time relations, then it is no different for human existence. If the supposed "objective" world is comprised of forces and impacts, the same holds true for the "mental" world of which it is a part. Thus physical *bodies and* mental *bodies* matter together in their semiotic and phenomenological entailments.

Investigating *ellipse* has proven to be a good entry point into Korzybski's epistemological project concerning language and discourse. As an "event" of discourse, i.e., as an embodied space-time configuration, *ellipse* allows us to make a perceptual shift in our thinking about what our living logic actually entails. For it highlights the lived-body's complicity in shaping time (consciousness) and space (experience) relations into meaningful "events" (Korzybski, 1994, p. 232) of speaking and listening. Whether invoking a negative or positive discursive economy, *ellipsis* signifies the *tropic* or "poetic" nature and function of discourse (Jakobson, 1971) that operationalizes our *psycho-logic*, as Korzybski conceptualizes it. On the poetic nature of Korzybski's *psycho-logic*, Bois (1963, p. 264) claims, "*psycho-logics* considers poetry as an adequate vehicle of human communication. . . its purpose is to trip off a learning experience, to induce an insight, to bring about an organismic reaction that will be an event in the life of the recipient." This "organismic reaction" is nothing less than a semiotic phenomenology. Viewing our *psycho-logic* as only an intellectual exercise thus proves short-sighted. By expanding our awareness of this *tropic* process we may avoid so many of the discursive pitfalls or economies that, according to Korzybski, so often thwart our efforts to live productive lives.

Above all, understood as more than merely a "sign of omission" (Eicher-Catt & Sutton, 2010) that appears to be an empty container, *ellipse* offers a productive moment in discourse and action by providing an interlocutor with the ability to render his/her own semiotic and phenomenological "version" (Peeren, 2008) of events. Derived from the Latin root *vertere,* versioning means "to turn" and it provides another *tropic* space-time from which to embody alternative discursive practices. Unlike the notion of translation (Benjamin, 1991) which implies an essence or original from which we work to model or reproduce (based upon modernist assumptions and reflective of Aristotle's law of identity), versioning views texts, discourse, and action as "no more than preliminary drafts" (Peeren, 2008, 215-216) from which we might discursively arc forward—creating new space-time, embodied relations. Ultimately versions "are first and foremost subjective accounts, developed by a particular person from a particular spatiotemporal coordinate. As such, versions mark agency without claiming truth or totality" (Peeren, 2008, p. 208). Versioning thus describes an important epistemological adjustment in our thinking about discourse and action, in general, which articulates postmodern sentiments.

So, while the writings of Korzybski address a number of topics for those interested in improving our understanding of "the science and art of human nature," (2008, p. 38), his use of *ellipse* and promotion of the rhetorical expression, *et cetera,* proves heuristic for those who desire to delve deeper into the philosophical and epistemological tenets that undergird General Semantics. From within the theory and methodology of semiotic phenomenology, we begin to appreciate a *tropic thematic* that runs through Korzybski's theorizing. We can view him as a precursor to more postmodern approaches to language and discourse that focus on the "events" of speaking and listening as embodied constitutive space-time relations (for an example see, Eicher-Catt & Catt, 2010). The "new language" or "structural understanding of language" that he proposes we need, is found in the developing postmodern approaches to language and discourse, like semiotic phenomenology and the concept of versioning.

For Korzybski, this productive (versioning) side of discursive practices is both humankind's bane and cause for celebration (Hayakawa, 1962). For he understood that "man[sic] in society 'secretes' his[sic] symbolic environment, i.e., his[sic] culture, in which he[sic] must continue to live. This symbolic environment is instrumental in shaping man's[sic] natural environment, and is, in turn shaped by it" (Rapoport, 1955, 183-184). So, regardless of its positive or negative manifestation, the key is to become more aware of our reflexive *tropic logic.* Thereby, we eliminate viewing language as a mere representational tool to grasp a fixed and stable external world. Unlike normative approaches to language and communication that presuppose communication as mere instrumentality, viewing our *psycho-logic* as *tropological* we start to recognize an emerging "new science of embodied discourse" (Eicher-Catt & Catt, 2010) that radically shifts our epistemological ground. As a physicist/engineer, Korzybski knows that the supposed "objective" world is anything but a static, given entity to a perceiver. Rather he recognizes our *tropic logic* that better matches the multi-dimensionality inherent in our mediation process. Our capacity for time-binding is our very capacity *to turn* the events of the past into memories for the future in order to grow and change within the present. The *psycho-logics* represented within the discursive operations of *ellipse* keep us focused on the *figural* or multi-dimensional qualities of our creative embodied expressions and perceptions rather than any literal or one-dimensional appearances. Such a stance creates an on-going awareness of the healthy *and* destructive powers inherent within our "symbolic secretions" (Rapoport, 1955, 185). It is the development of this awareness that, for Korzybski, is the first step in manifesting our distinctive human genius.

REFERENCES

Anderson, R.D., Jr. (2000). *Glossary of Greek rhetorical terms connected to methods of argumentation, figures and tropes from Anaximenes to Quintilian.* Leuven, Belgium: Peeters.

Anton, C. (2002). Discourse as care: A phenomenological consideration of spatiality and temporality. *Human Studies,* 25, 185-205.

Anton, C. (2008). The thing is not itself: Artefactual metonymy and the world of antiques. *ETC:A Review of General Semantics,* 65(4), 365-371.

Bakhtin, M. (1981). *The dialogic imagination.* Austin: University of Texas Press.

Bateson, G. (1972). *Steps to an ecology of mind.* New York: Ballantine Books.

Bateson, G. (1991). *Sacred unity: Further steps to an ecology of mind.* (R. Donaldson, Ed.). New York: Harper Collins.

Bateson, G. & M.C. Bateson. (1987). *Angels fear: Towards an epistemology of the sacred.* NewYork: Bantam Books.

Benjamin, A. (1992). Translating origins: Psychoanalysis and philosophy. In L. Venuti (Ed.), *Rethinking translation: Discourse, subjectivity, ideology* (pp. 18-41), London and New York: Routledge.

Bois, J. S. (1963). Logic and psycho-logics. *ETC : A review of general semantics,* 20 (3), 261-267.

Bois, J. S. (1975). Korzybski's living logic. *ETC : A review of general semantics,* 32 (2), 165-168.

Burke, K. (1969). *A grammar of motives.* Berkeley: University of California Press. (Originally published 1945).

Cassirer, E. (1969). Mythic, aesthetic, and theoretical space. *Man and world,* 2(1), 3-17.

Cassirer, E. (1979). Reflections on the concept of group and the theory of perception. In D. P. Verene (Ed.), *Symbol, myth, and culture.* New Haven: Yale University Press.

Cassirer, E. (1996). The metaphysics of symbolic forms, In J. M. Krois & D. P. Verene (Eds.), *The philosophy of symbolic forms, volume 4.* New Haven: Yale University.

Cole, Michael. Message from the Dr. Sanford I. Berman Chair in General Semantics, Universityof California, San Diego, Department of Communication, Retrieved January 26, 2010 from http://communication.uscs.edu/berman/

Detienne, M. (1996). *The masters of truth in archaic Greece.* J. Lloyd (Trans.). New York: Zone Books.

Dupriez, B. (1991). *A dictionary of literary devices, a-z.* A. W. Halsall (Trans.). Toronto: University of Toronto Press.

Eicher-Catt, D. (2010). What E-Prime "is not": A semiotic phenomenological reading. *ETC: A Review of General Semantics,* 67(1), 1-18.

Eicher-Catt, D. & Catt, I. (Eds.). (2010). *Communicology: The new science of embodied discourse.* Madison, NJ: Fairleigh-Dickinson University Press.

Eicher-Catt, D., & Sutton, J. (2010). A communicology of the oval office as figural rhetoric: Women, the presidency, and a politics of the body. In D. Eicher-Catt & I. Catt (Eds.), *Communicology: The new science of embodied discourse,* (pp. 200-234). Madison, NJ: Fairleigh-Dickinson University Press.

Foucault, M. (1972). *The archaeology of knowledge and the discourse on language.* (A.M. Sheridan Smith, Trans.). New York: Pantheon Books.Foucault, M. (1973). *The order of things: An archaeology of the human sciences.* New York: Vintage Books.

Hayakawa, S. I. (Ed.) (1962). *The use and misuse of language.* Greenwich, Conn: Fawcett Premier Book.

Jakobson, R. (1971). The dominant. In K. Pomorska & L. Matejka (Eds.), *Readings in Russian poetics* (pp. 82-87). Cambridge, MA: MIT Press.

Johnson, W. (1946). *People in quandaries: The semantics of personal adjustment.* New York: Harper & Row.

Kellogg, E.W., III. (1987). Speaking in E-Prime: An experimental method for integrating general semantics into daily life. *Et Cetera,* XX, 118-128.

Kellogg, E.W., III (1992). The good, the bad, and the ugly: Comments on the E-Prime symposium. *Et Cetera,* XX, 376-392.

Korzybski, A. (1994). *Science and sanity: An introduction to non-Aristotelian systems and general semantics.* Forth Worth, TX: Institute of General Semantics. (Originally published in 1933).

Korzybski, A. (2008). *Manhood of humanity: The science and art of human engineering.* UK: Dodo Press. (Originally published in 1921.)

Lanham, R.A. (1991). *A handlist of rhetorical terms, 2nd edition.* Berkeley: University of California Press.

Lanigan, R.L. (1988). *Phenomenology of communication: Merleau-Ponty's thematic in communicology and semiology.* Pittsburgh, PA: Duquesne University Press.

Lanigan, R.L. (1992). *The human science of communicology: A phenomenology of discourse in Merleau-Ponty and Foucault.* Pittsburgh, PA: Duquesne University Press.

Lausberg, H. (1998). *Handbook of literary rhetoric: with a foreword by George A. Kennedy.* (D. E. Orton & R. D. Anderson, Eds.; M.T. Bliss, A. Jansen, and D.E. Orton, Trans.). Leiden, Netherlands: Brill.

Lee, I. J. (1994). *Language habits in human affairs: An introduction to general semantics.* (S.I. Berman, Ed.). Concord, CA: International Society for General Semantics. (Original work published 1941).

Lefebvre, H. (1991). *The production of space.* (D. Nicholson-Smith, Trans.). Oxford: Blackwell.

Merleau-Ponty, M. (1962). *Phenomenology of perception.* (C. Smith, Trans.). London: Routledge Classics. (Original work published 1945).

Murray, E. (1978). Perceiving our perceptions of structure. Alfred Korzybski Memorial Lecture presented at New York University, April 29, 1978. Retrieved June 21, 2010, from http://www.generalsemantics.org/misc/akml/akmls/44-45-murray.pdf

Peeren, E. (2008). *Intersubjectivities and popular culture: Bakhtin and beyond.* Stanford, CA: Stanford University Press.

Peirce, C.S. (1955a). The principles of phenomenology. In J. Buchler (Ed.), *Philosophical writings of Peirce* (pp. 74-97). New York: Dover. (Compilation of original texts published 1940).

Peirce, C.S. (1955b). Logic as semiotic: the theory of signs. In J. Buchler (Ed.), *Philosophical writings of Peirce* (pp. 98-119). New York: Dover. (Compilation of original texts published 1940).

Quintilian. (1921). *The institutio oratoria of Quintilian, Vol. 4.* (H.E. Butler, Trans.).

Rapoport, A. (1955). The role of symbols in human behavior. *ETC: A review of general semantics,* 12(3), 180-188.

Read, A.W. (1983). The semiotic aspect of Alfred Korzybski's general semantics. *Et Cetera,* XX, 16-21.

Read, A.W. (1985). Language revision by deletion of absolutism. *Et Cetera,* 42(1), 7-12.

Read, A.W. (1987). The relation of semiotics to general semantics. *Et Cetera,* XX, 291-292.

Ricoeur, P. (1973). *The rule of metaphor: The historical imagination in nineteenth-century Europe.* Baltimore: Johns Hopkins University Press.

Sachs, J. (1995). Aristotle's physics. In H.M. Flaumenhaft (Ed.), *Guided studies of great texts in science.* New Brunswick, NJ: Rutgers University Press.

Sebeok, T.A. (1982). Pandora's box: Why and how to communicate 10,000 years into the future. Alfred Korzybski Memorial Lecture presented at the Yale Club, New York, November 6, 1981. Retrieved June 21, 2010, from <http://www.generalsemantics.org/misc/akml/akmls/49-sebeok.pdf>.

Sloan, T.O. (Ed.), (2001). *Encyclopedia of rhetoric.* Oxford: Oxford University Press.

Sutton, J., & Mifsud, M. (2002). Figuring rhetoric: From antistrophe to apostrophe through catastrophe. *Rhetoric Society Quarterly,* 32(4), 29-49.

Taylor, S. (2002). Right reasoning: S.I. Hayakawa, Charles Sanders Peirce, and the scientific method. *Et Cetera,* 59(2), 141-147.

Vassallo, P. (2008). Holes in the earth and in the photos: Of signs, signifieds and signifiers. *ETC: A Review of General Semantics,* 65(4), 332-336.

White, H. (1978). *Tropics of discourse: Essays in cultural criticism.* Baltimore: Johns Hopkins University Press.

White, H. (1999). *Figural realism: Studies in the mimesis effect.* Baltimore: Johns Hopkins University Press.

ABOUT THE AUTHORS

Ramiro J. Álvarez (1951, Lugo, Spain) is a clinical psychologist concerned with the language-thought-behavior-context relations and their implication in the issue of personal values and choice. Author of several self-help books in Spanish and in Portuguese.

Corey Anton (Ph.D., Purdue University, 1998) is Professor of Communication Studies at Grand Valley State University. With wide research interests in communication theory, phenomenology, semiotics, media ecology, communicology, and stoicism, Anton is author of *Selfhood and Authenticity* (SUNY Press 2001); *Sources of Significance: Worldly Rejuvenation and Neo-Stoic Heroism* (Purdue University Press, 2010); *Communication Uncovered: General Semantics and Media Ecology* (IGS, 2011); and editor of *Valuation and Media Ecology: Ethics, Morals, and Laws* (Hampton Press, 2010). A Fellow of the International Communicology Institute, he currently serves as the Vice-President of the Institute of General Semantics.

Thierry Bardini, Agronomist (ENSA Montpellier, 1986) and sociologist (Ph.D. Paris X Nanterre, 1991), is full professor in the Department of Communication at the University of Montréal, where he teaches since 1993. His research interests concern the contemporary cyberculture, from the production and uses of information and communication technologies to molecular biology, or, in other words, everything that concerns the fictions of science and the science fictions of code. He is the author of *Bootstrapping: Douglas Englebart, Coevolution and the Genesis of Personal Computing* (Stanford University Press, 2000), *Junkware* (University of Minnesota Press, 2011) and *Journey to the End of the Species* (in collaboration with Dominique Lestel, Éditions Dis Voir, Paris, 2011).

Isaac E. Catt (Ph.D., Philosophy of Communication, Southern Illinois University, 1982), is President of Semiotic Society of America, Visiting Scholar at Simon E. Silverman Phenomenology Center and Department of Communication and Rhetorical Studies, Duquesne University and Fellow, International Communicology Institute. He is co-editor of *Communicology: The New Science of Embodied Discourse*, and author of many articles and book chapters on communicology, semiotics and phenomenology.

319

John S. Caputo is Professor and Chair of the Master's Program in Communication and Leadership Studies at Gonzaga University and the Walter Ong S.J. Scholar. Dr. Caputo earned his Ph.D. from the Claremont Graduate School and University Center. His areas of expertise include communication theory, philosophy of communication, intercultural and interpersonal communication, and media and social values. He is the author of five books and written more than 25 articles in professional journals, and been honored as a Visiting Scholar In-Residence at the University of Kent at Canterbury, England and directs the Gonzaga-in-Cagli Project, a study abroad program in Cagli, Italy. He has received numerous teaching awards and has served as a consultant and communication researcher with a number of organizations. He also directs the Northwest Alliance for Responsible Media.

Heather M. Crandall is an Assistant Professor in the Masters Program in Communication and Leadership Studies at Gonzaga University and the Associate Director of the Cagli Project --a cultural immersion digital storytelling experience for students located in Italy. Her Ph.D. is interdisciplinary from Washington State University. Her areas of concentration include American Studies, Communication, and Rhetoric. Heather teaches courses in theorizing communication, visual rhetoric, organizational communication, public speaking, small group communication, and interpersonal communication.

Deborah Eicher-Catt (Ph.D. from Southern Illinois University at Carbondale, 1996) is Associate Professor of Communication Arts and Sciences at the Pennsylvania State University, York. As a Fellow of the International Communicology Institute, she is current Chair of the Philosophy of Communication Interest Group for the National Communication Association. An award winning-author, in addition to several book chapters, her publications appear in such journals as *The American Journal of Semiotics, The Review of Communication, The Journal of Contemporary Ethnography, Women and Language, The Atlantic Journal of Communication,* and the *International Journal of Communication.*

Geraldine E. Forsberg (Ph.D., New York University, 1991) currently teaches in the English Department at Western Washington University. She teaches courses on media and culture, researching workplace culture, and professional writing.

Dr. Jean-Yves Heurtebise is a Fellow Research Member of Aix-Marseille University Research Center on Comparative Epistemology (CEPERC) and currently a Visiting Professor at National Dong Hua University in Taiwan. His research aims at evaluating the validity of contemporary French Philosophy conceptual apparatus when applied to other disciplinary fields: biology and ecology, cultural studies and comparative philosophy. For now, he has published eight book chapters (Ashgate Publishing, Presses Sorbonne Nouvelle, De Boeck, …), eleven articles in peer-review journals (Philosophia Scientiae; Transtext(e)s, Transcultures: Journal of Global Studies; Cinergon; Taiwan Sport Studies; …) and delivered forty three invited lectures all over the world (University of Stanford, University of Turin, Paris 7 University, Peking University, Tsinghua University, National Taiwan University, …).

Bruce I. Kodish —widely-acknowledged as a veteran scholar-teacher of 'general semantics' (GS)—wrote *Korzybski: A Biography*, the first comprehensive book-length account of Korzybski's life and work, awarded the Institute of General Semantics (IGS) Book Prize in 2011. One of the small number of graduates of the IGS's former Teacher Certification training program, he earned a PhD in General-Semantics/Applied Epistemology (Epistemics) from the Union Institute and University in 1996. Bruce lectures on Korzybski's life and work; has taught advanced university-level seminars on *Science and Sanity* and on "The Scientific Roots of GS"; and gives presentations and seminar-workshops on the GS approach to Epistemics and the Art of Awareness. A practicing physical therapist in Pasadena, California, Bruce has specialist certifications in Mechanical Diagnosis and Therapy (MDT), and in posture-movement education (the Alexander Technique).

Martin H. Levinson serves as the President of the Institute of General Semantics, Vice-President of the New York Society for General Semantics, and Book Review Editor for *ETC: A Review of General Semantics*. He has published three GS-related books and many articles on general semantics. He holds a PhD in Organizational and Administrative Studies from NYU.

322 ■ KORZYBSKI AND . . .

Bini B. S. is the academic fellow and program officer of Balvant Parekh Centre for General Semantics and Other Human Sciences in Baroda, India. Her Ph.D. was on Michel Foucault and Historiography. She has contributed her articles and poems to national and international journals and magazines.

William Henry Sharp has been a student of and applied the principles of general semantics to his work in project planning, management and education for four decades. As the Director of Transition Centre he now works to develop models of sustainable local economies. He is working on a general semantics handbook drawn from the writings of Alfred Korzybski which will be used in project and leadership development.

Lance Strate is Professor of Communication and Media Studies and Director of the Professional Studies in New Media program at Fordham University. He is the author of *Echoes and Reflections: On Media Ecology as a Field of Study*, and *On the Binding Biases of Time and Other Essays on General Semantics and Media Ecology*, and co-editor of several anthologies, including *The Legacy of McLuhan*, and two editions of *Communication and Cyberspace: Social Interaction in an Electronic Environment*. He is currently working on a book entitled, *Amazing Ourselves to Death: Neil Postman's Brave New World Revisited*, due to be published in 2013. One of the founders of the Media Ecology Association, he was the MEA's first President, serving in that capacity for over a decade, and is a partner in NeoPoiesis Press.

Zhenbin Sun received his Ph.D. from New York University and pursued his postdoctoral research at Harvard University. He teaches communication studies at Fairleigh Dickinson University. He is mainly interested in Chinese and Western philosophy of language.

Robin Wynyard is a sociologist. Before taking very early retirement, he worked for several British universities and was visiting professor at universities abroad, particularly in Pakistan and the United States. Still very much involved in writing and journalism, his interests include cultural transmission theory and its relationship to popular culture, and the sociology of art and literature. He is currently Honorary Research Fellow at the University of Greenwich UK and Visiting Research Fellow in Education at the University of Derby UK.